England Test Cricket
1981 – 1992

England Test Cricket

The Years of Indecision

1981 – 1992

NEVILLE SCOTT and NICK COOK

The Kingswood Press

This book is dedicated,
with gratitude,
to Peter and Cynthia Cook
and to Audrey Scott.

First published in Great Britain in 1992
by the Kingswood Press
Michelin House, 81 Fulham Road, London SW3 6RB

A CIP catalogue record for this book
is available from the British Library
ISBN 0 413 66820 7

Photoset by Deltatype Ltd, Ellesmere Port, Cheshire
Printed in Great Britain by
Clays Ltd, St Ives plc

Contents

Acknowledgements

Our sincere appreciation is due to Patrick Eagar (nos. 1–6, 8, 11–15, 17, 18), Graham Morris (no. 7) and David Munden (nos. 9, 10, 16, 19, 20) for their generous assistance with photographs. We are equally grateful to Bob Sedgwick for the author photograph; to Jacqueline Blair for her invalulable research and editorial contributions; and to Christine Forrest for providing the England batting and bowling averages set out in the appendix and for her tireless scrutiny of the text.

Between 13 February 1981 and 19 February 1992, ninety-five players represented England, with varying degrees of success, under the uniformly intense, and often unfair, scrutiny of the media. To those cricketers is owed the principal debt.

Introduction

In February 1991, I completed a book, *The Narrow Line*, with Geoff Cook, which attempted to outline the principles that underlie contemporary professional cricket. Now, a year later, Nick Cook and I have, in some senses, sought to apply basic principles to a specific practice: England Test cricket through a period of just over ten years. Why, we ask, were adequate resources of natural talent not translated, for most of the time, into achievement on the field itself? A recurrent theme in our examination is that of the England cricket team's failure to do justice to the playing abilities at their command. While that necessarily involves the notion of specific cricketers repeatedly falling short of their potential, this alone does not explain why authority, and especially the climate in which authority operated, allowed this to be so. Undoubtedly, it is far simpler to write history along such neat lines, ignoring those difficult areas which complicate the account. There will certainly be occasions, unintentional but probably avoidable, when we have erred from analysis into the dynamics of story-telling.

At the opposite extreme, when dealing with the factual weight of 119 Test matches involving ninety-five England players, lies the danger of merely annotating scorecards to provide potted résumés of every passing series. A certain amount of fact is essential, both to illustrate the issues under consideration and to remind the reader of what actually took place. But it is impossible to record all the salient performances; and since any selection of highlights may tend towards bias, the book is perhaps best read in conjunction with full match details.

The hazard of which I have been most acutely aware is that of slipping into the tone of wisdom after the event. There is an important difference between perspectives confirmed by passing years and the implication, for example, that specific selection decisions had predictable outcomes. The text tries to recall how things appeared at the time and thus distinguish culpable error from misconceptions which were widely shared. Issues are most often clouded by attitudes which are only eventually understood as conflicts of interest rather than as matters of mere disagreement. To offer a still-controversial example: the 1980s echoed to the debilitating argument that politics and sport should not mix. The fact that this line was orchestrated, at the political level, by a lobby which was staunchly pro-South African escaped general attention in the media. It is now quite obvious that only political developments could ever have resolved the issue of contact with South Africa, a fact it would have been helpful to acknowledge from the start.

More directly pertinent is the fact that the causes which, ever more palpably, contributed to England's decline were ignored – or at least left unexplored – by those who alone had the power to act, because their prime concern was not to arrest this slide and address key deficiencies. Rather their concern was with a spurious idea of what constituted 'entertainment' and with pursuing 'success' at a purely county level. The central question of why England were failing in Tests was thus subordinated to what, in essence, were matters of commercial self-interest. Though the debate was hardly couched in such explicit terms, they were the very crux of the issue and probably, alas, remain so still.

One final introductory point needs to be made. No history is ever neutral; it will always entail a certain angle of attack. Unless wedded to the dictates of propaganda, however, this need not imply any conscious distortion or omission of fact. But the ways of seeing and explaining a process are many. It is an illusion, perhaps invited by the very spectacle of sport itself, that events on the field must be interpreted by reference to the physical participants alone. Thus it is that the popular press, most notably, seeks all its answers in the shortcomings of the particular players engaged in a given match. These will certainly have some relevance, and where such shortcomings demand it, this book has offered comment. But too often in the 1980s, players were attacked simply because they were the most conveniently identifiable targets – for criticism, at best, and virulent abuse at worst. If this analysis is informed by a certain perspective, then, it is avowedly one in sympathy with the professional outlook.

I believe, moreover, that this has far more in common with the view of the genuine devotee than is generally realised by those who administer the game.

May 12 1992 Neville Scott

1
The Roots of Decline

On 1 September 1981, at the end of one of the most exhilarating Test series in the game's history, the mood among England cricket followers, and indeed in the nation at large, was almost euphoric. England, now under the captaincy of Mike Brearley, had entered the third Test at Headingley already 1–0 down. After the Australians had batted first, England, following on, found themselves at 135–7 on the fourth afternoon still 92 runs short of preventing defeat by an innings. In eighty minutes, Botham and Dilley then added 117 for the eighth wicket. Botham went on to total 149 not out, on the final day, before Bob Willis, bowling like a man in a hypnotic trance, took 8–43 as Australia, requiring just 130 to win, were dismissed for 111.

Batting last again in the next Test at Edgbaston, Australia, this time seeking 151, had reached 87–3. The remaining seven wickets then crashed for 34 runs and England led the series 2–1. In a final spell of twenty-eight deliveries, in which he conceded only a single run, Botham removed each of the last five Australian batsmen. Lightning had struck twice. When the scene shifted to Old Trafford, England collapsed in their second innings to 104–5 midway through the match. As Botham came to the crease, his side's lead was 205 and the game was still in the balance. Two hours later he fell for 118, the last 90 of his runs taken from only forty-nine balls, and another Test had been completely transformed. With an hour and a half to spare, England went on to complete victory by 103 runs and so retain the Ashes.

The bare facts of that summer are so astounding in themselves that they refuse embellishment still. Ten years later, it is as difficult to find adequate words of description as it was at the time. In the glow of these events, cricket became not merely exciting or fashionable but positively chic; a conversational acquaintance with cricket was a requisite social grace. It was inconceivable then that by the end of the decade England cricket might be deemed suitable only for jest. By 1989, and through at least the three years before that, everything had altered. Mockery and scorn were now the standard accompaniments to any reference to the national side.

It is this question of popular perception which governs the breadth of our survey. Logically, perhaps, a review of the modern era should begin earlier – with the return of one of England's banned players (Underwood) for the three-Test series in Australia, in 1979–80, which marked international cricket's post-Packer settlement. Unquestionably, though, the high point against which England's subsequent decline came to be measured – fairly or otherwise – was the triumph of 1981. And since part of the drama of that triumph turned on the apparent rejuvenation of Botham, we include the West Indies series two months earlier, his last as captain, as a necessary prelude.

For about three years, relative optimism prevailed before things began to sour. Statistically, at least, much evidence can be adduced that the period from February 1986 to September 1989 represented the worst interval in English cricket since the first-ever Test match of March, 1877. Moreover, it was a period preceded by a further two years (1984 and 1985) of evident, if far less pronounced, decline. But results are only part of the story. If we are to understand fully the demise of England's cricket through the decade, and the sense of disaffection and lack of direction which seemed to afflict it, then it is the public response to those results which is as significant as the factual record. It is ironic that the watchword of the era was the ever repeated refrain 'politics and sport should not mix'. Cricket has never been divorced from the social forces which have determined the world in which it is played. Certainly we cannot begin to offer the fullest account of England's decline without reference to the cultural and political climate within which it occurred.

Whether or not the tables below can be said to prove that cricket was at its lowest ebb is less important than the fact that, by 1989, it was universally felt to be so. In the 1980s failure was not excused, it was despised. In so far as this intolerance eventually swept away the amateur regime which tried to manage and guide English cricket, perhaps it proved beneficial. But in contributing to the insecurity and irrationality of the time, it helped change the attitude of almost a generation of cricketers both to the game itself and to its highest, Test match form.

In the table below, England's standing at the end of the decade is compared with previous periods of intense decline. From the start of the 1981 series until the end of 1983, the record was P28 W11 L6 D11. Through 1984 and 1985, the element of failure crept in: P23 W5 L9 D9. Thereafter the descent was catastrophic. Exactly how helpful such comparisons are is open to dispute. Though the ratio of wins to defeats in 1986 to 1989 (1:6) contrasts bleakly with each of the earlier three eras (1:2), it can be argued that the only half-appropriate comparison will be with results against Australia or, since 1945, with West Indies. Victories over the other, weaker, nations in earlier periods must be discounted. Yet if we compare only results against the strongest sides, the record against West Indies from 1986 to 1989 (P10 W0 L9 D1) is equally discouraging. Even if we pursue a more favourable gloss by excluding these West Indies games, the overall record (P30 W3 L10 D17) remains meagre.

PERIODS OF DECLINE

1897–1902	P	W	L	D
v Australia	20	3	11	6
v South Africa	2	2	0	0
Overall	22	5	11	6

1920–1925	P	W	L	D
v Australia	15	1	12	2
v South Africa	10	5	1	4
Overall	25	6	13	6

Nov. 1946–Jan. 1951	P	W	L	D
v Australia	15	1	11	3
v South Africa	10	5	0	5
v West Indies	8	1	5	2
v New Zealand	5	0	0	5
v India	3	1	0	2
Overall	41	8	16	17

21 Feb. 1986–29 Aug. 1989	P	W	L	D
v Australia	12	2	5	5
v West Indies	10	0	9	1
v New Zealand	6	0	1	5
v India	3	0	2	1
v Pakistan	8	0	2	6
v Sri Lanka	1	1	0	0
Overall	40	3	19	18

The point, of course, is that it was precisely because England were now losing to sides which hitherto they had been expected to beat that discontent was so intense. England had lost a home series to both New Zealand and Pakistan for the first time in their history. Indeed, they had failed to win any of their previous three series against either side. By August 1989, England had been victorious in only one of nine successive series and had now lost their last 'result' series against every other nation, a uniquely humiliating record.

The disarray in which the England team floundered as they passed through eleven defeats in the twenty-five games during the final three years of the 1980s – for the slender consolation of a solitary victory over Sri Lanka – was reflected in the home series of 1988 and 1989. Twenty-three cricketers, and four separate captains, were employed against West Indies and, after the intervening tour of India was cancelled by the host government, twenty-nine cricketers faced Australia in the six Tests of the following summer. On 1 August that year, a second 'rebel' tour of South Africa was announced, thus neatly providing, with impeccable timing, the final straw. Hope, apparently, consisted in no more than the thought that things could not get any worse.

It was the peculiar misfortune of English cricket that its deterioration from the start of 1984 took place in the context of an era which not only desired success but demanded it. Indeed, it seemed to many of the participants that this was part of the problem. Failure was unwelcome enough in itself, but the atmosphere created by much of the coverage of this period left the impression that players were accused not simply of losing cricket matches but of flagrant moral crimes. Personal media attacks on cricketers were not new; even in earlier years of comparative success, reports which could denigrate rather than applaud were clearly more attractive to sports editors. The same Botham who was made a great British hero after his century at Leeds had been considered a disgrace to his country only thirteen days before. In previous eras of cricketing decline, the nature of comment upon the game was infinitely more sympathetic and reasoned, its function to assist with constructive assessment. Now, for the contemporary popular press, the chance to villify or ridicule appeared all.

The reasons for this shift are complex, but seem to owe much to Britain's long fall from international significance. Gradually, through the course of the last twenty or so years, sportsmen in all fields have become scapegoats for a wider decline. Just as sporting success seems to be translated by the popular press into the message that 'Britain is great again', so sportsmen who fail can be made to bear a profound weight of national frustration.

More specifically, we can point to the effects of the redefinition of the sport which the Packer ethos has entailed. Sensationalism, wilful controversy and the presentation of cricket not as a team game but as gladiatorial combat are the dubious bequest of Packer cricket. A popular press which, embracing this version with delight, deals always in personalities, and reduces complicated issues to matters of individual right or wrong, personal praise or blame, is particularly unsuited to the subtleties of cricket. The culmination of this approach was surely the infamous headline in 1987 which could label an England captain 'Gatt the Pratt'. English cricketers will claim, for the most part quite honestly, that they do not expect to open a newspaper and find praise for their play when they have performed poorly. Yet there is a vast distinction for the player between accepting such criticism and discovering a cartoon of himself in the sports pages with an axe drawn through his head, under the headline 'Time for the chop'.

In its implicit denial of the game's dignity and in its relish for abuse, the tone of such coverage – for the player as much as for the public – could hardly fail to erode the respect in which cricket was held. At one, no doubt, with the new values of the 1980s which, at their most strident, would hail success indiscriminately and pillory failure, it was an approach which continuously undermined the self-belief and self-confidence of cricketers. More than that, it was changing the very nature of the game they had entered. The lure of South African money was undoubtedly all the more enticing for those who felt that their efforts at home, far from being acknowledged, would be derided, often quite viciously. Crudely, the question which faced many players was, 'If Test cricket is not particularly enjoyable, why not accept a lucrative escape?'

It is a pity, to say the least, that, with a handful of laudable exceptions, the media's relentless drive to reduce cricket to spectacle contributed to a wider failure in the game to analyse how events were moving. For there were clear cricketing issues which underpinned England's decline. If these were recognised at all at the time, they were certainly not addressed with any consistency or rigour. The critical problem here concerned the lack of a spearhead for the England attack, a matter which to a large extent entailed the question of who was to support Willis in his final seasons and, more importantly, who would take over when Willis retired.

The other periods of decline rested, quite crucially, on this absence of a wicket-taking England attack. In the aftermath of both World Wars, this situation reflected the fact that, with domestic cricket in abeyance, the process of replenishment had been interrupted. New bowlers, with the opportunity to develop and test their skills in the county game, took time to come through. As a generalisation, continuing success at international level is determined not by the runs which are scored (which enable a side to stay in the game and compete through five days) but on the cheapness of wickets and the frequency with which they are taken. While the spearhead which can deliver these wickets has not always exclusively involved fast bowling, in the long term that element has always been pre-eminent and today, on covered pitches, it is more important than ever. The post-war sequence which had seen Trueman give way to Snow and Snow to Willis had now reached a hiatus. It can be seen with hindsight that the lack of a firm and strong-minded strategy to tackle this problem, through at least the six years to 1989, was at the heart of England's demise.

It is a fact that throughout the decade in question, England Test teams have been fashioned by a body of selectors whose choice of captain and team members appears to connect with no settled game plan or strategy for a series. Since the selectors, individually and collectively, play such an important role in any Test series, their names have been included with those of each squad in the pages that follow.

An inherent problem in English cricket has been that, for the most part, selection is not a matter of distinguishing between the great and the average but between the good and the better. That is to say there will usually be several excellent, reliable county bowlers, two or three of whom must be nurtured into Test cricketers. The key here is to make the choice early, keep faith with the decision and offer every support to the player concerned.

If asked to nominate the two bowlers who should have been consistently prominent in England cricket through much of the 1980s, the majority of county professionals would unhesitatingly opt for Dilley and Foster. Dilley they would identify as, initially, an out-and-out fast bowler with an awkward action. In time he developed into a county performer who retained considerable, worrying pace but consistently swung the ball away in the air. Foster would ideally be seen, at Test level at least, as a first-change bowler whose intelligence and improvisation would complement the strike attack.

Far from pursuing continuity in its fast-bowling policy, however, England's Test selection was characterised by two elements: an increasingly unjustifiable and unfair reliance on Botham as the core of the attack, and a vacillation and experimentation in the choice of those bowlers to accompany him. We will return to this first point later. Some statistics are appropriate to illustrate the second. Until he withdrew from Test cricket after 16 July 1984, Willis played in thirty-three of the forty-one matches in the period under review. In contrast, Dilley played in only forty-one Tests from his début, at the age of twenty in December 1979, to his defection to South Africa ten years later. Foster, who also opted for 'rebel' cricket in August 1989, at the disappointingly early age of twenty-seven, had played in only twenty-eight of a possible sixty-three Tests, since his début in August 1983. The two played as team-mates in the same Test side just eight times.

Prior to the announcement of this second 'rebel' tour, England had also, at various times but equally briefly, employed Capel, Ellison, Jarvis, Lawrence, Lever, Newport, Radford, Sidebottom, Les Taylor and Thomas. Others were used to fill the fast-bowling breach of the decade at greater length: DeFreitas twenty-six Tests (to August 1991); Pringle twenty-five; Cowans nineteen; Malcolm eighteen; Small seventeen; Allott thirteen. What is absent here is the kind of record of longevity – in an age when more Tests are played than in any other – which might indicate a decisive and aware attempt to establish the bowling spearhead so integral to international success.

It needs to be conceded immediately that part of the problem for England's selectors in the decade was a continuing difficulty both with injury and what might be termed 'attitude' in its chosen faster bowlers. We will consider both aspects shortly. Injury apart, though, it is debatable whether at any stage either Dilley or, more especially, Foster felt genuinely secure in his Test place. The point was also often raised that helpful pitches in county cricket distorted the picture and misled onlookers as to the international potential of English bowlers. This argued for precisely the kind of long-term exposure to Test conditions, under sympathetic guidance, which England players were denied. Neil Foster, for example, was brought to the fore, with the expert assistance of Keith Fletcher, in the context of a fine Essex attack which invariably enjoyed the cushion of innumerable, quickly-made runs. That England failed to get the best out of Foster suggests not that this domestic background flattered his abilities, but that England lacked exactly the kind of foresight and planning which are the hallmarks of team success at county level. Not only did England bowlers lack confidence in the selection process, they were deprived of long-term goals and of settled national captains in whose strategic thinking they could consider themselves to figure. In short, cricketers, and particularly spearhead bowlers, could not feel part of any established, far-sighted plan. On the contrary, the selectors seemed merely to react, usually in haste and often in fright, to short-term failure.

The changes which have been belatedly brought about under the galvanising influence of Gooch have involved working to an outlook which embraces more than a single Test or even a single series. Gooch's approach, supported by Micky Stewart and Ted Dexter, reflects the realisation that players must be given every chance to play in an uninterrupted number of Tests. The reality which informs this attitude is that an England Test side will not in the main comprise exceptional talents – which effectively select themselves – but good county players who must be granted an opportunity to develop.

Before the resignation of Peter May in November 1988, after seven years as chairman of selectors, the English way was not only literally amateur but, more damagingly, amateurish in its lack of method and philosophy. Those empowered to choose England teams earned their livings outside the game. To county professionals, their visits to watch potential Test players appeared both random and infrequent; the opinions which they sought were more likely to be those of press men and administrators than of players, coaches and umpires. Once chosen, a bowler had perhaps two Tests in which to make his impact before the selectors would bow to the chorus of acid comment in the popular press and seek a fresh candidate. This, in itself, would make it less likely that the discarded player would do well on his eventual return. His brief exposure to cricket at the highest level was less a benefit to the advancement of his game than a debilitating and inhibitory warning of what to expect next time, should success again prove elusive.

In direct contrast was a contemporary Australian determination, in the period of England's decline, to keep faith with the players whom Border began to assemble after receiving the captaincy in 1985. These he identified as the nucleus of his future team and, despite bitterly discouraging early results, the Australians were prepared to back the wisdom of their approach and wait for the corner to be turned. Such an admirably rational attitude undoubtedly reflected the Australian selectors' belief and confidence in their own fitness to judge. They were able to maintain this resolve because the Australian press and public, though critical of specific shortcomings at specific times, were very evidently behind their team and clearly wished it well. For England players, such support was altogether less assured. The Test side began to play more in fear of the attacks it would incur than in the hope of understanding or encouragement.

The 1980s were a decade characterised by new money and by economic depression in those industrial areas which had historically provided the wealth of Britain. The caricatures of the age became yuppy foreign exchange dealers who, a generation earlier it was suggested, would have been hawking their wares from market barrows. Even at the level of government, those who generated and promoted the attitudes of the new Britain were no longer patricians but of a middle-class, or humbler, origin. Within this aura, the selection processes of the England Test teams, so redolent of amateur worthiness, were a rather odd reminder of a bygone age. For some time, as counties became preoccupied with making money of their own, the selectors were allowed to persist almost by default. And it was probably money which, in the end, led the counties to act: if English cricket had become a laughing stock, it was unlikely to retain either corporate sponsorship or spectator support.

While it would be false to pretend that the passing of the old guard was for even a moment mourned within England's professional ranks, the selectors' task was rarely made any easier by the prevalence of injury in the contemporary game. This is especially true of fast bowlers and, given their centrality to Test success, injury had a further undeniable bearing on England's decline. Nor is it a problem which the new régime has managed to evade: the absence of Angus Fraser, for example, caused plans to be redrawn in 1991.

Bowlers of previous decades often express some amazement at

the levels of present-day injury. There are several reasons why this should have become a peculiarly modern phenomenon. The amount of domestic one-day cricket now places such different demands on the bodies of bowlers that rhythm, the secret of avoiding stress and strain, is forever disrupted. The volume of overs completed in a season is less relevant in this regard than the types of different cricket between which these overs are spread. Moreover, this very diversity of competitions also ensures that the amount of play which retains a genuine bite, 'pressure cricket' as it is often labelled, is greater than in the past. The attempt to bring a consistent match contribution to three separate one-day tournaments and to a Championship which rewards each of the top five counties, as well as to Test cricket and one-day internationals, involves a greater intensity of endeavour if not a quantitatively greater workload. It is also the case that injuries which formerly curtailed or blighted professional careers are now far more likely to be diagnosed and treated. Thus the bowler who today appears to break down several times in his ten or so years at the top might in the past have retired early, or forever carried a problem which limited full effectiveness.

The fact is that neither of the two bowlers who were the essential spearheads of England sides from the late 1960s to the early 1980s, Snow and Willis, was particularly renowned for his services to his respective county. Snow more than once fell foul of his Sussex committee for an alleged lack of all-out effort in the domestic game. Willis, with altogether more accommodating employers, famously took only thirteen Championship wickets for Warwickshire in the same 1981 season in which he achieved twenty-nine invaluable successes during England's victory over Australia. To approach the issue from another perspective, it is doubtful indeed whether Foster, for example, would have been physically able to perform for Essex with quite the devotion he so admirably displayed in 1990 and 1991 had he at the same time been engaged in Test cricket. Both Snow and Willis were established England forces, their places in the side largely assured. For younger men trying to break into the team, or regain a place after being dropped, the requirement to maintain consistent performance on several fronts is altogether more severe.

Unavailability due to injury, then, undoubtedly played its part in the absence of a regular, settled front-line attack through our period. It is unfair to place the entire weight of criticism on the selectors for the instability and uncertainty which attended England's decline. And just as there were fitness problems with most of the spearhead bowlers cited above so, too, many would raise questions about their attitudes as they sought international careers. With the exception, perhaps, of the admirably stable Gladstone Small, the early efforts of, for example, Dilley, Cowans and DeFreitas were characterised by levels of inconsistency which in part derived from a lack of maturity.

Why some modern players should fail to bring a level-headedness and resolve to their cricket at an early age – in contrast, allegedly, to the professionals of earlier times – again invites a debate more appropriate to social history than to a cricket book. In a rather woolly, and certainly irresoluble discussion, all kinds of factors are variously cited, from the ending of National Service to contemporary consumerism, many of which reflect political prejudice rather than calm analysis. From a purely cricketing perspective, and in defence of the players of the period, there are surely objective reasons why Test cricket in the 1980s did invite both an insecurity and a tension which prevented some from doing themselves justice. Prime here was the apparently haphazard selection and the absence of any evident prospectus, far less any blueprint, for England's future.

The question of individual attitude and character, without which sustained Test success will fail to materialise – whatever a player's level of innate ability – is less straightforward than it is often presented to be. The inability to handle the pressure of Test cricket derives as much from a lack of organisational support for the player as from his own personal deficiencies. Similarly, growth into a mature, hardened Test professional can be understood only in the context of the background against which he develops. To refer again to Neil Foster, we find a cricketer who seems to exude confidence but perhaps lacks, deep down, the assurance his demeanour would suggest. Never at a loss for a word in the dressing-room, he none the less needs to be convinced of his value to a side and of his place in its thinking. As such he was peculiarly unsuited to the haziness of England cricket. An apposite contrast here would be with the transition of DeFreitas from indifferent, desultory performer – just one of several hopeful seamers – into the outstanding Test bowler of the 1991 West Indies series. Perhaps more than anybody else, DeFreitas, whom many were prepared to consign to permanent under-achievement, has responded to the clarity of Gooch's outlook and to his inclusion in his captain's plans.

If the lack of a spearhead to the England attack after Willis is the prime cricketing reason for decline in the 1980s, then glaringly absent from the discussion so far has been Ian Botham. Until August 1987, Botham was effectively the core around which the attack was built, appearing in sixty-three of the seventy-six Tests which had taken place since the start of 1981. He was the man upon whom the side relied for the bulk of its wickets and who would typically bowl more overs than any other member of the attack. But the bare facts of Botham's bowling record speak volumes. From his début in July 1977 to the end of the 1981 Australia series, Botham took 202 wickets in forty-one Tests at 21.20. On seventeen occasions he achieved five wickets in an innings. Through the ten years from that series until September 1991, however, his subsequent fifty-eight Tests produced 178 wickets at 36.28. Only ten times in this period did he take five wickets in an innings.

With the unfair benefit of hindsight such figures would seem to establish that the absolute primacy of Botham, as a bowler, in England's cricket was an error. From the period of his greatest triumph, the 1981 series, Botham's bowling potency, while certainly not disappearing, greatly declined. To build a side's hopes around such sharply diminished returns necessarily invited problems. For long periods, the belief in Botham regaining his old touch was near total. Willis had seen Botham at his best and thus forever carried the expectation that crucial match-winning analyses would at some stage be rediscovered and turn a series. To a degree this was also the attitude of Gower when he succeeded Willis as captain. The selectors, also, retained the memory of Botham performances which had brought England many of their earlier victories. When eventually it began to be conceded that perhaps he was not the decisive bowling factor he once was, Botham's role as the side's all-rounder inherently made for further difficulties. Unless the nettle was to be grasped and Botham was to be selected purely as a batsman, or as a batsman with a fifth bowler's function at best, then the balance of the England attack would always be upset. To go into a Test with often only four bowlers, and effectively guarantee that Botham would be one of them, both reduced the force of the attack as a unit and narrowed the remaining selection options.

Were the figures for Botham's earlier career inflated? Though often directed at teams which lacked their Packer players, Botham's bowling in that time, in terms of swing and movement off the seam at lively pace, was great by any standards – consistently, in short, he produced deliveries which would take wickets against Test opponents of the highest calibre. Rather, the key to his subsequent decline is perhaps in the fact that the younger Botham played within excellent bowling units which ascribed to him a particular role. His attacking readiness to pursue wickets, even where this entailed conceding runs, complemented the varied all-round abilities of his colleagues. The later Botham, now as the linchpin of the attack, arguably failed to adjust his game to new requirements and concentrate more on what would be termed 'percentage' bowling.

This is hardly surprising. If certain methods have served you spectacularly well, there is no immediate incentive to alter your mental approach. Sustained by popular affection and his status as a superstar, and invariably able to reassert himself with consistent batting and fielding contributions, Botham perhaps too belatedly examined his bowling returns. It can be argued that he persisted with ultra-aggressive, strike-bowling methods even when, manifestly, they were not bringing the rewards they hitherto offered. While batting genius can be maintained almost intuitively, few bowlers will gain continuing success if they fail to think about or practise their game. Gradually, Botham's mind began to turn from the development of his cricket. He was, quite understandably, distracted by scandalous levels of press intrusion into his private life, and increasingly he escaped into an entourage of minders and friends who were not best placed to assess his game.

Periodically, the magic of old would return with some heroic bowling feats, his 8–103 against the 1984 West Indians at Lord's being outstanding as a magnificently sustained performance. Set against that, however, might be his attitude earlier in the year at Christchurch when New Zealand humiliated England by an innings and 132 runs. Declaring immediately that the pitch was woefully substandard, Botham, rather than bowling careful line and length, pitched short and indulged in endless experimentation. Willis apart, the attack contained Cowans, in just his ninth Test, and Pigott, drafted in for his one Test cap owing to widespread injury in the squad. Botham's seventeen overs conceded 88 runs for the sole wicket of Martin Crowe, and New Zealand achieved a match-winning 307.

Genuinely decisive analyses had become more infrequent and fewer wickets were gained against the opposition's top order. In the face of this, Botham could adopt a curiously fatalistic attitude at times, arguing that the wheel of fortune was turning against him and trusting implicitly in the approach which had served him so superbly in the past and which, he believed, would eventually serve him again. While there is scope for that outlook in the context of an experienced and talented Test attack, which can regain lost ground should aggressive methods prove expensive, there was less justification in an England side which lacked Willis, its leading strike bowler, say, or contained impressionable and inexperienced young newcomers. For too long Botham failed to come to terms with the fact that the attitude which had made him one of the most feared opponents in the game needed to be rethought in different circumstances.

Part of the problem here was that others in positions of influence on the England scene effectively deferred to Botham's own estimate of his strengths. They, too, recalled matches won by inspired bowling performances and, unsurprisingly, were reluctant to steer his efforts in a different direction. The effect of such thinking was to delay English cricket's self-examination. This situation can hardly be seen as a failing in Botham alone; though a senior player, it was not Botham who was charged with the game's future. If England teams were to be given game plans which entailed changing Botham's role from focal all-rounder to batsman, then the decision could hardly reside with the man himself. Moreover, if the model which Botham offered – of success through infinite self-belief – was deemed inappropriate for newcomers of altogether lesser ability, it was for others to point this out and provide such newcomers with guidance.

Botham's awesome talents, and his status as the greatest all-rounder England has produced this century, are beyond dispute. But in the decade under discussion, Botham was consistently a less formidable bowler (and, let it be added, a considerably better batsman) than any of his three great contemporaries, Richard Hadlee, Imran Khan and Kapil Dev. And, as a generalisation, it is bowling, not batting, which will win a Test series. For most of the six years until 1987, with the soundest of reasons at first, England placed pivotal reliance on Botham as a bowler, even as his powers waned. To a degree, England also failed in consequence to promote the careers of likely alternative bowlers and develop them for the years to come. From this failure to resolve the Botham question followed, perhaps to a quite critical extent, many of the specifically cricketing difficulties of the decade.

It may be thought by some that the analysis to date has tended to let off England cricketers rather lightly. Expressions of press reproof in the 1980s were often accompanied by the complaint, implicit or otherwise, that cricketers cared rather too much for financial reward and rather too little about their game. Before the intervention of Packer cricket, professionals had never been particularly well paid. The history of their status is largely unchanging: in the depression of the 1930s, for example, they were better rewarded than the average skilled worker, and they did at least have employment. For its part, the abolition of a distinction between amateur and professional in 1963 brought with it a greater security, but until the Packer incursion of 1977 to 1979, there had been no significant shift in the purely material attractions of the game. Thus in the immediate aftermath of the Packer period, the player's perception of his profession changed more in the space of about five years than in the preceding hundred. It is hardly astounding, in retrospect, that this should have occasioned changes in attitude which, in most cases perhaps, lacked balance and perspective. Money, both in society and in cricket, began to dominate conversations as never before. The abiding, if false, impression was that the game was awash with the potential for gain and that this could not last forever.

Rumour and a sense that the gravy train should not be missed fed this new perception. As stories circulated that given individuals had gained inordinately, so others were the more moved to seek some of this elusive, and often illusory, largesse. It was a feeling all the more acute for those whose span in the game was coming to its end and for whom the fear of just failing to catch the tide of history quite naturally loomed large. English cricketers required some time to come to terms with these changes. Where all would agree in principle that the moment an England side had gathered in its dressing-room thoughts of money should be put aside, in practice this did not, and probably could not, always occur. While the future structure of English cricket was still perceived to be in the process of formulation, and the place of the England cricketer in relation to this structure was only slowly emerging, it was undeniably the case that financial issues could distract sides from the game in hand.

The English cricketer's search for a new identity, however, his balancing of allegiances to bank balance and game, only accompanied decline; it did not begin to explain it. The key cricketing causes which we have already identified were altogether more decisive. Yet in a way, of course, all these elements were inextricable. If you distrust the consistency of selectors, doubt the good faith of the media and fear that the game lacks direction, your thoughts will more readily incline to self-interest. Moreover, it is easy to underestimate the influence which a legacy of unbroken failure begins to exert on a side. On one level, the enforced changes dictated by the second 'rebel' tour brought to prominence a generation of players with a rather less confused sense of their relationship to a much altered game. In addition, it introduced to the side those who had not been caught up in the cycle of demoralisation which the process of prolonged defeat tends to feed.

It is altogether easier to fight for a cause if you have experience of having done so with success in the past. The more a side's experience, despite its best efforts, has been one of failure, so the prospect of further failure seems to become almost inescapable. More graphically, perhaps, the sting of defeat is not quite so bitter for a side which has tasted if often before. The demoralised state of English cricket in the Australian series of 1989, played against the background of yet another round of imminent defections to South Africa, had become so endemic that the only solution seemed to lie in wholesale change and with it, more importantly, the regeneration of self-belief and of the will to win. The departure of sixteen cricketers, half of whom had played in the series, made the turn to new blood unavoidable. In itself, this fact could hardly ensure rejuvenation; necessity does not automatically become a virtue. But for the first time in years, England selected a tour party with a coherent game plan in mind. Moreover, the captain and manager gained the authority and resources to give this party a clear sense of what was expected.

Most of the new players had come into the game after a period of change which had transformed the levels of financial reward available to Test cricketers. The side which was to play the third Test in Bridgetown the following April had won, on average, just 12.64 caps per player – the most inexperienced team put into the field in the period under review. For these players, the money-making opportunities which international status implied were now a settled feature of the game; the disorientating changes of the early 1980s had run their course and present scales of payment were, in effect, all they had ever known. They perhaps did not feel so insistently, therefore, the urge to make the most of new prospects. Lucrative prospects were now no longer new; they were the assured accompaniment of consistent endeavour and commitment on the international stage. Players could better distinguish between the time to talk money and the time to think cricket.

It is perhaps appropriate to say something more here about the cricketing effects on the decade of the loss of players, first to Packer and then to 'rebel' tours. On the face of it, at least, it is a factor which would appear to have an inevitable bearing on both inconsistency and decline. Logic might seem to suggest that the greater the availability of eligible players, the better the chosen England side. Perhaps instructively, the statistics indicate the contrary. If we divide the interval since the end of the Packer years into periods of availability and non-availibility, we find the following figures:

a) All available (post-Packer)	13/12/79–21/2/82	: P26 W5 L8 D13
b) Players absent (first 'rebel' tour)	22/2/82–29/3/85	: P32 W9 L12 D11
c) All available	13/6/85–1/8/89	: P45 W7 L19 D19
d) Players absent (second 'rebel' tour)	2/8/89–10/2/92	: P26 W8 L8 D10

The players who were ineligible for England selection at various times were:

i) 22/2/82–29/3/85: *First 'rebel' tour to South Africa*:
Amiss, Boycott, Emburey, Gooch, Hendrick, Humpage, Knott, Larkins, Lever, Old, Sidebottom, Les Taylor, Underwood, Willey, Woolmer.

ii) 2/8/89–24/2/95*: *Second 'rebel' tour to South Africa*:
Athey, Barnett, Broad, Chris Cowdrey, Dilley, Ellison, Emburey, Foster, French, Gatting, Graveney, Jarvis, Maynard, Tim Robinson, Thomas, Alan Wells.

(*Given South Africa's return to world cricket, it seems probable that the ban will be lifted before 1995.)

It is worth noting that Amiss, Knott, Underwood and Woolmer had also been banned between 31 August 1977 and 13 December 1979 for their allegiance to Packer. The fact that the loss of these players did not materially affect results – indeed results became relatively more encouraging following each series of defections – perhaps confirms two points: that most England selection is invariably made from a wide group of players of similar ability, and that consistency of selection from this group is therefore of the essence. In the early 1980s, a key problem was that support bowling for Willis did not deliver sufficient wickets. Tempting though it might have been to call up Hendrick, Lever or Old periodically, each of these 'rebels' was thirty-three by the time he reached South Africa. None of them, at that stage, could realistically be thought better bets than those (Allott, Jackman, Cowans, Pringle, Dilley, Foster and Ellison) who fulfilled the same role. Indeed, it is arguable that their availability might only have encouraged yet further the selectors' propensity to change bowlers so readily. If one problem in the decade was that England did not nominate and keep faith with a limited number of fast bowlers, then defections to South Africa did at least limit the options.

Similarly, of those bowlers banned since 1989, only Foster, perhaps, would have lent a significantly wider dimension to the thinking of selectors Dexter, Stewart and Gooch. Indeed it would have been fascinating to see whether the twenty-seven-year-old Foster, under the leadership of his county captain and with security of tenure at last, could have confirmed at Test level the ability his county cricket always indicated. Fearing that injury might blight his future, however, Foster opted for the 'rebel' tour. With Dilley – now thirty and regularly sidelined by back problems – Jarvis, Ellison and Thomas ruling themselves out, selection possibilities narrowed further. Again this appears to have been to the side's benefit, not its detriment. The players' feeling of security was enhanced and, interestingly, the team was not subject to unfair levels of expectation. For once in the 1980s, the media did not clamour for success; if anything, there was an air of genuine sympathy for the thanklessness of England's predicament!

Perhaps the single undoubted cricketing liability of the 'rebel' tours was in the removal from the scene of quality opening batsmen – Gooch (and to a far lesser extent, the forty-one-year-old Boycott) in 1982 and Broad in 1989. Again, the selectors wholly failed to come to terms with these losses. Rather than deciding which batsmen should be earmarked as replacements, they chose nine different openers in the three years of the ban to 1985. And, though the tactical thinking was much more upset by injury here, England played eight different openers in the two years after the second set of defections in 1989.

If the prospect of unauthorised foreign tours was, at an individual level, an undoubted distraction for England cricketers, the actual loss of playing resources which these tours entailed was not, then, a prime element in decline. An altogether more crucial factor, and one which, sadly, had been all too little addressed until the end of the 1980s, was the narrowing of the social base for the game. The near-disappearance of cricket in state education has had an incalculable effect on the year-by-year provision of fresh talent to county staffs. Anybody who spent any time in New Zealand, for example, soon encountered the question, 'How can a country of fifty-five million people fail to find a better team than a country of three million?' Part of the answer, quite simply, is that the number of players coming into the game over the last fifteen to twenty years bears little relation to the size of Britain's population. Where the great majority of children in New Zealand will play cricket in their youth, very few taught in Britain's state schools will automatically have the opportunity to play cricket at school.

If this serious problem for the game has at last been acknowledged, there is still little cause for complacency. Through the admirable efforts of the National Cricket Association, initiatives have centred on sponsoring Kwik Cricket in primary schools and ensuring that a greater number of representative county teams are fielded than ever before for all age groups between twelve and eighteen. Several county clubs, moreover, have instituted coaching schemes and founded centres of excellence. Whilst this provides the incentive for young cricketers to strive for recognised standards, it cannot in itself bring children into the game. There remains a perhaps insurmountable distinction between embedding cricket in the national culture through exposure at school and providing laudably wide-ranging opportunities for those who have already found a way into the game.

Consider, for example, the difference in background between the team which contested the first Test of the decade under discussion, against West Indies in 1981, and the side which played West Indies at Leeds ten years later:

February 1981: Gooch, Boycott, Brian Rose, Gower, Botham, Willey, Miller, Downton, Emburey, Dilley, Old.

June 1991: Gooch, Atherton, Hick, Lamb, Ramprakash, Robin Smith, Russell, Pringle, DeFreitas, Watkin, Malcolm.

The former side contains two players (Gower and Downton) of a public school/university background while the remaining nine are very much in the model of 'traditional' county professionals. The 1991 team, in contrast, fields two of a public school/Oxbridge background, three who were born in Southern Africa and two more who were born in West Indies. The state-educated, English-born category has narrowed to four, including both Gooch, who appeared in the first side, and Ramprakash, who played no cricket whatever at school. Of players of immigrant parentage, Ramprakash is in fact all too unusual in being born in Britain. For the most part, the black players who have brought so much to the England team in our period have spent some part of their formative years in another country. Their introduction to cricket was not, then, a product of British education but of a childhood elsewhere.

Ramprakash apart, the only British-born black cricketer to have represented England has been David Lawrence. Indeed, without the graduates of the excellent Haringey Cricket College (an example which, alas, has not been copied elsewhere), even county cricket would include very few black cricketers who have emerged from a specifically British education. The sole exceptions in 1991 were Gregory Mike (Nottinghamshire) and Paul Weekes (Middlesex). The contrast with football or athletics here should be alarming indeed. At present, England has the nucleus of a good Test side for the medium-term future. Given, however, that up to seven potentially key players in the wider squad were born outside Britain and that the social base for the game continues to dwindle, the prospect is that England will again suffer from the fact that significant sections of its population lack the chance to participate in cricket.

The discussion so far has sought to isolate symptoms of the malaise underlying England's decline which we might broadly term cultural. They relate to the attitudes and outlooks which administrators, players and, to a degree, even the public brought to the game in the 1980s. Other commonly identified, and perhaps overstressed, problems are rather more structural. The influence of one-day cricket or the inadequacy of Championship matches as a preparation for Tests, for example, has been widely debated elsewhere and will not be examined in any depth here. Such concerns are largely now a matter of consensus. The great majority of professional cricketers would argue that, in the interests of the Test side, the Sunday League could beneficially be scrapped and the Championship played over four days rather than three. What prevents such helpful change is, in essence, the financial self-interest of the clubs, a loud echo, again, of the culture of the time.

To re-state, in brief, what are all-too-familiar arguments, we may say that one-day cricket places its emphasis on a lack of specialism where Test success is critically determined by specialists. The prime one-day bowling skill – relative containment – is directly alien to the need in Test cricket to take wickets. Equally, one-day batting prowess, typified by the value of a rapidly improvised 40 against defensive fields, has little to do with the Test requirement to withstand assault and then craft a lengthy hundred. The stereotyped patterns of thought, inherent in the limitation of overs which define one-day cricket, are similarly at odds with the obligation in a Test match to remain fluid and alive to minute shifts of emphasis. In so far as three-day cricket on good batting pitches too often simply replicates the one-day game by consigning the first seven sessions to formal manoeuvring and placing all emphasis on the last-day run-chase, it, too, fails to offer an adequate proving ground for Tests. More to the point, the art of creating victory as a team unit by remaining alert to key moments of opportunity is devalued when so much Championship cricket proves predictable and contrived. The Ashes series of 1990–91, for example, was primarily lost because England failed to turn critical periods to their advantage. The technical skills nurtured by domestic cricket were adequate to the task, but the habit of reading a game and anticipating its fluctuations was no longer second nature.

The fact that these shortcomings at the heart of English domestic cricket have been remarked upon so often to so little material effect says much, alas, about the attitudes which have prevailed in this period. Embracing an age which has made annual balance-sheets more important than long-term investment, counties have pursued a local self-interest to the detriment of the national game. It is only proper that criticism should continue to highlight this. Analysis should always begin at home. If it is unhelpful to look first for excuses, it would be equally unfair not to conclude this survey with reference to something external: the rise of England's opponents. Though, even by its own standards, England cricket did indeed decline – almost terminally – through the 1980s, the cricket of other countries, in general, was stronger than ever before.

Ironically, the exception to this was Australia, the other senior power. Yet by the end of the decade, under a captain, Allan Border, whose efforts were backed at the top by a continuity of leadership and outlook, Australia's rebuilding had produced an authentic Test side. In their batting they were better than for fifteen years. Of the other nations, the New Zealand and Pakistan teams throughout the 1980s were consistently the best either had ever fielded. And if India's side in the decade was arguably not better than Wadekar's team of the early 1970s, it was certainly its equal and remained competitive for a far longer period. For their part, the West Indians had, from 1976, not only the finest team in their own history but the strongest in the history of the game. Other teams bear comparison with West Indies but only in terms of given series or limited sequences of series. It is true that, since 1987, Pakistan have been able to dispute the title of unofficial world champions. No other country, however, had hitherto known such a period of almost unassailable supremacy as that enjoyed for eleven years by the side under Lloyd and, latterly, under Richards.

The present West Indies team, as it undergoes a transition, is perhaps in relative decline. But it remains a measure of their power that the performance of Gooch's side in squaring the 1991 series was arguably the finest English achievement since regaining the Ashes in 1970–71 under Illingworth. The 1992 England series against Pakistan, one of the most eagerly awaited in years, may throw further light both on the quality of Gooch's team and on Pakistan claims to the succession. Only Sri Lanka, who acceded to Test status with an inaugural match in February 1982, have failed to maintain at least rough parity with England through the period under review, losing three of the four games contested. It seems to be one of the very few immutable laws of cricket that, though international-calibre batting can be developed by a new Test nation inside a handful of series, similar bowling ability tends to lag by at least some twenty years. This has been palpably true of Sri Lanka in their first decade. Several very highly rated batsmen have emerged but, largely deprived by political unrest of the chance to develop their spinners at home, few bowlers of better than average county standard have come through.

Such developing strength abroad essentially speaks for itself; it would be pointless to seek an assessment of the relative weight to be attached to England decline as against overseas advance. In their defence, most county professionals would add that the new-found ability of advancing sides to compete on level terms, specifically in England, owes much to the unique opportunities which English cricket presents to overseas players. This is of particular relevance to bowlers who, through their exposure to English conditions and pitches at county and league level, no longer spend much of their first tours coming to terms with an alien environment. While this does not begin to account for the decline of the 1980s, it remains the case that most of the bowlers who won series in England during the decade had enjoyed considerable earlier experience there. A significant advantage held by the home teams of other eras has thus disappeared.

England cricket would do itself an injustice, however, if, in the final analysis, it allowed either overseas developments or the prevalence of injury to distort its reading of the period. The best sides, at all levels, take blame upon themselves. In cricketing terms, the central problem of the decade was that of the Willis succession. For initially quite understandable reasons, it was a problem which, at first, was simply transferred to the accommodating shoulders of Ian Botham. This remained England's solution, despite continuing evidence of its failure, for more than three years and some forty Tests. Whether or not the domestic resources of county cricket could significantly have ameliorated matters is quite another debate. The fact is that no determined organisation and direction of those resources ever took place. Under a variety of captains, and with a constant, bewildering change of personnel, England came merely to pass from one Test to the next.

The 1980s were no time in which to lack purpose. For a virulent press, indecision simply promised the gleeful prospect of further easy prey. In the face of an age whose venom they could not understand, the England selectors appeared to make ever more arbitrary and panic-stricken attempts to placate ignorance. It was a tendency which compounded not only the crisis itself but the confusion of cricketers in a decade which had changed their identity. That they were no longer mere sportsmen was altogether evident; what they were being turned into, in the national mind, was less straightforward. Too often, as the very momentum of decline overwhelmed even the outlines of a way forward, players perceived themselves as no more than fodder for a media which neither wished to explain the disorder nor particularly cared about recovery. And in so far as the media had created a new, non-cricketing audience for its soap opera, this was a public response too. The history of England's decline on the pitch through the decade under discussion was simultaneously, then, a descent into siege mentality and disillusion in the dressing-room. If the fresh hopes of the 1990s are to be sustained, they rest as much, perhaps, on the attitudes which pertain outside cricket grounds as on the fields within.

2
A Prelude: 1981 Revisited

WEST INDIES v ENGLAND, 1980–81

Average England total: 259 *Average West Indies total: 430*

Date	Venue	Result	Caps per Eng. Player
13–18 Feb	Port-of-Spain	*West Indies* by innings and 79 runs	25.91
28 Feb–5 Mar	Georgetown	Cancelled	
13–18 Mar	Bridgetown	*West Indies* by 298 runs	20.64
27 Mar–1 Apr	St John's	Drawn	20.73
10–15 Apr	Kingston	Drawn	21.64

Tour party: I. T. Botham (captain), C. W. J. Athey, D. L. Bairstow (wicket-keeper), G. Boycott, R. O. Butcher, G. R. Dilley, P. R. Downton (wicket-keeper), J. E. Emburey, M. W. Gatting, G. A. Gooch, D. I. Gower, G. Miller, C. M. Old, B. C. Rose, G. B. Stevenson, P. Willey; A. C. Smith (manager). (Because of injury, R. D. Jackman was added to the party later.)

Selectors: A. V. Bedser (chairman), K. F. Barrington, D. B. Close, C. S. Elliott.

In the light of subsequent England performances against West Indies, it is ironic that Botham's brief tenure of the England captaincy was, at the time, thought to be unsuccessful. Admittedly the main public concern was not with the results but with the effect of captaincy on Botham's all-round cricket. Nevertheless Botham himself clearly conceived that his task was to match his opponents, and it did not then appear unrealistic to him that England should seek to do so. Nine of the twelve games in which Botham led

England were against West Indies. More than once at the end of the home series which preceded the Caribbean tour of 1981, he remarked that the challenge should be viewed in its entirety: the home leg was over, and West Indies were marginally ahead, but the contest was not yet finished.

Within only three years it was odd to recall such defensiveness. Though defeated, Botham's side achieved the kind of results later captains would have accepted with open arms. The five-Test series between the two sides in England over the summer of 1980 had seen England do well to lose just 1–0. If it is true that England were assisted in this by appalling weather – without the aid of rain they might have lost by three clear Tests – sides can be judged only against the actual conditions which prevail and in that context England had repeatedly fought with great character.

Botham had not yet captained at county level. When, three years later at Somerset, he did succeed his fellow 1981 tourist, Brian Rose, the most consistent criticism was that his approach was too attacking. Off-spinner Vic Marks, for example, might be given three or four close catchers on an unresponsive pitch, and bowl poorly owing to the pressure this placed upon him. At international level such objections were hardly appropriate. Against West Indies, objective opportunities to attack were necessarily limited and England, like so many sides before and since, found themselves fighting more for survival than for any advantage. In fact, in the Centenary Test against Australia at Lord's in August 1980, the claim had been that Botham was too cautious in refusing Greg Chappell's challenge to score 370 in about ninety overs on the final day.

Botham's aggressive thinking was evident, however, both in the selection policy for the 1981 tour and in the strategy which it implied. It was an approach which was to be critically compromised by the forced return of Willis with injury before the first Test. Indeed, the choice of Robin Jackman, perhaps England's steadiest seamer, as replacement for Willis, indicated that the plan was being rethought and gave the first sign of the side beginning to fall between two stools.

Initially the tour party had coupled Willis and Dilley with Graham Stevenson, a Yorkshire fast bowler who, on his day, was as sharp as anyone in the Championship. From this it was apparent that the Botham approach would be to 'fight fire with fire' rather than seek to restrict the West Indian batsmen and thereby frustrate them into error. Not only do West Indies teams tend to play several strokemakers who favour attack, their strategy in some senses requires this if the accompanying quartet of fast bowlers is to be allowed sufficient time to dismiss opponents twice. An element in Gooch's successful policy ten years later, for example, was a concentration on precisely this desire to contain the West Indies and thereby invite injudicious play. In 1981, such an outlook might have entailed a more central role for Old (who was selected) and the choice of, say, John Lever and Jackman from the outset. Mike Hendrick, another who could have assisted a containment strategy, had declared himself unavailable.

Given the resources at the captain's disposal, the difference between the two approaches, in terms of likelihood of success, was probably minimal. Conditions in the Caribbean are not particularly conducive to an England medium-pacer's ability to swing the ball in the atmosphere and move it off the seam on dampish pitches. The surfaces are invariably bone hard and the amount of swing which can be achieved is limited. Moreover, Botham was not to know that Willis would be injured, nor that this would effectively undermine the stock-bowling role envisaged for Emburey.

Though attack was attempted in the first Test, this policy came to be abandoned for an uneasy combination of initial attack followed by attempted consolidation. The same aggressive approach seemed also to underpin Botham's choice of Roland Butcher for his middle order, despite a batting average the previous (1980) season which, at 39.60, had been unspectacular and placed him only twenty-fourth in the list of those qualified for England. Butcher, the first Englishman of West Indian birth to be selected, was asked to complement the counter-attacking intentions of Rose and Botham himself in contrast to the methods of, say, Boycott or Willey, who were to play a more obdurate role, in the hope of blunting the key West Indian strike weapon of unremitting pace.

Through the course of the last fifteen years, the prime batting demands in any attempt to compete with the formidable power of West Indies have, in theory, become simple to state. Putting such theory into practice has been an altogether different prospect. The fact that West Indies would customarily bowl about thirteen overs an hour, and – in part for that reason – offer very few bad balls to hit, meant that a side needed to bat for approximately one hundred overs per innings to stay in the game. Depending on how well the side's own bowlers then curbed the speed of West Indian scoring, this entailed a match aggregate of perhaps 550 to 600 runs. The problem which sides found, of course, limited though these ambitions may sound in theory, was to bat for longer even than a day. Relatively fresh at all times, West Indian fast bowlers are of such a quality, and achieve such a daunting strike-rate, that the key attribute of the team has been an ability to induce the collapse. Thus, at no point can an opponent's job ever quite seem complete: 200–3 in this context has a repeated tendency to become 225–7.

If a critical score against West Indies is around 250 plus, the typical total of the era was perhaps between 160 and 210. Such was the supremacy which the West Indians so long maintained that they took the field confident in their own minds that the opponent would generally fall those crucial 50 or so runs short. For that reason the West Indian over-rate remained largely immaterial to the side. The scores in the first two Tests of the 1980–81 series, which left England 2–0 down with only two to play, must have seemed all too dismally familiar to the visitors: 178, 169 (which, due to rain, held off defeat until an hour from the close in Trinidad), 122 and 224. Thereafter, on good batting pitches, and with appreciable assistance from the rain in the fourth Test – but principally due to high-quality centuries from each of Willey, Boycott, Gooch and Gower – the tour was completed with considerable cause for pride. The readiness to toil for long periods to save an individual Test, though a series already be lost, was still part of the English game. So indeed was a determination to turn any weather assistance to the side's advantage. The capitulation which would be almost second nature to England teams even four years later had largely not yet appeared.

With England's plan for the series upset by the injury to Willis, hopes were probably terminally dashed as early as the opening Test. Given the strength of West Indies, the rule of thumb which argues, 'If in doubt, play the extra batsman', was probably all the more relevant here. Yet, hoping for the turn traditionally associated with Port-of-Spain, England went into the match with two front-line spinners, leaving a middle order and tail on the scorecard of Botham at five, Willey at six and then Miller, Downton, Emburey, Dilley and Old. Moreover, the attacking option was taken and Gatting omitted, even though Willey was there to act as a second spinner. The revised, alternative approach was only gradually taken up by the fourth and fifth Tests when Willey, operating as an effective stock bowler, completed twenty-eight overs, at 2.21 runs each, in the two West Indies innings possible. For his part, Emburey bowled ninety-one overs at 2.12, which helped prevent West Indies gaining a winning position. Since the second Test had been cancelled, however, West Indies were by now assured of their series victory.

Realistically, after heavy defeat in the first Test, England's sole chance to come back into the reckoning arrived in the next game at Bridgetown. Batting first, West Indies had reached 65–4 when, as invariably they did if the top order failed, Lloyd and Gomes, with the help of dropped catches, combined in a stand of 154 and repaired the bad start. Events in a match subsequently lost seemed of little importance, though, after the second day. During the night, Ken Barrington suffered a fatal heart attack. His death, at the age of fifty, overshadowed all else in the remainder of the series and left a gap in England cricket which, with hindsight, was even more profound than was realised at the time.

Barrington was very much in the mould of his former Surrey team-mate, the later England manager, Micky Stewart. Staunchly professional in outlook, and fiercely loyal to those prepared to give their all in an England cause, he had been one of those cricketers who would not concede that a match was lost until the last ball was bowled. He was of course part of the match-to-match selection process on the tour but was designated assistant manager and was sometimes even known by the older, and, at Test level, now largely outdated title of 'coach'. Unlike Stewart he had no permanent selectorial function.

Barrington's actual role was to explain things to people and listen to their complaints and fears. In this way he acted, to a degree, as an intermediary between the commanding ranks of the game and the players who were supposed to realise the selectors' hopes. He offered an ear to talk to and a store of wisdom which could be drawn upon; in short, he was an experienced and sympathetic figure in whom a player could confide. During a period which saw the characteristic stance of the England professional become one of uncertainty and disaffection, such a function would have been all the more valuable through subsequent years. In fact it was not a position filled on a regular, thought-out basis until Micky Stewart went to Australia in 1986–87 as the specifically cricket counterpart to Peter Lush's office as tour manager.

The potential problem with such a role is either that it has too little genuine power or that, if combined with a selector's remit, it can have too much. Where the function is purely pastoral it runs the risk of being thought merely a token, offering the illusion of sympathy while being in reality ineffectual. But if the role is associated with authority, the player may be reluctant to confess his doubts or concerns for fear this will be construed as weakness. When a cricket manager is also a selector, then, he needs a keen sensitivity to the delicacies of his position if it is to be fulfilled adequately.

Undoubtedly, it was to the considerable detriment of England cricket that, for six years, the vacuum which Barrington so tragically left was filled neither one way nor the other. Moreover, when Stewart was eventually appointed, it understandably took him some time to come to grips with his position and project himself to the game as the figure with whom any professional should feel able to confer. Initially he tended to veer too much towards the untenable position of off-field captain, though he came later to relate to players far more as cricketers with an advanced sense of their own game and less as one who issued instructions. On the practical side, he holds the same responsibility carried by Barrington to relieve the captain of such tasks as supervising nets, ensuring practice facilities are acceptable and so on. More than this, he seeks to be the focus of discussion about a match and, on a wider plane, the barometer of feelings and attitudes in the English game.

It may be wondered whether some of this does not usurp functions which might more properly rest with the Test captain, and in ideal terms the captain should seek absolute control. This is no longer practically feasible, however, a fact England might have acknowledged at this early stage. For example, the captain on a modern tour has to contend with nightly press meetings and television interviews. He has a variety of official engagements to fulfil and sponsorship obligations to meet. Whatever hopes he may have to keep minutely in touch with the development of his side or to monitor individual moods, the full breadth of the task will be beyond him. Prior to the productive alliance which Gooch came to forge with Stewart, no doubt Test captains in our period could have achieved a far more certain feel for the pulse of the English game.

The spirit which Botham's side showed in drawing the final Test of the 1981 tour indicated that the English game was still, at this time, relatively sound. But captains could unquestionably have been assisted in an ever more difficult task had the legacy of Barrington's contribution been built upon.

ENGLAND V AUSTRALIA, 1981

Average England total: 264 *Average Australia total: 265*

Date	Venue	Result	Caps per Eng. Player
18–21 June	Trent Bridge	*Australia* by 4 wickets	30.64
2–7 July	Lord's	Drawn	32.27
16–21 July	Headingley	*England* by 18 runs	37.27
30 July–2 Aug	Edgbaston	*England* by 29 runs	38.55
13–17 Aug	Old Trafford	*England* by 103 runs	39.55
27 Aug–1 Sept	The Oval	Drawn	37.64

I. T. Botham (captain for the first and second Tests), J. M. Brearley (captain for the third, fourth, fifth and sixth Tests), P. J. W. Allott, G. Boycott, G. R. Dilley, P. R. Downton (wicket-keeper), J. E. Emburey, M. W. Gatting, G. A. Gooch, D. I. Gower, M. Hendrick, A. P. E. Knott (wicket-keeper), W. Larkins, C. M. Old, P. W. G. Parker, C. J. Tavaré, R. W. Taylor (wicket-keeper), P. Willey, R. G. D. Willis, R. A. Woolmer.

Selectors: A. V. Bedser (chairman), D. B. Close, J. H. Edrich, C. S. Elliott.

The first three weeks of the 1981 Ashes series were dominated by doubts over the captaincy. By 7 July, when Botham withdrew from consideration on the grounds that speculation had placed intolerable strains upon his family – only for the chairman of the selectors to announce, rather ungraciously, that he would have been replaced anyway – England were 1–0 down with four to play. At Trent Bridge, in a match which at the time seemed tense but would later appear almost soporific, Australia had taken the first Test by four wickets with more than a day to spare. By any objective criteria, the Nottingham pitch, like most of the surfaces in this series, had not been of an adequate Test standard but, in part for that very reason, had produced much enthralling cricket.

Botham undoubtedly had a very good cricket brain to accompany his vast natural ability, but was arguably far better suited to the role of vice-captain. Periodically, he could offer a valuable idea to the bowler or captain and express his thoughts well, but the requirement to concentrate his mind at all times tended to stifle a feel for the game which, to his later detriment sometimes, was largely instinctive. Granted the licence to stand back from play and allow notions to suggest themselves, Botham would provide frequent helpful advice. In short, his thought processes dealt more in flashes of incisive understanding than in constant analysis. Monitoring developments ball by ball is quite another activity. To ask of a man that he should be what, demonstrably, he was not, lacks a certain justice – Botham could produce such astonishing feats precisely because he was the perfect natural cricketer. To demand that, in addition, he should keep a methodical or contemplative eye on events was effectively to deprive him of his unique strengths.

Later in his career, these strengths would sometimes place a severe and largely unsustainable burden upon Willis and Gower. For now, the key concern was with the influence of captaincy on Botham's own individual game. Though he repeatedly repudiated the conclusion himself, it seemed that, in retaining Botham as leader, the England team was effectively denying itself its greatest, single playing resource. Botham's bowling had not in fact been markedly undermined at this stage. In the preceding two series against West Indies, his twenty-eight wickets in all had been taken at 31.32 with 3.17 runs conceded per over – an acceptable, if not startlingly good, return given the strength of the opposition. Specifically on the Caribbean tour, his bowling had not been notably effective and, even in the context of an attack whose faster bowlers were conceding runs quickly, it had not been particularly tight either. But it was the deterioration of his batting which produced most alarm.

In West Indies, a Test average of 10.42 had followed one only marginally more impressive, 18.77, the previous summer. Now, against the Australians, Botham reached the end of the second Test with innings of 1, 33, 0 and 0 behind him. To an extent, Botham was a victim of his own earlier success here. The expectations his record had come to invite made average bowling seem mediocre. But his batting genuinely warranted disquiet.

More significant than such uninspiring statistics alone, perhaps, was the subjective impression which his batting now left. Botham's game began to betray the tentativeness and uncertainty of a man whose natural inclinations were being made to fit a theoretical version of how a captain should play. Intuition and zeal gave way to inference; there was a diffidence about Botham's approach which had never before seemed remotely possible. Moreover, however much he might affect self-assurance, the very fact that his scores continued to be so poor would necessarily have eroded even his confidence. It was not Botham's way to confess to doubt – even though he might know his touch was missing or that his timing was off, he would attempt to bluff his way through with bravado. This series more than any was to prove the extent to which Test cricket rests on psychology. If Botham was concerned, he would not for a moment reveal this even to his team-mates, far less the opposition.

Botham's native exuberance and flair with the bat, then, was shackled by captaincy. A player of immense natural talent, to whom things have come relatively easily, is often slower to understand the nuances of thought and emotion which underlie a less gifted player's approach to his game. For this reason the best players are by no means always the best captains. If this is not an inviolate rule of cricket, as is shown by the example of Greg Chappell, amongst others, it did have a real bearing on the decade ahead. More to the point, when a hitherto untroubling game seems suddenly to go wrong, the naturally gifted player is often less aware of how to fight his way back than the man whose limitations have made cricket a matter of more permanent torment.

If Brearley's part in the events which followed 7 July were ostensibly flattered by Botham innings which twice resurrected England, he takes the fullest credit for giving him his head in opportune circumstances. Brearley related to those around him as separate and particular individuals with distinct identities of their own. When England's position was impossible, he urged Botham not to caution but to glory. Under Brearley, Botham returned once more to being the outstanding all-rounder, indeed the outstanding player, in world cricket. The evident turning point of this series was thus not a dropped catch or even a specific innings. It hinged on the fact that Botham was relieved (and the verb, on this occasion, is entirely apt) of the England captaincy.

It is in no sense our wish to deny the events of the 1981 summer even a moment of their splendour. The displays which the England side came almost routinely to offer, it seemed, from mid-July until September will stay in the minds of those who witnessed them for probably longer than any other feats they will see in a lifetime following the game. Yet it is always helpful to view cricket from the perspective of the opponent. For England players, these games were akin to their finest hour. For Australians, visited by a repeated dislocation of the expected, they were like a recurrent nightmare.

If our question, then, is not, 'How did England win?' but, 'How did Australia lose?' – the question which any self-respecting side must always pose in defeat – the emphasis shifts to a critical loss of nerve at vital times. Australia had beaten England in each match of a three-Test series only sixteen months earlier. Their bowlers performed with remarkably similar records in both 1979–80 and 1981. Moreover, with one exception, the individual batting contributions for each position in the order can be seen to cancel each other out almost exactly. That exception, Greg Chappell, who chose not to tour in 1981, was quite crucial. Rationally, on two of the three occasions when Botham brought England back into the game, his staggering performances, from the Australian point of view, should have been like the passage of a meteor, no more. Thereafter the skies should have resumed their comforting normality and Australia their path to victory. Shattered by the assault, however, they lacked the calm, composed ability of a Chappell to applaud what had gone before and then settle to the sanity-restoring task of easing his side home.

Allan Border, who was to pass his twenty-sixth birthday during the series and had already gained twenty-seven caps, probably came closest to the qualities Australia so sorely missed. At the end of the summer, he recorded scores of 123 not out, 106 not out, and 84 in his last three Test innings of the tour. By this time, though, the series had been lost. Far from the memory of Botham's fight-back at Leeds being erased, the knowledge that Australia had thrown the game away there was to return in each of the following two Tests and blight their ability to compete. Border's wicket in the fourth Test, caught off the glove for 40 when an Emburey delivery bit and lifted to leave Australia 46 runs short at 105–5, was as vital as any of the numberless key events in so desperately close a contest.

Arguably this series had a greater effect on Border's psychology than it did on any of the other individual participants. The future

Australian captain grew up more in the impact of this one set of games than he had done in several successive earlier series. It was appropriate indeed that it should be Border who, eight years later, brought to England an Australian side which inflicted a 4–0 defeat, thus equalling the best-ever win in an Ashes series in England. The mental supremacy which his team was to hold in 1989 was altogether similar to that which England came to achieve in 1981. The professional unit's pride in performance, which England had exhibited in the Caribbean, was again evident in the repeated contribution of essential late-order runs and in a general refusal to surrender. Long before 1989, this was to disappear. England would come to carry a certain unconscious resignation into most of the games they played.

As Botham brought to his team-mates an inspiration which encouraged tailenders to stay with him while he blazed away, so, day by day and session by session, he came to annihilate the self-belief of the Australian side. Indeed, perhaps because it was notably low-scoring, this series was one of the very few in recent times which was arguably won more by batting than bowling. Or, to be exact, batting, in terms of bravura on the one side and periodic disintegration on the other, had an unusually influential bearing. Though Willis's frenzied 8–43 at Leeds, for example, was integral to success, it did not explain victory in the way that, on their own, such Test analyses so often do. Botham's batting made resurgence possible not only in its statistical effect on a match but in its emotional effect on the Australians. In a state of near shell-shock, the Australian bowlers, and the side in general, lost all semblance of confidence. Theirs was perhaps the classic example in the decade of the insidious process of self-doubt, a process which in cricket seems to assume a dynamic of its own and which is often not so apparent from the boundary.

The Australians came to be overwhelmed by a state of mind which the England team properly relished at the time but which would so often, within the next four or five years, afflict their own game quite agonisingly. The psychological dominance which England, and Botham especially, exerted over Australia in that series – a dominance which, in many ways, it is the precise object of sides to achieve in Test cricket – was almost absolute. In truth Australia did most things right in 1981. But it is exactly when a team knows that, in general, it is playing well and each player is doing his job, that defeat becomes so destructive. On two more occasions after Leeds, good all-round Australian cricket had once again achieved winning positions. But as soon as the apprehension that history might repeat itself began to intervene, so this made failure more likely. The specific elements of such a process may be innumerable – a captain will set the wrong field, a bowler's mind will race ahead of him and lose track of the simple option, a batsman may fail to play deliveries on their own particular merits – but the cumulative effect is one of helpless dread. Events, it seems, are inexplicably passing out of the team's control before players realise what is occurring. The process of defeat envelops a side, all the more remorselessly, it appears, for having been been endured before. It is a condition akin to trauma; the Australians could hardly believe what they were witnessing, almost as though it were happening to somebody else.

Experience and a tough, battle-hardened determination to regain command showed through in the attitude of the old campaigner, Lillee, in the third Test. Joining Bright at 75–8, still 55 from victory, he tried to hammer the bowling to all parts of the ground and so turn the pressure back towards his opponents. Yet even Lillee was not immune to the air of inevitability which began to accompany Botham's performances. Perhaps the single most indelible memory of this unforgettable series was that of the sixes which Botham, with his head turned away and his eyes therefore averted, swatted into the Old Trafford crowd when Lillee bowled bouncers in the fifth Test. The fact that reason had by now apparently fled the Australian camp after their two devastating reverses was plain to all. Rather than trying to restrain a man whose utter refusal to be checked might conceivably have brought his dismissal, Lillee found himself drawn into a confrontation which, by this stage, Botham's surges of adrenalin would never permit him to win.

All of this was exploited in a quite masterly fashion by Mike Brearley, a rare captain who remained ever aware of the balance to be struck, in a given situation, between saving runs and taking wickets. Brearley was appointed by the selectors, after the resignation of Botham, for what could effectively be just four Tests at most. They knew already that he would not be available for the coming Indian tour and, as it proved, he was to retire at the end of the following, 1982, season.

It seems entirely reasonable to assume that, even at this stage, the selectors also had Keith Fletcher in mind, however vaguely, not only for the winter but, beyond that, for the period to April 1984 at least. That Fletcher was not drafted in immediately, and that Brearley's mission was so dramatically short-term, says much about the weight which is still attached – perhaps over-romantically today – to Ashes series. Brearley's worth was already proven and he enjoyed the unreserved admiration of Botham, a man from whom he had coaxed the best so often in the past. No doubt there was also a desire to let Fletcher take on the job afresh, without the impediment of an agenda which had now been set by Australia's 1–0 lead.

The Australians were largely unable to cope with Brearley, a man they respected but found themselves disliking, both in his decided Englishness and in his intellectuality. If cricketing feats of the kind which a Botham could display commanded unqualified esteem, even awe, the Australians' response to Brearley was more akin to resentment. Cricket teams can willingly defer to superior playing skills; they take rather less well to being out-thought.

The grasp which Brearley so consistently maintained, and which other captains so rarely achieve, is quite easily stated: he knew when to attack and when to defend. How you pursue each of these approaches becomes a critical refinement, but the first art of captaincy is the facility to sense exactly when the one is more appropriate than the other. After Brearley, England captains were to lack either the ability to develop such awareness or the time and encouragement to discover it. Gooch has begun to discern the requisite Test balance, and he has certainly learned when to defend, but in our period Brearley's touch was unique. Though he averaged only 17.62 in the series, his tactical acumen effectively made him an all-rounder. The way in which he habitually handled spin bowling – knowing when to introduce the spinner and whether to employ him aggressively or containingly – is perhaps the hallmark of his feel for the game.

Moreover, he manipulated his attack as a unit, understanding which bowler to bring on against which batsman. In this he enjoyed a crucial advantage in 1981 over Kim Hughes, his Australian counterpart. During the fourth Test, for example, defending a first-innings total of just 189, the pressure which Brearley exerted, by his constant changing of bowlers and his careful field placing on a poor pitch, not only helped to bring about the run-outs of both Wood and Hogg but prevented four other batsmen reaching 50 after they had passed 25. In contrast, in the next Test, with Australia now 2–1 down, part of the blame for England's vital first-innings recovery from 137–8 to 231 rested with Hughes's strange decision to employ the young Whitney, rather than Alderman, against Allott and Willis.

Captaincy such as this had a major influence on countless individual moments, which together determined one of the great Test series. Yet, no series can have one explanatory theme. In 1981, the combination of factors involved was probably exceptional. It is tempting, therefore, to place the summer in a category of its own, with no particular relevance to the years which followed. Certainly the lack of coherence in the post-Packer Australian camp, so stunningly exposed by Botham and pitilessly probed by Brearley, presented unusual opportunities. But opportunities are not exploited mechanically. To seize the advantage, and indeed to defy disadvantage, a team must comprehend situations as a unit and retain the desire to do itself justice both individually and collectively. It was exactly these attributes which, over future series, were allowed to dissipate, at first imperceptibly and later quite culpably.

INDIA v ENGLAND and SRI LANKA, 1981–82

Average England total: 343 *Average India total: 405*

Date	Venue	Result	Caps per Eng. Player
27 Nov–1 Dec	Bombay	*India* by 138 runs	43.36
9–14 Dec	Bangalore	Drawn	39.73
23–28 Dec	Delhi	Drawn	45.27
1–6 Jan	Calcutta	Drawn	46.18
13–18 Jan	Madras	Drawn	37.00
30 Jan–4 Feb	Kanpur	Drawn	39.73
17–21 Feb	Colombo	*England* by 7 wickets	36.82

Tour party: K. W. R. Fletcher (captain), P. J. W. Allott, I. T. Botham, G. Boycott, G. Cook, G. R. Dilley, J. E. Emburey, M. W. Gatting, G. A. Gooch, D. I. Gower, J. K. Lever, C. J. Richards (wicket-keeper), C. J. Tavaré, R. W. Taylor (wicket-keeper), D. L. Underwood, R. G. D. Willis; R. Subba Row (manager).

Selectors: A. V. Bedser (chairman), D. B. Close, J. H. Edrich, C. S. Elliott.

The England tour of the subcontinent was about as far removed in tone and intensity from the series which had preceded it as it is possible to imagine. If the immediate illusion was that all was now right with the world, the extreme tedium of the six Tests against India presented the severest of antidotes. It was in some senses almost the archetype of the modern, attritional tour of the subcontinent in that the general blandness of the pitches ensured that all would effectively hang on one, or at most two, Tests; or even on but one or two sessions.

Since tours of New Zealand in the 1980s tended to be similarly resistant to conclusive cricket, there is a case for dividing international cricket in the period between England, Australia and West Indies, where, weather permitting, crowds might usually anticipate a result, and India, Pakistan and New Zealand where the draw would be much more prevalent. The distinction demanded markedly different kinds of mental preparation from the players concerned.

Certainly in this series, crucial enterprising runs from Kapil Dev, for example, as India added 70 for their last two wickets in the third innings of the first Test were to prove immensely influential. Equally critical was England's subsequent batting failure when left to score 241 for victory in that game. More relevant still, as the players saw it, was the infamous role of the umpires both in that innings and in their collapse from 95–1 to 166 all out at the first attempt.

It was hard for the side to dispel the thought, after Bombay, that there would be precious few chances to come back into the series in the length of a protracted tour thereafter – and, in this, though their attitude could have been rather more positive, they were essentially correct.

Before the tour had begun, the first question to be resolved was who would become the year's third captain. Brearley's decision, in 1980, to devote himself to his psychotherapy studies prevented him from taking winters off. As we have already suggested, it seems highly probable that the England selectors had begun to consider Fletcher during the previous summer. With the recent example of Brearley in mind, both in 1977 to 1980 and again in 1981, the prime need was considered to be for a captain who could steer the side through a second era and ensure that its character and its best collective qualities were retained. This was, anyway, the traditional England approach – first pick the captain and then construct the team, in contrast to the general Australian policy of selecting the best side and then asking which of the chosen players should be made captain.

If Fletcher was not thought of in this light, it is hard to see why Willis, or somebody else, was not appointed at this stage. And, logically, at least, it follows that the selectors' apparent change of heart by the summer of 1982 resulted from transgressions of which Fletcher was deemed guilty in India. Indisputably, his captaincy there did not live up to the perhaps unrealistically high expectations which his Essex record had encouraged. This alone, however, could not justify so radical, and ultimately very harmful, a revision of plans, a point to which we shall return.

It was also argued at the time that Fletcher was not the greatest player of quick bowling and, therefore, should not realistically figure in England's medium-term strategy. Yet it was two and a half years before West Indies were due to be confronted again and the probable assumption was that, by then, Gower or Gatting would have become established captains at county level and have demonstrated their fitness or otherwise to take over. In that sense the seat was being kept warm for men who, at this point, were both still only twenty-four.

There seems to this day a great deal to commend such thinking and, if the proposal was to find someone to steer England productively through an interim period, then Fletcher was precisely the kind of man for the job. He was in no sense a lightweight as a player and few would therefore resent his inclusion on grounds of ability. It was entirely reasonable to assume that he would maintain in the England set-up exactly the kind of continuity of intelligent captaincy and team development which Brearley's successes had confirmed as paramount. In professional circles, Fletcher was almost revered, because his efforts had apparently injected such enterprise into the surly, lacklustre character of Essex cricket.

He had brought Essex a reputation for combining humour and good-heartedness with an unfailing instinct for turning the moment of opportunity into victory. In short, his Essex teams were much more than the sum of their individual parts. Even in adversity they would play positively and their attitude was the envy of the circuit.

If, unfairly, this county reputation made all the more stark the disappointments of Fletcher's one series as England captain, the reasoning behind his appointment looked eminently sound, and indeed still seemed convincing in 1982. In the light of the slow fracturing of team consciousness which, we now know, was to take place later, the rather mysterious discarding of Fletcher appears all the more premature. It was a decision which would deny England one of the domestic game's best influences for some eight years to come.

To a large extent Fletcher was tainted by, and probably took the blame for, the inherent sourness and inertia of the tour itself. His role in this was not above reproach but, for the most part, events were beyond his control. The central features of the tour were umpiring decisions, in the first Test, which the visitors considered appalling (so much so that an official complaint was lodged by Fletcher and the manager, Subba Row, the day after it had been lost); the drear, bat-dominated nature of the second, third, fifth and sixth Tests; and a pedestrian rate from both sides of thirteen overs an hour. Willis found only twelve wickets at 31.75 in five Tests and Botham, playing all six matches and bowling twice Willis's number of overs, gained seventeen at 38.82.

While it was not lost on the England team that the moribund pitches which followed the first Test at Bombay could only be to the advantage of a home side seeking to preserve its lead, such a dawdling over-rate could hardly be of any logical benefit to the visitors. Almost certainly, it made no material difference, in fact, but England could obviously get back into the series only by bowling their opponents out twice. Slim though the chances of a result were to prove after Bombay in all but the crucial fourth Test, this apparent cussedness in Fletcher's response to the frustration and enervation of an Indian tour was held against him. Cussedness in Test cricket is often a supreme virtue; in this context it appeared manifestly misplaced. To be cynical, a more superficially impressive vigour would no doubt have better served Fletcher's interests; although it would not have altered results.

Not only was it an Indian tactic at this time to slow the game down, but their team typically turned to its own advantage much of the peripheral lethargy associated with Tests on the subcontinent. Drinks intervals may take ten minutes out of a session, hours of play are not rigorously observed and crowd commotion can offer a repeated opportunity to break the continuity of play. For a side which is winning, such interruptions are no doubt welcome: most professionals, in truth, would offer grudging admiration for the players who can enlist them to their cause. For a side trying to fight back, however, frustration over umpiring, complaints about hotels and the stop-start nature of much of the play can all too readily distract from the task in hand. The instinct to indulge in tit for tat, though clearly of no benefit, may mislead even the most sage and experienced of tourists.

Since Fletcher had toured India both in 1972–73 under Tony Lewis and in 1976–77 under Tony Greig, it is certainly true that he should have been aware of what to expect. Perhaps he was all too well aware: though they might attempt to convince themselves otherwise, England feared very strongly within the first fortnight of a three-month tour that the loss of the opening Test would decide the series. In the context of games which seem unable ever to progress, the attitude of a side which so soon appears to lack realistic hopes of revival will tend, if not to defeatism, then to a certain resignation. Moreover, the players know that a second defeat will unquestionably settle the issue and are accordingly all the more prone to caution. That said, the one clear hope of an England victory which subsequently arose was not only pursued keenly by Fletcher but largely set up by his own positive batting. This brought England quick runs for a declaration in the fourth Test and, disenchanted or not, they did their best to win it.

Many outside observers will argue, with some justification, that, whatever their legitimate grievances, it is the captain's task to maintain his side's evident application. The challenge of overcoming adverse circumstances must at least be attempted, however slender the chance of success. There remained, though, a further highly significant cricketing reason why the loss of the first Test was so demoralising. Again making the error, perhaps, of playing a five-man attack and omitting the extra batsman (Emburey went in at seven and Dilley at eight), even though the Wankhede Stadium provides one of the few Indian venues likely to produce a result, several of the England players were to be given out playing the sweep.

Over the last decade, the sweep in England has become essentially *the* safe method by which to negotiate spin. Where once umpires would tend to respond to lbw appeals against the stroke almost as though applying an unwritten rule which punished any failure to execute the shot successfully, it has largely become accepted that, on the front foot, the batsman will gain the benefit of the doubt on the basis that it cannot be known with certainty what the ball would have done after hitting the pad. Accordingly, excellent players of the sweep developed and for many batsmen, against good spinners in tight games, the shot became almost the equivalent of the forward defensive. On slow pitches, when scoring opportunities have been limited by accuracy, it is the stroke relied upon both as an escape – a means of late correction if defeated in the flight – and as the source of a high proportion of runs.

In discovering that the sweep in India had become a liability because so often resulting in an adverse decision (either lbw or caught), players were particularly disconcerted. Effectively a major element in the armoury of the batsman schooled in English county cricket was instantly rendered redundant. In the England first innings at Bombay, three batsmen in succession were given out attempting the shot. It was not only a matter of losing faith in the quality of the umpiring but of doing so in respect of a key area of their game. In a series where much of their work would inevitably be directed at countering spin, this proved especially disruptive to the side's thinking. The second-nature English method of trying to upset an opposing spinner and deny him the initiative was being disallowed in advance. Statistically, the surface evidence of the series suggests that the slow left-armer, Dilip Doshi, was the key to India's success. Rightly or wrongly, the England batsmen's knowledge of Doshi as a very worthy, but far from insuperable, opponent in the Championship (first for Nottinghamshire and, by this time, with Warwickshire) confirmed for them that India were benefiting from a novel, if not partial, interpretation of the lbw law.

After the failure in Bombay, the one genuine chance of an England come-back was at Calcutta in the fourth Test. Largely owing to the enterprise of Fletcher in scoring a rapid 60 not out, England declared to set India 306 for victory in what would realistically be some ninety-five overs at most. Thwarted initially by the loss of much of the first session on the last day to smog-induced bad light, they were then denied by a supreme display of application and self-control from Gavaskar, which helped ensure that only three wickets were taken. His innings was of such a quality that, with or without smog, it is doubtful if England could have won. Yet it is important to note again that they made every attempt to do so in the only match after Bombay where a result was even remotely possible.

Though Fletcher at no time knew this, the last stages of the tour were played out against the background of clandestine attempts to recruit 'rebels' for the forthcoming, first unofficial tour of South Africa. This, in conjunction with the growing disappointment of the side, brought a reprehensible lack of commitment to the England team as they entered their seventh Test of the winter, the solitary game against Sri Lanka. Attempts to recruit the final members of that 'rebel' party were being made even as the Test got under way. In truth, Fletcher had every reason to feel aggrieved at the duplicity of some of his team-mates, and it is difficult to avoid the conclusion that this final unsavoury contribution to the tour's atmosphere of sterility cost Fletcher his post. Having gained a first-innings lead of just 5 runs after two low scores, England allowed Sri Lanka to reach 140–2 at the second attempt. In danger of the ignominy of defeat against a side in its first-ever Test, England responded to scathing comments from vice-captain Willis in the dressing-room and swept forward to victory by seven wickets.

Willis's attempts to stir his colleagues to a belated sense of duty (five of the 'rebels' who were so swiftly to take to a South African field had been on the tour and three played in this match) may have had only a marginal bearing on his elevation to the captaincy. The single incident which was thought to count most, though, occurred in the second Test. There, Fletcher had tapped down a stump with his bat as he departed after being given out caught behind while attempting the sweep. It was an uncharacteristic lapse and, from an England captain, perceived to be more serious than it is easy to credit today in the light of all too commonplace dissent. It can be wondered whether the gesture betrayed less a sense of immediate frustration than the pressure generated by the high hopes for Fletcher's reign. The 1981 series was by no means an enviable act to follow and Fletcher's presentiment, even at this stage, of how the tour would unfold may have induced a certain anxiety. Beyond this, his general part in what had been a notably vapid series left him guilty by association. Mitigating circumstances were appreciated with altogether less sympathy from Lord's.

It remains mysterious, however, that these reasons alone should have counted so heavily against him. It has sometimes been suggested that the scales were crucially tipped by the fact that Allan Lamb would become eligible for England the following summer. To find a place for Fletcher in the middle order would entail either the omission of Gower or Gatting or the failure to include Lamb. This does not now seem quite the obstacle it has been assumed to have been, for Gatting was not by any means yet an automatic choice and there were at least as many voices opposing the immediate elevation of Lamb as there were urging his case. And if this was seen as a genuine problem, it is difficult to explain why Fletcher was appointed in the first place.

The initial thinking behind Fletcher's selection was that England results benefit most from a continuity, at the top, of good planning and strategic awareness. If the selectors believed in this principle, then success would presumably carry its own validation. Few had argued, after all, that Brearley's lack of runs outweighed the evident sense of purpose and direction which he brought to the side. The fact was that England's selectors, having made the correct choice in Fletcher, immediately allowed the disappointments of one series to deflect them from the wisdom of their reasoning. It was the first sign of the irresolute thinking which was so to bedevil the decade. Though results in the next period under Willis, to 1984, were better than they proved thereafter, it was during this time that the drift first began to become so apparent in England teams. Many of the difficulties which were to accompany the side's subsequent plummet emerged – and were left untreated – in the Willis years.

Though the selectors showed a change of personnel at this juncture, and Peter May replaced Alec Bedser as chairman, committee thinking was doubtless still significant. While we have no way of knowing the precise lines of argument which attended either the decision to discard Fletcher or the debate over his successor, we can be reasonably sure that the tendency towards safe options and compromise, inherent in committee deliberation, now came to the fore. For those who had expressed reluctance over the comparatively bold move of appointing Fletcher initially, there was evidence to support his removal. And for each advocate of a given replace ment, there would be those around the table entering reservations. Committee structures are neither universally desirable nor universally damaging, but only appropriate to particular circumstances. In the workings of democracy, for example, where the issues of representation and accountability are paramount, committees are a necessary expedient. But unless informed by common agreement over means and principles, a committee entrusted with the leadership of English cricket will tend to shift between opposing perspectives, or seek a middle ground which reflects no clear perspective at all.

As the most experienced member of the touring party, Willis had been number two to Fletcher in India, although at no stage hitherto does he seem to have figured prominently in the captaincy question. Within a selection committee now retreating from the principled position which the Fletcher appointment had indicated, the fact that Willis was theoretically next in line may itself have had some influence. But more significant was almost certainly the fact that only Willis, of the central characters left in England cricket after South African defections, had experience of captaincy at county level. The England norm has long been to appoint only incumbent county captains to the leadership of the Test team, though the memory of bringing in Illingworth so successfully after just seven games in charge of Leicestershire might helpfully have counselled a rethink. Any inclination to depart from this rule could be plausibly deprecated by the example of Botham.

Thus it was, apparently, that a policy of elevating existing county captains alone was adhered to, despite fears which would certainly have been felt over giving the task to a fast bowler. Even more than most of his type, Willis would inevitably find it difficult to bring his mind to bear on captaincy at the same time as he was developing his own bowling plans. It is rightly acknowledged that the two categories of player who necessarily devote to their own games too great a degree both of physical effort and concentration to be effective captains are fast bowlers and wicket-keepers. But if this was a deterrent to the choice of Willis, other factors clearly overcame it. Neither Gower nor Gatting was yet a county captain and Gatting, moreover, after nineteen Tests with a batting average of just 25.40, was taking a surprisingly long time to establish himself in the side. Ironically, when Gower did succeed Willis in 1984, he had only just taken on the job with his county.

In retrospect we can see that, rather than pursuing further the sound arguments which had suggested Fletcher as a captain in the Brearley mould, England came to move from one of the central performers of the decade to the next, almost on the principle of Buggins's turn. Thus, in sequence, Botham gave way – after eleven Tests under Brearley and Fletcher – to Willis, Gower, Gatting, Emburey, Gooch, Gower again and finally Gooch once more. Of the England-qualified county captains in 1982 (four of the seventeen were overseas players) with what appeared to be requisite skills for the job, neither Roger Knight (Surrey) nor John Barclay (Sussex), both of whom were championed, was of quite the ability to merit a place. For his part, Geoff Cook (Northamptonshire) had only just gained his first cap in Colombo. If the desire was to discard Fletcher, then the line of reasoning which had first brought his elevation might next have suggested Chris Tavaré.

Tavaré was not to captain Kent until 1983 and had played his Oxford cricket under Vic Marks. But he was tactically astute and strong-minded enough to insist on the best from those under him. Given the waywardness so often associated with the kinds of natural ability around which England's team was built, the need was for a captain who would impress upon players a responsibility to fulfil their own talent. Tavaré might well have encouraged the kind of sensitivity to the varying demands of different Test situations which, under Willis, England players often seemed to lack. He also had the advantage of being, at Test level, an opening batsman who, after the defection of both Gooch and Boycott, might remain an England regular for some years to come. Certainly, his eleven Test appearances to this point had provided many encouraging signs.

Our reference to Chris Tavaré is intended to show that, in the context not of hindsight but of contemporary debate, there was a credible alternative to Willis if Fletcher was to be prematurely eliminated. Whether the suggestion is thought convincing or fanciful is not really the point. The factors involved, at a key juncture in the decade were complex and numerous; the decision which faced the England selectors was in no sense easy. But it did require both a firm basis in cricket reasoning and a vision of the kind of identity the side was supposed to seek. Increasingly, from this stage in the narrative of decline, both elements became lost. The process was by no means uniform or even; it contained troughs and misleading peaks. Yet the trend was undoubtedly downwards and its key starting point was here.

3
The Willis Years, 1982 to 1984: A Distant Professionalism

Anybody who ever played with Bob Willis, or watched him from the boundary, would agree that the new England captain's absolute dedication and commitment were never in doubt. Not only was he a world-class fast bowler, with all the single-mindedness and painstaking honing of energy that that implies, he was also a man for whom Test cricket required extraordinarily intense levels of concentration and mental preparation. During play, Willis tended to bury himself in a mental cocoon; before a match, whether in private isolation or in trying to sort out his run-up in the nets, he channelled thoughts quite rigorously towards the Test ahead. To assist this process he even enlisted the aid of a psychologist whose tapes he could play to himself in hotel bedrooms. As a player, this utter professional integrity was entirely to his credit. But as a captain – indeed as a reluctant captain who, again to his great credit, had not evaded the burden placed upon him – such detachment was inevitably a disadvantage.

Initially, the problem was at most only latent. Results were generally not too disconcerting: England could undoubtedly have done better but their approach was not apparently blemished by any radical flaw. Deficiencies in the team's collective grasp of their cricket were implicit – both during the 1982 Pakistan series and on the Australian tour which followed – in a tendency to collapse at certain times or let the opponents back into the game. If seeds were sown in this period, however, it was not until the winter of 1983–84, and the tours of New Zealand and Pakistan, that such departures from the best standards became worryingly persistent.

Willis was not able to bring to his task as captain the ability to monitor the particular development of individual players under him, and ensure thereby that such development was always directed towards a unified sense of purpose within the team. There was in this an expectation, wholly understandable, that professional cricketers at this level would take most responsibility upon themselves. Certainly, outside the game, the widespread sentiment would probably be that appearing in a Test should itself provide all the stimulus a player requires. Yet such a blanket conclusion is both too crude and manifestly contradicted by innumerable examples throughout cricket's history. By the end of Willis's term of captaincy, doubts could rightly be expressed over the extent to which key performers sometimes simply allowed their games to drift untended. Influenced by this, players in general began to enter each Test as it came, with too little thought, either to the way in which specific situations would demand differing attitudes of mind, or to team objectives as a whole. This was a process undeniably enhanced, let it be said, by fears over selection for most of the players. More contentiously, there was at the same time, perhaps, too great a complacency over selection from others in the side.

With Lamb's qualification by residence now settled, the core of the England team was built around three players in the middle order – Lamb himself, Gower and Botham – of similar cricketing outlooks and inclinations. Positive, attacking and supremely confident, each was a prospective match-winner. Such qualities, such prodigious talents indeed, are perhaps intrinsically allied to a certain carelessness and an inability to wed prudence to potential at all times. Unless outside intervention, most obviously by the captain, can regularly provide the focus for ability which a player lacks, inconsistency arguably will be inevitable. In cricketing terms, the same fervour which can sometimes carry a team forward to the psychological advantage in a blaze of strokeplay can also produce middle-order collapses. Moreover, those in the tail who follow such occasional collapses not only now fear that survival has become difficult, but confront a newly invigorated attack. To a degree they also arrive with an advance excuse for failure.

It would be a gross simplification to accuse a batsman such as Lamb, with the steel and courage of six centuries against West Indies behind him, of a lack of application. Yet there is enough about his record, with a relatively poor series so often succeeding a good one, to suggest that, like Gower and Botham, he did not fully rise to the same challenge in every Test. And if a decade granting plentiful reward and frequent distraction to the celebrated sportsman sometimes also expressed itself through the approach of these players, it was for the leadership in the game to interpose.

Disabled by a commendable preoccupation with his own cricket, Willis was not able to fulfil this duty frequently or consistently enough. Indeed, it is doubtful whether he consciously perceived a problem until it was beginning to take hold. That Willis, as the side's key bowler, would lack the capacity to execute his captain's mandate to the full was always foreseeable. His leadership was characterised by selfless levels of devotion to the England cause which he trusted others to match. For much of the time his approach was rewarded, but ultimately England cricket began to develop a certain sense of drift. This in turn was to be inherited by Gower under whom it continued, masked, unfortunately, by two good series whose important lessons were not learned. Four years later, in 1986, the side was in a state of aimlessness which Willis, of all cricketers, would have shuddered to imagine as he now embarked upon his first series as captain.

ENGLAND v INDIA, 1982

Average England total: 475 *Average India total: 340*

Date	**Venue**	**Result**	**Caps per Eng. Player**
10–15 June	Lord's	*England* by 7 wickets	23.81
24–28 June	Old Trafford	Drawn	26.73
8–13 July	The Oval	Drawn	25.73

R. G. D. Willis (captain), P. J. W. Allott, I. T. Botham, G. Cook, P. H. Edmonds, D. I. Gower, A. J. Lamb, G. Miller, D. R. Pringle, D. W. Randall, C. J. Tavaré, R. W. Taylor (wicket-keeper).

Selectors: P. B. H. May (chairman), A. V. Bedser, N. Gifford, A. C. Smith.

A three-match half-series is both unforgiving and potentially distorting. This India series, though, provided the first Test cricket in England to be bound by the kind of minimum-overs requirement which can lessen this tendency. It was an idea enthusiastically accepted – indeed promoted – by the Indian captain, Gavaskar, and welcomed by all in the light of the preceding winter's dull cricket. To a cynical observer, this response also reflected the fact that India lacked the box-office clout to pose any obstinate objections. Fixed overs or not (and the figure set, at ninety-six a day, was higher than the present stipulation), the side which wins the first Test will often go on to take a short series and are certainly unlikely to lose it. In cricketing terms, there is every argument against such brief tours. Until the 1970s, at least, they took place because England would typically outclass weaker opponents and make longer engagements pointless. Now, perhaps misguidedly, the main concern is that a full series may generate too little revenue.

This particular encounter was decided by a single Indian batting failure in their opening innings of the summer. When followed by rain in the second Test and an Oval 'belter' in the third, this effectively settled the issue. It was not the first time that India, undone by their fear of crucial early errors and failing to acclimatise quickly enough, had let themselves down. This was all the more true in 1982, since Indian strength was so decidedly with their batting. That one failure, importantly – and inevitably, as it seemed at the time – was against Botham, who returned an excellent 5–46 to complement his violent, first-innings 67. With the addition of a century at Manchester and 208 at the Oval, it was immaterial that he bowled poorly and expensively thereafter. His limited impact as a spearhead bowler had implications which were evident only in retrospect. In the context of a three-Test series, he had done everything necessary to ensure victory: he had overrun India at the first opportunity and scored so well thereafter that they could never come back.

Willis certainly showed himself to be a hard-bitten professional from the outset in his pursuit of batting in apparent depth, a stance which at this stage spoke of realism more than caution. Equally, he sought the ballast of one spinner and steady seamers to support the thrust bowling, as it was still interpreted, of Botham and himself alone. The twenty-three year-old Cambridge student, Derek Pringle, made his début, accompanied first by Allott against India and then by Ian Greig against Pakistan. Ultimately, as the summer drew to a close, Jackman played this role on his own, in what had effectively become a three-man attack, with Marks, as the stock spinner, hardly employed at all.

Less convincing, in this desire for depth of batting cover, was Willis's leaning away from specialists and towards bowlers who could bat acceptably in domestic cricket. Though this English affection for 'bits and pieces' players did not begin with Willis, it was certainly endorsed by him. A singular victim of this attitude was Dilley, who was omitted from the team.

Interestingly, Willis also opted for the return of Randall, out of the side since January 1980, ahead of Mike Gatting. Willis did not share the general opinion in the professional game that Gatting was a batsman of unusual quality, a fact which perhaps helps explain why Gatting did not approach doing himself justice until Gower took over. Willis's choice of Randall, and his high appreciation of Tavaré, also tell us something about the kind of men he wished to have around him. Like the new captain himself, Randall was a fighter and ready to do whatever was asked of him in the England cause. It was an amenability which brought Randall various roles in the order, including (with success at this time) that of opener. There was already a hint in this, and especially in the later use of Randall to come in behind Lamb, Gower and Botham at six or even seven, that Willis acknowledged a potential for fragility in England's line-up. It may be argued that this reliance upon Randall's readiness to do whatever was asked tended to evade the problem itself. At this stage, though, criticism would have been unfair: if there was a difficulty, it was not really to be seen until the second series of the summer, against Pakistan.

ENGLAND v PAKISTAN, 1982

Average England total: 270 *Average Pakistan total: 298*

Date	Venue	Result	Caps per Eng. Player
29 July–1 Aug	Edgbaston	*England* by 113 runs	27.82
12–16 Aug	Lord's	*Pakistan* by 10 wickets	20.18
26–31 Aug	Headingley	*England* by 3 wickets	27.09

R. G. D. Willis (captain for the first and third Tests), D. I. Gower (captain for the second Test), I. T. Botham, G. Fowler, M. W. Gatting, I. A. Greig, E. E. Hemmings, R. D. Jackman, A. J. Lamb, V. J. Marks, G. Miller, D. R. Pringle, D. W. Randall, C. J. Tavaré, R. W. Taylor (wicket-keeper).

Selectors: P. B. H. May (chairman), A. V. Bedser, N. Gifford, A. C. Smith.

The side selected to play Pakistan saw a change in the opening partnership. Geoff Cook was dropped, though his last three innings against India had been 66, 50 and 8, thus providing the first evidence of an almost unwavering inability in England to grant the confidence of lengthy tenure to the two openers thought best able to fill the position at international level. Thrown by the loss of both Gooch and Boycott to South Africa, England were rightly anxious over the prime importance in Test cricket of the solid foundation. But they undermined their desire to achieve this by lack of faith in their own selections. Given the ever-present lurking possibility that the volatile middle order might fail *en bloc*, England became rather desperate about the opening pair. In cricketing terms it was one of the recurrent themes of the decade and the indecision it characterised was to become perhaps the central debilitating factor. Though, admittedly, often affected by injury, Willis's teams started with a different opening pair from one match to the next no less than twelve times in his nineteen Tests as captain.

Perhaps influenced by uncertainty over the openers, the sides for the Pakistan series still, in theory, reflected a desire for batting in depth. And the heavy reliance on Willis himself and Botham to take wickets was further underlined in the replacement of an attacking spinner, Edmonds, first by Miller and Hemmings and then by Marks. In the Lord's Test, Willis was absent through injury, but we can presume his influence on selection was considerable and, certainly, vice-captain Gower's side showed no change of direction despite its consequent toothlessness in attack.

The first objective, to ensure safety by volume of runs, continued to be somewhat impaired by the fact that the presence, respectively, of Miller and Greig at seven and eight in the opening Test, Pringle and Greig at seven and eight in the next and then Marks at eight in Leeds was in truth a largely theoretical strength. These were bowlers who could bat reliably at county level but were regularly found out in Test matches. Such players could not, with consistency, provide cover for the middle order's tendency, on occasion, to play injudicious cricket. Indeed, they seemed something of an ill-conceived substitute for addressing the main problem. Since they were not expected to gain strike bowler's analyses, their inclusion effectively demanded useful runs if the strategy was to be justified.

Three times, the failure of the middle order threatened to lose the series. At Lord's, needing 229 to save the follow-on, England subsided from 157–3 to 227, each of Lamb (33), Gower (29) and Botham (31) falling when well set. In the second innings, and at Leeds, the point was made rather more graphically by the bowling of Mudassar Nazar, a gentle seamer whom England sought to dominate both too soon and with something approaching fatal contempt. The result was that he dismissed both Lamb and Gower for 0 at Lord's and then took 4–55 at Leeds where England, at 168–1, needed just 51 more for victory. In succession, Lamb, Gower and Botham fell to his medium pace for 4, 7 and 4, and England were relieved to get home, with only three wickets standing.

The actual implementation of the bowling plan, and specifically Botham's part in it, seems equally significant. Complementing Willis in the opening Test, he achieved the vital 4–70 which decided the match as Pakistan pursued their unlikely target of 313 to win. Similarly in the third Test, with Willis taking six wickets in the game, Botham returned 4–70 once more and then, after Willis had removed both openers in his first over, the conclusive 5–74 which left England requiring only 219 for the series. In the starkest contrast, with Willis absent at Lord's, Botham's analysis, as Pakistan won the toss and made an excellent 428–8 declared, was 3–148. Gower turned to him for forty-four overs against the seventy-five delivered by his three fellow-seamers together and the twenty from Hemmings.

On the face of it, it is unfair to read too much into these instances: any bowler will obviously perform better when allied to a strike partner at the other end to form an authentic spearhead. In that sense it is perhaps debatable whether sufficient evidence was yet available. More to the point, Botham's figures, in contributing so much to the two victories, had again done most to secure the series. Here was still a quite formidable competitor whose efforts could evidently affect results. But, since the 1980 West Indies tour, Botham had several times been markedly innocuous, either on flat pitches or when Willis was not finding success at the other end. Of greater relevance was the fact that he had not on those occasions sought to adjust his approach by taking responsibility for denying fluent runs. And if this alone could not reasonably prompt a change in strategy, a weight of further evidence was soon to be offered which England remained reluctant to recognise – either in terms of grooming another bowler, Dilley most obviously, or in requiring Botham to think more about his central importance in all situations.

For their part, the Pakistanis have always insisted that this series was lost owing to umpiring. In the third Test, the fact that Sikander Bakht was given out caught at short-leg during their second innings has ever since been regarded by Pakistan as the principal cause of defeat. While any England team would undoubtedly have been aggrieved to feel that a vital error had been made, Sikander was the ninth batsman to fall and, critical though his support clearly was for Imran at this stage, the more crucial factor, by any cricket reasoning, could only be the earlier failure of recognised batsmen. Indeed, indiscipline in batting, despite Imran's tireless attempts to bring a sense of resolve to his ranks, was much the key to Pakistan's undoing.

The tourists' perception of that incident was clearly influenced by the fact that the umpire in question was David Constant, an official who has consistently taken a stand against any behaviour he deems unacceptable, though he might profitably have spoken to visiting Test players in a rather different tone to that used with England professionals. Ironically, the sense has grown amongst England players, since this series, that umpires have become all the more inclined to grant any benefit of doubt to the visitors; the feeling, paranoiac or not, is that England are at an appreciable disadvantage when playing at home. The general accusation has often been levelled that Pakistani complaints about umpiring are something of a smoke-screen, part of a wider wish to secure neutral officials in all Tests. This desire, in a rather convoluted way, probably owes most to a wish to have foreign umpires in Pakistan. This would then remove repeated allegations of bias in that country which have deflected attention from the growing quality of Pakistan sides.

While it owes little to arguments about decisions, however, the impression does remain that England were slightly fortunate to finish the 1982 series victorious. Or, more precisely, that though the results reflected a marginal superiority – in that Pakistan were more prone to error at key times than their opponents – the balance between the sides was such that 2–2 might have been the likeliest outcome of a five-Test series. As much as anything, England's slender edge over Pakistan had been psychological. There would be no such advantage in Australia where the desire to avenge 1981 was reportedly intense.

AUSTRALIA v ENGLAND, 1982–83

Average England total: 304 *Average Australia total: 371*

Date	**Venue**	**Result**	**Caps per Eng. Player**
12–17 Nov	Perth	Drawn	28.73
26 Nov–1 Dec	Brisbane	*Australia* by 7 wickets	29.09
10–15 Dec	Adelaide	*Australia* by 8 wickets	30.27
26–30 Dec	Melbourne	*England* by 3 runs	28.27
2–7 Jan	Sydney	Drawn	31.91

Tour party: R. G. D. Willis (captain), I. T. Botham, G. Cook, N. G. Cowans, G. Fowler, I. J. Gould (wicket-keeper), D. I. Gower, E. E. Hemmings, R. D. Jackman, A. J. Lamb, V. J. Marks, G. Miller, D. R. Pringle, D. W. Randall, C. J. Tavaré, R. W. Taylor (wicket-keeper); D. J. Insole (manager).

Selectors: P. B. H. May (chairman), A. V. Bedser, N. Gifford, A. C. Smith.

Selecting a party to visit Australia should in theory be somewhat easier than for any other tour. The probable characteristics of the five Test pitches can be anticipated with greater confidence than is usually possible for most series. Adelaide will provide the surface most welcome – perhaps even too welcome – to the batsmen; Sydney should turn; Melbourne, depending on the weather leading up to the Test, is likely to produce a result and will demand discretion; Perth has been consistently the fastest pitch in the world through the decade in question; Brisbane, with its moisture under the surface and sub-tropical humidity, will assist swing and seam and is also likely to bring a result. Such variation makes the notion of balance in the party, not only in terms of bowling breadth but in terms of batsmen who can adapt their game as circumstances dictate, more essential than for any other tour.

The actual squad assembled in 1982 was notable in at least three ways. It contained three off-spinners (Hemmings, who was a valid first choice in the role, Marks and Miller), two of whom could bat, but no slow left-armer – both Nick Cook (ninety wickets at 23.25 the previous summer) and, rather more significantly, Phil Edmonds (eighty at 22.1) being left behind. It included, interestingly, the twenty-one-year-old Norman Cowans, after only sixteen first-class games, in the role of raw, novice fast bowler, which Willis himself had once played and which has been almost mandatory on tours of

Australia and the Caribbean. And, though only six specialist batsmen were taken, the squad excluded Gatting.

If the choice of Cowans shows that Willis at least wanted cover for Botham as his spearhead, the absence of Dilley (64 wickets at 28.73), either in Cowans's place or, more boldly, in addition to him, remains baffling. Three years earlier, it was Dilley who was cast as unknown quick bowler and, logically, with sixteen caps now gained, this tour might have provided the next stage in his development.

The spinning options, together with the preponderance of bowlers and the remarkable choice of Ian Gould as reserve wicket-keeper, seem unarguably to point to the sad, if not woeful, influence of an agreement to include up to *sixteen* possible one-day internationals in the itinerary. All of these were to take place after the Ashes had been decided, which implies that the folly of trying to combine incompatible playing requirements had been justified on the basis of cost. In addition, Willis had always been ambivalent towards spin bowling. He was uncertain not only in his choice of spinner but also in his perception of the slow bowler's role in modern Test cricket. He did not have the highest regard for the proposition that slow bowling might win a Test and, before the previous series, had notably observed that Abdul Qadir should not be allowed to become a crucial factor.

Willis's reasoning – by no means unique to him – was that if pitches accepted spin then, by implication, they would either be rough or cracked. Therefore, he argued, a pace bowler should be able to achieve similar deviation but at greater speed. With that, and one-day cricket, no doubt in mind, the spinners selected for Australia were evidently seen in a containing, support capacity – one which Hemmings and Miller were indeed to perform well, though their contribution on a turning pitch in the vital last Test might perhaps have been more significant.

In respect specifically of Edmonds – at this stage the best available slow left-armer in the country – Willis's decision is perhaps most instructively linked with his regard for Randall. Where Randall was identified as the solid team man, Willis made little secret of his antipathy towards the oddity, even perversity, of the character of Edmonds. Edmonds's frivolous relish for provoking argument and playing the devil's advocate made him largely incomprehensible to

Willis, who thought he would be a liability on tour. There are different ways of dealing with the eccentricity of the talented and no fault can be attached to Willis for deciding that he wished to create a staunch, professional identity for his side.

That he should pursue this path rather than seeking means to blend more wayward elements into his unit was entirely his prerogative – Gooch adopted a similar, though more subtle, approach in the early 1990s with notable success. The approach does, however, demand a certain consistency, and it relies upon those who are chosen to maintain the best standards. When, later, this was not always apparent, the suspicion again arose that Willis was trying to accommodate the errancy of his core players by building the rest of the side around them.

Series under Willis certainly included a lot of very helpful team meetings which contained much good advice from the captain himself regarding game plans, for example, or the strengths and weaknesses of opposing players. He was less convincing at a personal level, indicating to team-mates how such general points might relate to their own specific contributions. Moreover, there comes a time in play when further comment is required if such plans are not being adhered to or if tactics are going astray. Willis was not a great initiator of minor changes in approach and was not markedly alive to those moments when the general rules of captaincy might profitably be amended. He relied considerably on his long-standing associates and present lieutenants, Gower and Botham, a fact which often gave a feeling of committee captaincy to his efforts.

If this was to result in error in the third Test where, against his own judgement, Willis was persuaded to insert Australia after winning the toss, the subsequent defeat – which left England 2–0 down with two to play – owed far more to batting failure, once again, than to any single poor decision. In principle there is nothing inherently wrong in a joint, consultative approach to leadership. It does, however, demand that everyone is equally alive to his responsibilities and can discharge them, even when distracted by playing problems of his own. The only man who, in the final analysis, has any formal obligation to unite the two remits of player and leader, each onerous enough in itself, is the official captain. He must therefore be sufficiently engaged in reading the game to have clear views of his own on the appropriateness of ideas suggested to him, and to realise when the preoccupations of others have reduced their attentiveness to play.

Willis's captaincy was perhaps shown at its weakest on this tour in resolving the role of Norman Cowans. In retrospect, the greatest historical significance of the series was that it provided now quite unequivocal evidence of Botham's bowling decline. This, in turn, should necessarily have shifted the emphasis on to careful and sensitive treatment of Cowans. Perhaps inevitably, Willis by-passed the unenviable dilemma of how to expose Cowans while at the same time not risking defeat, by reaffirming his faith in Botham. In the first Test, Botham was given forty overs (2–121) in the first innings while Cowans bowled only thirteen. In the second Test, where England's injudicious batting had led to a score of 219, it was of the essence to restrict Australia's reply. Recovering from 130–5, however, they totalled 341; Botham's twenty-two overs conceded 105 runs for three wickets but Cowans, whose first salvoes had also been dishearteningly expensive, was not permitted to bowl again. His six overs (in a total of 111) had been calculatedly savaged by Greg Chappell, in a shrewd and perversely complimentary piece of captaincy, for 36 runs.

In the second innings of that Test, with Australia needing only 188 to take the lead in the series, Botham was given sixteen overs (0–70) to Cowans's nine (1–31). Soon to be dropped for the following match, Cowans cut a forlorn and rather bewildered figure fielding in the deep. To his immense credit, he returned to win the fourth Test and bring England hope with 6–77 in the second innings (Chappell dismissed in both innings for 0 and 2), but it was only after this that he was given the new ball and Botham became the third seamer. Revealingly, in this new role Botham now achieved 4–75, his one significant analysis of the series.

It is only with extreme reticence that commentary, even ten years after the date, should venture criticism of England players who, in the past, had so often brought victory to their side. If that is still true today, how much more true must it have been for Willis at the time in assessing how his side's cricket had unfolded through the previous three years. Whether or not one agrees with his apparent choice of Cowans rather than Dilley for England's key future role, he had at least faced the decision and, in so doing, had allowed responsibility to override caution. But that was before the tour. In the heat of the campaign itself, when once more overtaken by the demands of his own integral playing role in the bid to retain the Ashes, Willis lost sight of long-term requirements.

Part of those requirements, part of the constant obligation of Test cricket, is that every participant should play to his fullest capacity within the context of given match situations. In that sense the argument should rarely be about an individual player's statistical place in Test records, but all about the player's consistent desire to meet his own unremitting standards. If it is harsh to highlight the inconsistency of England's batting again in this series, when, after all, three players did average above forty, then it reflects a harshness which is intrinsic to Test cricket itself. The more pertinent fact, perhaps, is that five of the Australians bettered 45 and no specialist fell below 35.

When comparing two teams' batting, one usually looks at the respective spread of scores through an innings or for genuine, crease-occupying performances which at least prevent defeat. Though, on paper, England's batting was not markedly inferior to Australia's, on neither count did England compete well enough. Man for man, Australia's side was probably just better than England's. That this was made to count, however, owed more to their grasp of a game's key intervals, and of their determination to emerge with the initiative, than to any disparity in skill. Thus, this series was most decisively lost because of low England totals at Brisbane (219) and Adelaide (216). If, for the most part, England had fought well, this was the first series for some years where a loss of direction at certain times had an appreciable bearing on the overall outcome.

We should emphasise again that, by this stage, the results of the England team under Willis remained fairly good. If his reliance on the personal professionalism of those he led had already betrayed hints of future problems, it had for the most part served him well. The home series against India and Pakistan had been won, the Ashes had been surrendered but not by any catastrophic margin, and now the New Zealanders were about to be comprehensively beaten – though hardly for reasons which Willis could have anticipated.

ENGLAND v NEW ZEALAND, 1983

Average England total: 314 *Average New Zealand total: 254*

Date	Venue	Result	Caps per Eng. Player
14–18 July	The Oval	*England* by 189 runs	31.36
28 July–1 Aug	Headingley	*New Zealand* by 5 wickets	33.64
11–15 Aug	Lord's	*England* by 127 runs	28.91
25–29 Aug	Trent Bridge	*England* by 165 runs	33.36

R. G. D. Willis (captain), I. T. Botham, N. G. B. Cook, N. G. Cowans, G. R. Dilley, P. H. Edmonds, N. A. Foster, G. Fowler, M. W. Gatting, D. I. Gower, A. J. Lamb, V. J. Marks, D. W. Randall, C. L. Smith, C. J. Tavaré, R. W. Taylor (wicket-keeper).

Selectors: P. B. H. May (chairman), A. V. Bedser, P. J. Sharpe, A. C. Smith.

To the extent that Botham would be used as a change bowler in this series, first behind Willis and Cowans and then, by the second Test, behind Willis, Cowans and the returned Dilley, a lesson had been bravely acted upon. Moreover, when Dilley was unfit for the third Test, Neil Foster gained his first cap after just nineteen first-team appearances for Essex. Ascribed a new role in a re-conceived attack, and arguably all the hungrier for being 'demoted' (itself a tribute to good captaincy), Botham twice took four wickets in an innings in support of match-winning performances.

Willis was still unsure, however, about what he expected from slow bowlers. Having employed four different spinners the previous summer and taken three off-spinners to Australia, he now opted to readmit Edmonds. When Edmonds was injured before the Lord's Test, Nick Cook, who was not performing to any great effect for Leicestershire at the time, was called up, and bowled as well, by the Nottingham Test, as he was ever to do in his career.

At the season's outset, spin was hardly the prime concern. Belatedly, the fast bowling was being adjusted and, by the third Test, Gatting was restored, thus breaking up, by chance or design, the concentration in the middle order of Gower, Lamb and Botham. In the same match, with Fowler injured, Chris Smith became the fifth opener to be employed by Willis in fourteen months. Within a year, two further openers were to supersede him.

New Zealand's tactical deployment was rather more settled. In Hadlee, who at thirty-two had cut down his run-up and become so ruthlessly efficient, they possessed the finest bowler in the world. Nevertheless, their greater strength was evidently in batting and their unexpected failure in that department, perhaps partly induced by the intimidating prospect of an historic first series success over England, had much to do with the overall result. During the 1980s, New Zealand began to make very canny use indeed of limited domestic resources and played very closely to an astute game plan. Thus it was appropriate that their first victory in England, in the second Test, should have owed so much to the lesser lights. The assiduous and hard-working medium-pace swing and seam of Lance Cairns, Chatfield and Coney – rather than the unlucky, wicketless efforts of Hadlee – dismissed England for 225 and 252 in helpful Leeds conditions which Botham, most notably, failed to exploit.

England, too, batted disappointingly, their lack of application at key times once more resulting in a series of capitulations which were becoming uncomfortably familiar. In sequence, England declined from 154–5 to 209 in the first Test, from 175–3 to 225 in the second, and from 288–5 to 326 and 195–5 to 211 in the third. Against that, significantly, the side were able to rediscover their resolve – prompted by an angry Willis – to bat through a full day's play for 194 runs in the second innings at the Oval, which helped produce a match-winning total in the opening Test. Then, in the final encounter at Trent Bridge, centuries in each innings (one from Botham, the other from Lamb, whose place in the team was now being questioned) ensured that New Zealand would have no chance to square the series.

If a scoring-rate of 1.98 per over on the Saturday at the Oval hardly made for riveting viewing, it certainly did make full cricketing sense. It also confirmed that, whatever else Willis might be as a captain, he was relentlessly hard in his grasp of the attitudes which enable teams to succeed at Test level. In the last match, with England 2–1 up, he not only insisted on the uncompromising insurance of an extra batsman (Randall, at seven, was to make 83) but also declined to enforce the follow-on. There were sound reasons for this decision in the specific context of the game, but it carried the further merit of denying New Zealand any possible chance of fighting back. Willis was implacable in his desire to defeat the opponent and an unfailingly stern task master where his own cricket was concerned. In this he might be compared with Hadlee, who was conspicuously disregarded for the New Zealand captaincy on at least three occasions. What Willis could not do so readily was to communicate these attributes to his players, lacking the space, and perhaps even the temperament, to relate to individuals with the right balance of exhortation and sympathy.

It should be added immediately here that the key stand in that all-important Nottingham Test, Botham and Randall's 186 after England had slumped to 169–5, needed just thirty-two overs. Botham, with an exhilarating hundred from 99 balls, thus not only helped determine the series, he did so once more with those uniquely personal methods which rightly brought him such awed acclaim and respect. But the sense that remains is rather of England doing just enough. Botham, with his unparalleled feel for the occasion, fired in the nick of time. Resolute batting performances would follow inappropriate ones which owed too much to one-day attitudes. Willis rescued the opening Test with 4–10 in his first twelve overs, removing each of John Wright and the two Crowe brothers for 0. And, unexpectedly twenty-six of the sixty-nine New Zealand wickets which fell in the series were taken by slow bowlers.

It can, of course, be argued that such opportunism, the priceless ability to fight back, is definitive of the best international sides. Results still tended to obscure the fact, however, that performances could have been appreciably better. While certain problems were acknowledged – the issue of the attack was addressed, though the response was once again to become desultory and muddled – others were left untackled. To what extent this relative success helped entrench qualities which would later prove harmful, it is difficult to say. We now know that a demeaning winter awaited English cricket. Even then the habit of losing – or of ceasing to be dismayed by defeat – was to be at least two years distant, and so many other factors fostered its emergence. But an air of negligence already attended affairs. Victory, certainly over sides like New Zealand, was perhaps too readily taken for granted, outside the game as well as within its professional ranks. England had lost but one series at home, after all, in the last seven years, and that by a single Test. As success was celebrated in Nottingham at the end of August 1983, it did not seem to anyone concerned that the date would mark a watershed.

NEW ZEALAND v ENGLAND, 1983–84

Average England total: 286 *Average New Zealand total: 404*

Date	Venue	Result	Caps per Eng. Player
20–24 Jan	Wellington	Drawn	33.73
3–5 Feb	Christchurch	*New Zealand* by an innings and 132 runs	35.27
10–15 Feb	Auckland	Drawn	31.91

Tour party: R. G. D. Willis (captain), I. T. Botham, N. G. B. Cook, N. G. Cowans, G. R. Dilley, N. A. Foster, G. Fowler, M. W. Gatting, D. I. Gower, A. J. Lamb, V. J. Marks, D. W. Randall, C. L. Smith, C. J. Tavaré, R. W. Taylor (wicket-keeper); A. C. Smith (manager). (A.C.S. Pigott was added for one Test.)

Selectors: P. B. H. May (chairman), A. V. Bedser, P. J. Sharpe, A. C. Smith.

If it is the case that England's fall from grace during the winter, with defeats against both New Zealand and Pakistan for the first time ever, could not realistically have been anticipated, then the critical question concerns the team's response to these events. Since the warning signs were now more evident, to what extent were they noted and responded to?

Undeniably, there were many objective external elements which helped explain failure. Though the England selectors made a wise decision in taking Cowans, Dilley and Foster on the tour, they were to lose Dilley through injury for the whole of the New Zealand leg, Foster was unfit for the débâcle at Christchurch and both Willis and Botham had to leave Pakistan after the first Test defeat. Excuses were also found by some of the players – too readily perhaps – in poor pitches, inadequate practice facilities and dubious umpiring. While these points were legitimate, and might even have made failure likely, it was the nature of defeat which was ignominious and the subsequent absence of self-examination which gave grounds for such concern.

Following a week flying the flag in Fiji, which might really have provided the ideal opportunity to discuss the demands of the series ahead, England seemed to approach the New Zealand matches with a curious lack of rigour. At net sessions, newcomers and those making a return to the squad were allowed to continue on their own without words of specific advice or direction from above. A solitary tourist, Willis in fact seemed more approachable on the field than off. During a game, he would welcome ideas from his team-mates and generally endorse their proposals encouragingly. Away from the action, though, opportunities to explore wider ideas on a more one-to-one basis were lost.

We have mentioned already how much more tolerable the burden would have been for a touring captain if granted a regular aide. On this trip, as in Australia, the man with the task might in theory have been Norman Gifford, the assistant manager. Yet Gifford was still a first-class cricketer himself and could largely afford to act only as coach, helping with specific problems when asked. In later years he executed a managerial role at Hove with some distinction, but here he lacked both the authority of a job description, which might have indicated his scope for intervention, and the assurance of any real long-term England role. Such appointments were still essentially one-off; they did not carry even the informal prospect of security.

At a team meeting a week before the opening Test, Willis expressed disappointment with the side's lack of bite and called for a hardening of approach. With some prescience, Tavaré urged the faster bowlers to concentrate more on line and length. As the Wellington Test arrived, there was a sense that the side were perhaps allowing things to happen rather than anticipating developments keenly enough. Certainly by the last day, which New Zealand entered just 91 runs ahead, with only three wickets standing after a first-innings deficit of 244, England were to a degree guilty of believing they need merely turn up to win.

It is true that the Basin Reserve in Wellington provides one of the most turgid pitches in the world (only one result was to be achieved in the eight years following England's visit) and that, at home, New Zealand have proved themselves the masters of the defensive rearguard. But this was the kind of situation in which Test sides should win. Botham, given the new ball again, had every right to expect that his huge match contribution, 5–59 in the first innings and 138, would be sufficient to secure the game; but with Cook, as the spinner, bowling poorly on the last day, New Zealand were allowed to escape.

Victory at Wellington could well have changed the complexion not only of the tour but of the winter. In fact it was followed by a performance in Christchurch which, but for mitigating circumstances, might be ranked with the most abject ever offered by an England side. If the previous game had shown Botham in his glory, this, a defeat in the equivalent of two playing days, represented dereliction.

Let it be said, the pitch, cut on the rugby field at Lancaster Park, was decidedly substandard and England now had only three fit fast bowlers. Given the certainty of uneven bounce, and betraying again his predisposition to pace, Willis called up Tony Pigott (who bowled reasonably well, in fact) from his off-season Shell Trophy cricket with Wellington. The choice was rather odd, not only because Neil Mallender, a much tighter bowler, was engaged with Otago, but because both spinners on the tour, whatever the state of the pitch, might at least have been expected to ensure accuracy. As it proved, England conceded 307 runs at 4.25 per over and the batsmen, whom Willis refused to blame, failed to pass 100 in either innings.

At various points in the game, Willis castigated his colleagues severely, but he allowed Botham to bowl for too long again, despite early successes for Cowans, and in a manner contrary to the established plan for Hadlee, whose 99 in eighty-one balls was devastating. Given the nature of cricket, disasters such as this can occasionally befall any team. But they should remain a matter for intense embarrassment, from which conclusions are drawn – the more so since it could now be quite correctly predicted that the Auckland pitch would guarantee a draw. In the aftermath of Christchurch Cook noted in his diary: 'Nobody can seem to give "Goose" [Willis] any help out of our bad patch; Botham, probably upset with his own bowling, is surprisingly quiet; Gower just seems to shrug his shoulders.'

Many of the strands we have been referring to in terms of the deficiencies of the team, and of the England set-up generally, were brought together on this tour. One of the further elements in an ever more sour winter was the role of the tabloid press. Well before Christchurch, indeed before the first Test, the morale of the squad had been appreciably affected by stories which marked a new phase in the widening of a sharp divide between players and correspondents. Digging for dirt about England teams now became an established feature of popular newspaper coverage.

The *Mail on Sunday* produced an article alleging the use of cannabis in England dressing-rooms and the *Daily Express* made reference to wild drinking parties. Analysis of the actual problems beginning to surface in English cricket, as opposed to exaggerations or fabrications designed to sell newspapers, had now clearly become secondary. Undoubtedly, there is some connection to be made between culture and sport, as such newspapers, however obliquely and unknowingly, testified. Ironically, the effect these stories had in the 1980s was to increase a sense of sport as show business; spectacle, it seemed, mattered far more than cricket. Even the game allowed itself to become confused about its audience. Unconsciously, it accepted the premise of the popular press that people cared about cricket only when scandal was involved. Any incentive to serious investigation of the game's ills was accordingly deflected.

PAKISTAN v ENGLAND, 1983–84

Average England total: 313 *Average Pakistan total: 331*

Date	Venue	Result	Caps per Eng. Player
2–6 March	Karachi	*Pakistan* by 3 wickets	34.55
12–17 March	Faisalabad	Drawn	23.09
19–24 March	Lahore	Drawn	23.45

Tour party: R. G. D. Willis (captain for the first Test), D. I. Gower (captain for the second and third Tests), I. T. Botham, N. G. B. Cook, N. G. Cowans, G. R. Dilley, N. A. Foster, G. Fowler, M. W. Gatting, A. J. Lamb, V. J. Marks, D. W. Randall, C. L. Smith, C. J. Tavaré, R. W. Taylor (wicket-keeper); A. C. Smith (manager).

Selectors: P. B. H. May (chairman), A. V. Bedser, P. J. Sharpe, A. C. Smith.

After two months in Fiji and New Zealand, England flew directly to Pakistan, where they were awaited both by news reporters (rather than sportswriters) and, within three days, by the game which was to determine the series. Cook, for example, was to find himself, in that Test match, bowling his first ball in anger for almost seven weeks. This, a uniquely poor piece of planning, provided perhaps the final ingredient in a winter which illustrated well the problems of English cricket. It was not that the party particularly wished for a warm-up period, in which illness was always likely to deplete their number, but that following an already lengthy absence from home, the prospect of a series in Pakistan would inevitably be approached in the wrong spirit.

It was the players themselves, of course, who repeatedly requested that overseas tours should be as brief as realistic Test preparation could allow. In an earlier era, England might be expected to take relatively weak sides to Pakistan or New Zealand and at least avoid defeat. Little thought had yet been given to the appropriate balance between travel and practice for tours whose outcome was now less assured. The present compromise of restricting time spent in distant hotels, but preparing conscientiously in England, was still some years ahead.

The same historical hangover implied in this lack of professionalism has undoubtedly also informed the attitude of cricketers through the decade under discussion. Heavily influenced, admittedly, by a well-founded mistrust of the umpiring they expect to encounter, England teams have approached Pakistan in a frame of mind which, if not defeatist, has been far more negative than any they would entertain in Australia or even in the Caribbean. In short, England teams did not bring the same impetus to do well which a West Indian side, for example, would routinely insist upon.

Adding all this to the disappointments in New Zealand, it is perhaps not surprising that England should lose the Karachi Test and with it most hope of even squaring the series. Confronted, albeit on a fairly flat pitch, by Abdul Qadir's leg-breaks and googlies, against which the batsmen had varying tactical policies, it is understandable that England were twice dismissed cheaply. Yet certain indications of a lack of grip were again detectable. However well a top-flight bowler performs, no side should regard as excusable a decline from 154–4 to 182 all out. Nor, having reduced Pakistan to 138–6 in reply, should a bowler drop a return catch, as Cook did, or a captain allow the seventh wicket to add 75 in twenty overs, as Willis did in persisting with Botham, on a pitch where the norm was 2.1 per over.

Before the inevitable draw followed at Faisalabad, events conspired rather melodramatically to reflect the disarray in the England camp. Willis flew home with a virus from which he was not fully to recover before retiring four months later; Botham also departed injured; Cowans strained a groin; Fowler became too ill to bat higher than six in the forthcoming Test; and Dilley was persuaded to rise from his sick bed only for fear that England would enter the game a man short. If these were omens then, with eyes grimly fixed on journey's end few were disposed to read them. It seemed only too absurdly appropriate that the team should spend its one day off between the second and third Tests signing affidavits, for Botham's hastily dispatched solicitor, to the effect that he had returned home for reasons of health not of discipline. By 1984, England cricketers, perforce, were looking as much to possible libel writs as to their next appearance in the middle.

Thus, without ceremony, Willis departed the England captaincy. Unable to play again for eleven weeks, he was to join the side for his last three Tests not as leader but as willing spearhead once more. The passage was observed with a notable absence of formal gratitude for a man who constantly gave his all yet had never really sought office. That the one fact might largely determine the other was no doubt pondered before his appointment. If blame is to be attached, therefore, for drift which, at this stage, still owed more to circumstance than personal error, it lies with those who asked him to discharge two incompatible functions.

In Willis's place for the last two Tests, and – it was soon confirmed – for the foreseeable future, came David Gower. The immediate signals were excellent. In his fifty-eighth match, Gower reached a Test 150 for only the third time in his career and, at Lahore, he added 173 not out in a total of 344–9 declared. Moreover, that declaration, prefaced by the announcement to the team that he would rather lose a series 2–0 than forsake a chance of drawing it, produced an equally positive response from his players. Set only 243 in 59 overs, Pakistan, cruising home at 173–0, were grateful in the end to reach 217–6. Far too much could be made of this, but it does not seem coincidental that, given the new ball and a clear part in the side's strategy, Foster, in his fifth Test, should take 5–67 and Cowans, at the critical moment, 5–42. Nor does it seem irrelevant to England's continuing decline that when the team next assembled in Birmingham, Cowans was playing for Middlesex at Lord's and Foster was made twelfth man.

4

David Gower, 1984 to 1986: 'I'm in Charge'

The two years of David Gower's first period of captaincy were characterised most notably by a startling disparity in results. Successive good series in the space of nine months against India and Australia were flanked, with a fearful symmetry, by defeats against West Indies which could not have been more comprehensive. That a side should beat other countries but lose to West Indies was not remarkable; the surprise was in the intensity of the contrast – absolute and humiliating failure in the one set of matches; commendable, even highly commendable, success in the others. To attempt a quantification of the vast difference between playing, say, India and playing West Indies, a team which could defeat the former might perhaps submit to West Indies by a margin of two or three Tests. Nobody, not even the players themselves, could have anticipated surrendering each of ten matches in sequence. And the shock of complete capitulation in the Caribbean in 1986 was all the more bitter for the illusion that England's spirit had been substantially revived in the intervening year.

Any process of decline in cricket will never be uniform or rigid. It is the game's most abiding attraction that the outcome of a match or of a series often appears to depend on a limitless combination of variables. Cricketers frequently enlist this fact – citing a specific dropped catch or a particular innings – to account for failure and provide security in a searching profession. While this is a largely self-protective mechanism, it is as well to concede that long-term analysis and explanation in cricket must deal more in tendencies and trends than in fixed patterns. There were reasons behind the perplexing unevenness of Gower's period and lessons which it was the province of selectors, far more than players, to explore.

At the playing level, the inexperienced and eager party which

Gower led to India in 1984–85 were given a freedom to prove themselves, against a side of comparable ability, to which they responded superbly. Gatting, who had been given only one match against the 1984 West Indians, was offered the confidence of the vice-captaincy and, unconfined by the presence of Botham or the doubts of Willis, at last put behind him an average of just 23.80 in his previous thirty Tests. The settled opening pair of Fowler and Robinson provided consistent foundations and Edmonds, who repaid the licence afforded him by his new captain, became integral to the side. Foster, granted the new ball again after a break of seven matches, took the eleven wickets at Madras which decided the series. The following summer, he was once more to be unaccountably left out of all but one of the four Tests for which he was fit.

There can be little doubt that the absence, on that tour, of Botham – characteristically honest enough, after appearing in seventy-three of the seventy-nine Tests since his début, to seek a rest – had a liberating effect on the side. Through little fault of his own, Botham, as the evident centre of attention, by now brought a certain claustrophobia to the England dressing-room. In his absence, players gained a readiness to express themselves, both in their cricket and in discussion, which it was the hallmark of Gower's captaincy to encourage. Much of the credit, therefore, for the happy and willing cricket England displayed against India and Australia lies with the attitude which Gower brought to bear. Sadly, it was allowed to camouflage a great deal.

When teams believe they can compete, and have an unconstrained keenness to do so, an approach which signally avoids cramping styles is all to the good; when they confront major problems, however, and are not given a lead by senior players, the natural inclination to retreat will be left unchecked. Teams with their own reserves of motivation, and the desire to demonstrate parity with opponents whom they knew to have similar ability, performed well for Gower. Those which began to be demoralised by defeat, or which started to enter matches anticipating failure, demanded qualities he could not supply.

The capacity to resurrect ailing causes is in many ways the authentic test of captaincy. Gower had the deepest respect for the professionals he led but, as another naturally gifted player, he was ill-equipped to empathise with their problems or assist in rectifying them. He was not an unapproachable man, but this inevitably lent him a detachment which his wide interest in activities outside the game tended to magnify. Believing sincerely in the benefit which relaxation and escape from cricket could bring, he would pursue his affinity for wildlife photography in India, for example, or his love for fine wines in Australia. He could not so readily understand those whose relationship with cricket and its difficulties was rather more fraught. In consequence many found it difficult to communicate with Gower and few, if any, could claim to know him well.

Moreover, the central needs in England cricket, for clarity in selection and strategy, were still not addressed under Gower. During the 1984 West Indies series, the sense of England players trying to get through each Test as it came in the desperate hope of easier pickings to follow began to assert itself. An inexperienced squad, in the context of a tour far from the nervous eyes of selectors, had acquitted themselves honourably in India only to return to indecision. While the Ashes were regained in that next summer, victory was decisively determined, in the last analysis, by three swing bowling performances from Ellison which, as is so often the case with this type of attack, were never to be repeated. Beneath the surface, team spirit and self-confidence, so badly eroded by a lack of pattern in either selection or philosophy, remained vulnerable. In the Caribbean, both qualities were to be destroyed utterly in an experience from which England spent most of the 1986 season trying to recover.

The widely differing fates of sides under Gower left a sense of inconclusiveness even three years after his dismissal. When, in 1989, the new chairman of selectors, Ted Dexter, a man not unlike Gower in temperament, found his preferred captain, Gatting, vetoed by the TCCB, he turned once again to Gower as second choice. Urged to be more demonstrably in command of his troops, Gower had printed a T-shirt which bore the ironic legend, 'I'm in charge'. Given the circumstances he took on in 1989, with eight of his players about to decamp to South Africa, he had, in truth, almost no hope of success. It was not without relevance, though, that in a further series where he needed to exert positive control, his side suffered a third massive defeat.

ENGLAND v WEST INDIES and SRI LANKA, 1984

Average England total: 226 *Average West Indies total: 423*

Date	Venue	Result	Caps per Eng. Player
14–18 June	Edgbaston	*West Indies* by an innings and 180 runs	31.82
28 June–3 July	Lord's	*West Indies* by 9 wickets	30.91
12–16 July	Headingley	*West Indies* by 8 wickets	26.64
26 July–31 July	Old Trafford	*West Indies* by an innings and 64 runs	21.18
9–14 Aug	The Oval	*West Indies* by 172 runs	22.55
23–28 Aug	Lord's	Drawn	23.55

D. I. Gower (captain), J. P. Agnew, P. J. W. Allott, I. T. Botham, B. C. Broad, N. G. B. Cook, N. G. Cowans, P. R. Downton (wicket-keeper), R. M. Ellison, N. A. Foster, G. Fowler, M. W. Gatting, A. J. Lamb, T. A. Lloyd, G. Miller, P. I. Pocock, D. W. Pringle, D. W. Randall, C. J. Tavaré, V. P. Terry, R. G. D. Willis.

Selectors: P. B. H. May (chairman), A. V. Bedser, P. J. Sharpe, A. C. Smith.

The first series under another new England captain began to the strains of a familiar theme. Having employed Tavaré, Geoff Cook, Fowler and Chris Smith as the main openers in the Willis period, England now offered Andy Lloyd the unenviable initiation of facing the West Indian attack. Lloyd, after injury, was replaced by Broad, while Paul Terry was also drafted in for the third and fourth Tests to bat at number three until he too was injured. Later, Moxon and Robinson were added to the stock of openers for the Indian tour.

Clearly, it is more difficult for a captain to insist on having his way in selection at the start of his tenure. Moreover, though Smith had played reasonably well over the winter, Tavaré had lost touch on tour and both, influenced by their demotion from the England ranks, were to have poor county seasons. Yet they had both shown proven qualities of resistance at Test level and confirmed the requisite attitude for the task. Against West Indies, where the inability to find either adequate runs or crease occupancy was again critical in the heaviness of England's defeat, such elements might have been thought paramount. As it was, the glare of a home series once more found England failing to abide by the principle of nominating certain batsmen in advance and keeping faith with them thereafter. In Broad, let it be said, they did produce a left-hander both strong on the back foot and resilient enough to hold the West Indian attack for long periods. Ironically, as the selectors bowed again to press pressure, Broad was to be discarded for allegedly batting too slowly against Sri Lanka, and another staunch performer in the Tavaré mould was lost for more than two years.

A key necessity in an attempt to repel the West Indian onslaught is to establish a nucleus of batsmen who will abide by a clear plan. This is obviously a strategy more readily expressed than implemented. But if theory was muddled over the personnel at the head of the line-up, it was compromised also by doubt over the batting order. At the heart of this problem was the desire to make best use of stroke-making batsmen, historically a real novelty for England, by protecting the middle order from the new ball. Though it contradicted Greg Chappell's dictum that the prime batsman should dictate developments from number three, the idea of keeping Gower down the order was sound enough, given that resistance did indeed materialise at the top.

Not until the fifth Test, however, when the grit of Fowler, Broad and Tavaré was eventually combined, did England apply the tactic effectively. First Randall, lacking the technique for pace, was used at three, then Gower himself and finally the débutant Terry. Gatting, the obvious other candidate in that by now he batted in that position for Middlesex, was disqualified by the media uproar which greeted the manner of his dismissal in his one Test – lbw offering no stroke to Marshall in both innings. This notorious technical aberration betrayed the anxiety over his England role which continued to inhibit his game. Undoubtedly, in the circumstances, it would have required some boldness to persevere with Gatting, but if his character and talent were not in question, it could only have benefited his poise to gain a first extended run since 1981.

If arguably inevitable against West Indies, the primary weakness in this series – as increasingly in those which preceded it – was with bat rather than ball. In addition, Botham's role was still unresolved. His 8–103 at Lord's was bowling on a titanic scale. But in the second innings, as West Indies successfully chased a target of 342 at 4.38, he conceded 0–117 in twenty overs in an overall England performance which, despite the breathtaking batting of Greenidge, was all too reminiscent of Christchurch. Similarly, at the Oval, Botham's 5–72 as first change was followed by 3–103 from twenty-two overs when given the new ball. In short, the awesome power of the old Botham still smouldered; but was too spasmodically glimpsed to justify his central position in the attack. If Botham lacked the perspective to gauge his own frame of mind, Gower, like Willis, proved reticent. Only in the third Test, where Allott bowled excellently to the Leeds conditions and took 6–61, did Gower insist on appropriate cricket and allow Botham a single spell in the match, 0–45 in seven overs.

With Willis retiring after the third Test and the injured Dilley missing the entire summer, England's room for manoeuvre was now more restricted than ever. In retrospect it seems that Foster should have been made the mainstay of the pace configuration, either with the new ball or, ideally, as first change behind an attacking Botham, who would be rested sooner rather than later. But the decision was for each of Foster, Cowans, Ellison and Agnew to make just one appearance in the series. To his credit, Gower took all of the fast bowlers who had worked for him, save Pringle, to India but, whether or not the future was thought to be with Foster, one of the unwieldy sextet, Pringle, Foster, Allott, Cowans, Ellison or Agnew should surely have been granted a full series?

England's playing policy was initially cautious, with Miller, Pringle and – as replacement for the retired Bob Taylor – Paul Downton in the late middle order. At 2–0 down, something of a halfway house position was then adopted at Leeds before a sudden swing to the offensive occurred in the last two Tests, four specialist bowlers being incorporated to complement Botham. There is an obvious temptation, and some real justification, for altering strategies in response to results, but the tendency revealed here, as so often in England, was of a side reacting rather than planning. Gower's sides brought a lot of thought to the question of how to bowl at individual opponents, but applied this more in the context of single games than of a series. If this hints only vaguely at a faith in inspiration rather than prudence, then the dramatic gesture of declaring the innings closed in the second Test, itself counter to the initial emphasis on consolidation, says much.

It is easy to sympathise with England's inclinations here. The first Test had followed a forbiddingly well-trodden path, via irresolute batting and a West Indian scoring-rate of 4.23 per over, to defeat by an innings and 180 runs. Despite a slow, flat Edgbaston pitch, Garner had contrived to make the ball cut back prodigiously and Richards had dispatched good balls on off stump over mid-wicket for six. Reacquainted with how formidable their opponents were, England now found themselves at Lord's with the rare luxury of parity at the start of a fifth day. The ball had swung earlier in the match, it could not be known how spectacularly Greenidge would play, and the desire immediately to square the series outweighed the risk of going 2–0 down and thus effectively conceding the summer.

Since England accepted bad light at Lord's on the fourth evening when 287–7, it seems only logical to assume that Gower had not yet decided to declare. In the circumstances, the prospect was of relatively comfortable scoring in the fifty minutes which remained. The closure came, in fact, twenty minutes into the last day after just 13 runs had been added. That, and the fact that nine wickets were now down, indicated a certain needless and urgent bravado. The sober question to be addressed at Test level was whether, in the light of likely pitches to come, risk at this stage represented England's best chance of competing in the series. It did not. Moreover, victory at Lord's was arguably more likely if, with due wariness, England had set about defending a final, all-out lead against a side in two minds over their tactics. Certainly it would better have secured the chance to fight another day.

The side deserves unreserved admiration for the fact that, despite Lord's, they held their own in the third Test until half the course was run. At this point, a batting collapse against Marshall, who had already struck an appreciable psychological blow by bowling at all with his fractured thumb, reduced the second innings from 104–2 to 159. It was the team's feeling that a lead of even 200, rather than the 127 gained, might have brought success in the conditions. For the second time in a fortnight England faced the frustration of failing to force their advantage home. Though, in marked contrast to the Caribbean eighteen months later, a new Test was still approached with optimism, doubt soon tended to take over. Even mild reverses saw the side beginning to succumb.

In the fourth Test, an inappropriate spell from Botham, after West Indies had lunched at 77–4 on the first day, began a slide compounded later when Winston Davis was allowed to carve his way to the single Test fifty of his career. At the Oval, where England competed well again until far into the West Indies second innings, Haynes made his one real contribution of the summer, helping to add 82 for the fifth wicket and then carry the side to 346 from 214–5. Small incidents often indicate a lot in cricket. At Old Trafford, with England on 278–9, 23 runs short of saving the follow-on, Lamb (98 not out) was joined by Terry who had earlier retired hurt with a broken arm. Lamb took 2 runs from the last ball of an over to complete his century and began to leave the field, believing that Terry had been sent out merely to see him to his landmark. Only then did Gower appear on the balcony to indicate that the batsmen should stay. Now facing a full over, and batting, in effect, one-handed, Terry was immediately bowled. On its own, such confusion was clearly not critical, but had England saved the follow-on in this match they would almost certainly have gained a draw.

Again, it seems uncharitable in the extreme to highlight apparently minor points. But if we are asking why England lost 5–0 to West Indies where other sides at least maintained dignity, it is in these elements that the answer lies. Together, they speak of a side which had now failed to play as a consistent Test unit for two years. On a wider plane we might cite the repeated tendency for the team's total to be built around only one significant score, for example. Or the slight all-or-nothing quality about Lamb's batting in an otherwise extraordinary series. It may be thought that the difference between losing 3–0 and losing 5–0 offers scant consolation. But the long-term effects, in respect of self-esteem and collective education, are considerable. To borrow from the county game, England, in failing to grasp in their entirety the demands of Test cricket, played very much like a Lancashire, a Hampshire or a Northamptonshire rather than an Essex or a Middlesex. They promised much but too often delivered less.

The sense of a side lacking a clear idea of what they were trying to achieve, and of how exactly, at this level, to achieve it, was evident again in the final Test of the summer, against Sri Lanka. In a game where much of the cricket was not matched to context, it seemed hard indeed on Broad and Tavaré to be castigated for scoring only 49 runs in the twenty-seven overs of the Saturday afternoon session. The implication in the press was that both were attempting too assiduously to secure a place in India. That England should reach late August, and a game of allegedly no great import, with players still in doubt over future selection was itself unsatisfactory. But since England needed 292 to save the follow-on, and both players had displayed equal stamina against West Indies, the approach of Broad and Tavaré, if excessive, was arguably well advised. It apparently conflicted, however, with the rather hazily understood priorities which English cricket, and English society perhaps, now entertained – so much so that Gower offered a public apology for its lack of 'fun'.

INDIA v ENGLAND, 1984–85

Average England total: 421 *Average India total: 427*

Date	**Venue**	**Result**	**Caps per Eng. Player**
28 Nov–3 Dec	Bombay	*India* by 8 wickets	19.64
12–17 Dec	Delhi	*England* by 8 wickets	20.64
31 Dec–5 Jan	Calcutta	Drawn	21.64
13–18 Jan	Madras	*England* by 9 wickets	22.73
31 Jan–5 Feb	Kanpur	Drawn	23.73

Tour party: D. I. Gower (captain), J. P. Agnew, P. J. W. Allott, N. G. Cowans, C. S. Cowdrey, P. R. Downton (wicket-keeper), P. H. Edmonds, R. M. Ellison, N. A. Foster, G. Fowler, B. N. French (wicket-keeper), M. W. Gatting, A. J. Lamb, V. J. Marks, M. D. Moxon, P. I. Pocock, R. T. Robinson; A. S. Brown (manager).

Selectors: P. B. H. May (chairman), A. V. Bedser, P. J. Sharpe, A. C. Smith.

England's victory in the second Test in Delhi was their first for almost sixteen months. That the side which won there could put behind them a record of eight defeats in their last thirteen matches and take a series in India was a striking achievement. Indeed, to Gower's party falls the credit, shared with Gatting's in Australia two years later, for arguably the most impressive all-round team performance in the twenty-three Test series of the 1980s. It is a large claim to make, and it is as well to acknowledge immediately that the quality of the opposition was not high. The Indian team which won in Bombay gained their first success since the defeat of Fletcher's side at that same venue thirty-two Tests before. If, in the interim, India had fought some creditable draws, notably against West Indies, their experiences in the previous three years had been even more disappointing than England's.

It cannot be emphasised enough, moreover, that facing the Indian attack was utterly different to confronting West Indian pace. A line-up led by Kapil Dev, who did not, as it proved, bowl well, and supported by Sivaramakrishnan, Yadav, Shastri and either Chetan Sharma or Gopal Sharma was significantly less menacing than, say, half a dozen of the county attacks typically encountered in England. On the other hand, the Indian batting was not only of daunting strength but of the highest technical proficiency and orthodoxy. We have already discussed at some length the difficulties faced by a touring side attempting to fight back, in India, after the loss of the first Test. To achieve this against so imposing a batting formation showed a level of spirit, commitment and unity in England's ranks on this tour unparalleled in our period before the accession of Gooch.

If the Indian attack was substandard, it was unquestionably not, in essence, less talented than the one which, with Kepil Dev again under-performing, was to defeat England twice in 1986. The key distinction, a year and a half on, was, as so often, in attitude. The side in India was disposed to ignore adversity and make the best of the opportunities their ability could create. But by Gower's last Test as captain in June 1986 – though six of his team-mates had been with him on this tour – the sense would be of an unregenerate England starting again from scratch. All conviction, in selection and strategy, had once more been lost.

The tone of the contest is conveyed well by the average scores of the two sides. In a subcontinent series marked by the customary dominance of the bat, crucial performances with the ball at vital times proved just enough for England. This was pre-eminently true of Foster's 6–104 and 5–59 at Madras, on a pitch so good that England had made their highest score (652–7 declared) against India. And earlier, India, leading by 93 at lunch on the final day of the second Test, were reduced from 207–4 to 235 all out by the specialist attacking spin of Edmonds and Pat Pocock. It was an instance of England inflicting precisely the kind of disorienting collapse on an opponent from which they themselves had so often suffered in previous series.

Such wresting of the initiative at decisive times is, of course, the essence of tense, competitive Test cricket between evenly matched sides. The advantage will usually pass to the team whose wish to prevail and whose common purpose is stronger. In recovering so unexpectedly and so soon from the loss of the first Test, England conceivably made possible their later victory in Madras. Not only had their own approach and enthusiasm gained swift reward, but the Indians had received the kind of affront to their confidence which England, of late, had but rarely delivered.

It was in no sense coincidental that the side which achieved this had, in Bombay, been the most inexperienced fielded by England in the forty-five Tests we have examined hitherto. Nor, perhaps, is it irrelevant that no more 'junior' eleven was to start a series until Gooch's novices won at Sabina Park in 1990. Innocent endeavour will undoubtedly not sustain a team which lacks the requisite international ability. Yet too frequently in the 1980s, England would display high talent which succeeded in some circumstances but lacked direction in others. If, to be cynical, naïvety helped, specifically in India, to avoid despondency after surrendering the opening Test, unjaded pride in performance was far more influential.

It conferred, for example, a readiness to accept hard labour and overlook minor ailment or injury to the extent that, astonishingly, only twelve players appeared in the five Tests. It meant also that the team maintained one of the most inspired England fielding performances of the decade. At Madras, where Fowler survived two chances before reaching 75 of the 201 he contributed to England's 380-run first-innings lead, this difference between the sides' fielding was clearly instrumental in victory. Even in Calcutta, with India batting for 200 overs to their first-innings declaration and the near-certainty of a draw, England remained attentive and disciplined in the field.

More pertinent still, the side played cricket which was attuned to Test rigours, yet remained adaptable to circumstance. Tim Robinson, who with Gatting and Fowler supplied the core of the batting, consistently played long opening innings to give the order stability. But when aggression was essential in the fourth Test, Gatting's 207, built on a first-wicket foundation of 178, required only 308 balls. And before tea on the fourth day of the final Test, with England 286–6 and needing 68 to save the follow-on, Edmonds joined Gower to fight for the critical runs which secured the draw and thus the series.

All this took place in the context of a series in which the captain, in theory the team's principal batsman, was to find no more than 167 runs at 27.83. Far from this providing even a subconscious excuse for failure, it seemed to increase the side's determination. In short, removed from the unnecessary pressures associated with performing at home, and confident in selection, players operated as a team rather than concentrating fragmentedly on surviving to the next Test. It may be observed that, in doing so, England simply re-embraced the rather obvious attributes of any good Test side. In an age invited to applaud the seductive attraction of overt and permanent assertiveness, however, this was by no means a negligible act.

Given the success which the party gained, one of only three series victories in the last six years of the decade, perhaps now with hindsight its overall selection looks good. The fast bowlers of recent matches had been retained. And though, in the light of his match-winning efforts, Foster's introduction for the fourth Test (his seventh cap) now seems belated, his colleagues had not let the captain down. In simple recognition of his work against West Indies, Broad should have toured ahead of Moxon, while the selection of Chris Cowdrey was, even at the time, a quite evident error. It owed all to the continuing fetish for 'bits and pieces' cricketers. Since it was largely predictable that Cowdrey, despite appearing in all five Tests, would bowl very few overs (sixty-one, as it proved, or 6.3 per cent of the series total), his role was always likely to be that of sixth batsman. In that sense, discussion should have centred, not on the merits of alternative county all-rounders (Colin Wells, most obviously), but on the choice between Randall and Tavaré as the additional specialist.

What remains more disconcerting, and entirely relevant to the history of decline, is the fate which awaited certain of the successful squad. Foster was omitted from three Tests the following summer, in effect giving way, though fit, to the hitherto uncapped Les Taylor, newly released from his ban. And Fowler, whose average after twenty-one Tests was now 35.30, made way for the return of Gooch, never to appear again. Undoubtedly Gooch's availability made for the most difficult of decisions. But if there is rightly no room in international cricket for sentiment – even for a batsman whose final England innings proved to be 49, 201, 2 and 69 – there is a place for justice if confidence is to be maintained in the professional game. Moreover, though the hard dictates of an Ashes series pressed with uncomfortable force, a player with Fowler's record, despite a woeful season for Lancashire, surely merited at least a place on the 1986 Caribbean tour?

England's immediate return, in a new domestic season, to the values with which 1984 had begun is important. Distance may certainly lend a clarity impossible in the glow of subsequent, rousing victory over Australia. But it remains difficult not to conclude that, by the time the team flew to West Indies a year after the Madras Test, evident lessons of the Indian tour had been forgotten, if not unlearned. Not only was another opener, Wilf Slack, to be brought in when Gatting was injured (ahead of Fowler, Broad, Tavaré or Smith); fast-bowling experimentation was also revisited. Greg Thomas, the latest pace discovery, was chosen before both Foster and Dilley. The latter failed even to make the party. Botham, after intelligent performances in a supporting role, was re-assigned to spearhead the strike bowling. And runs were expected to materialise without the positive direction of a batting plan.

In all, the general anticipation that talent will carry the day in any series was allowed to settle again on England's efforts. The relish to engage Test cricket which had so refreshed play in India would clearly never be appropriate to the grim truths of the Caribbean. But the Indian tour had confirmed that a side will explore their full potential only if they think about their game and develop the strongest team spirit. Both aspects of this truth were to be ignored a year later.

Before departure for the West Indies there was a further series which seemed to confirm that revival was in hand, one which involved not only the regaining of the Ashes but exalting volumes of runs. By the middle of the 1980s, the crux of the issue in England cricket was the relationship of other players to the established core – Botham, Gower and, to a lesser extent, Lamb. It was not even a question so much of how the selectors interpreted this triumvirate and the tone it imparted to England's play. It was more a matter of players perceiving themselves less as a team with given tasks to undertake than as individuals who needed to find an identity, a sense of alignment to a firmament illumined by certain fixed, and even dazzling, stars.

ENGLAND v AUSTRALIA, 1985

Average England total: 479 *Average Australia total: 316*

Date	**Venue**	**Result**	**Caps per Eng. Player**
13–18 June	Headingley	*England* by 5 wickets	31.91
27 June–2 July	Lord's	*Australia* by 4 wickets	32.64
11–16 July	Trent Bridge	Drawn	32.82
1–6 Aug	Old Trafford	Drawn	33.91
15–20 Aug	Edgbaston	*England* by an innings and 118 runs	39.91
29 Aug–3 Sept	The Oval	*England* by an innings and 94 runs	34.91

D. I. Gower (captain), J. P. Agnew, P. J. W. Allott, I. T. Botham, N. G. Cowans, P. R. Downton (wicket-keeper), P. H. Edmonds, R. M. Ellison, J. E. Emburey, N. A. Foster, M. W. Gatting, G. A. Gooch, A. J. Lamb, R. T. Robinson, A. Sidebottom, L. B. Taylor, P. Willey.

Selectors: P. B. H. May (chairman), A. V. Bedser, P. J. Sharpe, A. C. Smith.

At risk of becoming fanciful, the approach of a Botham or a Gower seemed to refer back to earlier days, to images of Woolley, perhaps, or Jessop. For his part, Lamb, raised on southern hemisphere pitches, embodied a heavy reliance on the cut, pull and, to his detriment sometimes, the flat-footed drive which was rare indeed in domestic cricket. Stylistically, the three were dissimilar but, in a common proclamation of their presence at the crease, each reflected an age of one-day cricket and of a three-day Championship based on bonus points and the absence of reward for draws. By contrast, an equally powerful batsman, like Gooch, who took far longer to impose his dominance on international play, was more quietly clinical, even severe, in his version of the modern approach.

It was precisely in relating to this attitude, as much as to their awesome ability, that English professionals could lose their bearings. Their immediate models, after all, were men like Amiss, Fletcher, Woolmer or pre-eminently Boycott, men more in the mould of Barrington or Edrich, whose conception of the dynamics of Test cricket was decidedly different. This is certainly not to argue that it was at all times more accurate. But, in strategic terms, the dilemma which English cricket in the 1980s largely failed to resolve

– or even recognise – concerned making the most of its altered personality and new strengths. And, albeit for the widest variety of quite additional reasons examined earlier, it is a matter of fact that the decade was not one of marked success.

With a certain irony, Botham and Lamb together, in sixteen innings, were to contribute just three of the nineteen scores in excess of fifty taken off the 1985 Australian attack. For this was the series in which their unspoken philosophy of cricket most ascendantly triumphed – arguably, at a team level, for the only time in the decade. Building on foundations consistently laid by Robinson and Gooch, the later cricket of Gatting and, especially, Gower achieved remarkable innings totals at even more remarkable speeds. In the first Test, 533 were made at 4.26 per over; in the third, 456 at 3.51; 482 at 3.41 in the fourth; 595 at 4.44 in the fifth; 464 at 3.92 in the sixth. When flair batting came off, it did so magnificently.

Since continuing batting failure, often associated with the desire of the middle-order to dominate too soon, had become such a feature of England cricket, it is important to ask why the batting succeeded here. One prominent element of the performance was that, though several contributions might be modest in themselves, when allied to a major innings they became impressive in combination. The batting was not uniformly effective – characteristic declines in the third and sixth Tests took England from 358–2 to 456 and from 371–1 to 464. But at Manchester and Leeds, for example, only three of the sixteen first-innings scores from batsmen in the top eight failed to reach twenty. Significantly, the only Test which lacked a long, foundation-laying innings from an opener was lost.

Rampant though it was in this summer, batting does not in itself win series. What was understandably overlooked, in the delight of seeing opposition bowlers brought to their knees, was that the balance of power between the teams remained roughly even until the last session of the fourth day of the fifth Test. Arguably, the loss of five hours in the fourth Test had been decisive in Australia's ability to draw, but they did finish 115 ahead with five wickets standing and Border on 146 not out. Only belatedly, at Edgbaston, was a quite limited advantage on points translated into a series lead. The final margin, after the last (sixth) Test was also won, overstated the difference between the sides. Once England had won the toss on a perfect Oval pitch, Australia soon conceded their inability to fight back for the victory needed to save the Ashes. Accordingly demoralised, they then showed the same key weakness evident in England sides for so much of the decade of failing to resist in adversity. While that reflected hearteningly well on England's recovered grasp of Test psychology, it betokened no fundamental reassessment of attitude. More to the point, though much had been admirable in the side's readiness to play as such throughout the summer, their victory depended substantially upon three bowling performances from Richard Ellison in the last two matches.

As with England's victory in India, we must be clear about the comparative strength of their opposition. Such analysis is always so difficult in cricket, because results depend on a broad conjunction of circumstances which may only exist for the duration of a particular series. The main consideration must again be with underlying trends and, specifically, with the ways in which problems are isolated and dealt with. In that respect, Australia provide a particularly helpful study, not only because they shared some of the wider difficulties of the decade but also because, in the profile of the 1985 team, were many of the imbalances we have associated with England.

Following their victory over Willis's party, Australia had defeated Pakistan 2–0 in their next domestic summer. However, from 6 January 1984, when Pakistan were beaten by ten wickets in the fifth Test in Sydney, until the regaining of the Ashes in England in 1989, Australia's eleven successive series (three of them against West Indies) produced one victory, two draws home and away to India and eight defeats. The complete match record in the five years, from 2 March 1984 to 7 February 1989, was P46 W7 L18 D20 Tied 1. The England record in the equivalent cricketing span (20 January 1984 to 30 August 1988) also with three series against West Indies, was P57 W8 L24 D25. England did not play again, after the 1988–89 Indian tour was cancelled, until the Ashes series in the summer of 1989 when Australia won the six-Test series 4–0.

If the measure of decline is less steep, and at no stage did it rival the bleakest England period of 1986 to 1989, Australia too were clearly going through one of their great historic troughs. To an extent, Australia's decline mirrored England's in respect of losing a sense of identity, direction and even, for a while, of commitment in the confused environment of the post-Packer era. Australia's team composition was far more severely hit by Packer: in essence a complete side defected only to re-emerge intact, in its central components, for a further four years. The disruption this occasioned was then compounded by the retirement, in quick succession, of several key players. Indeed a single game, the victory over Pakistan in Sydney mentioned above, marked the last international appearance of Greg Chappell, Dennis Lillee and Rodney Marsh.

On the critical bowling front, South African 'rebel' cricket had also hit Australia harder than England. For three years in the mid-1980s the attack lost Alderman and, with less impact at this point, the largely unproven Carl Rackemann and the thirty-four year-old Rodney Hogg. In response to crisis, Australia decided on a firm future plan and a reorganisation of the leadership. Assisted later by Bobby Simpson as team manager, Border was made captain on a stated long-term basis in December 1984, after the resignation of Kim Hughes. Abiding by essentially the same group of improving players through a time of travail not unlike England's, but not subject to the same tendency towards repeated false dawns, Australian cricket gradually reasserted itself.

The inexperience of Border, in what was his first full series in charge, was shown in his fidelity to a four-man attack despite the fact that the spearhead, Craig McDermott, was so raw and expensive. Conceding, in the six Tests, 3.84 per over, McDermott tended to be over-bowled in a strategy which, like England's over the past three years, had too uncertain a feel for defence. England, it is true, for all the evidence in India, remained spellbound in their affection for continual changes to the pace attack – a fact which Ellison's success, as one of the seven fast bowlers who accompanied Botham, also tended to obscure. They did, however, in deploying Botham with increased subtlety, at last seek the balance to which Willis had latterly been feeling his way. Employed in a variety of ways, and rejuvenated, perhaps, by the idea that an England team had done well without him, Botham was most effective as an attacking foil to either spin or swing. Statistically, his mature return of thirty-one wickets at 27.58, was his one sustained series contribution with the ball betwen 1982 and his extended absence from the team in 1987.

As well as providing hope that the attack had achieved a sense of balanced purpose, the summer also appeared to suggest that two other essential prerequisites of long-term success, opening runs and spearhead wickets, had been met. Given their importance to Test competitiveness, it is worth looking briefly at each in turn. In the case of Robinson, who had now supplied sensible, well-judged opening runs through two successive series, hope had every foundation in reason. In the case of Ellison, whose returns offered the tantalising prospect of that most critical of commodities – match-winning pace bowling – optimism, even at the time, was surely premature.

On the fourth evening in Birmingham, the series still 1–1 and only six playing days to come, Ellison (gaining his sixth cap) took 4–2 in a single five-over spell as first change. Australia, 260 behind on first innings following Ellison's 6–77 after they had been put in to bat, were suddenly 36–5. The next day, their remaining batsmen failed to survive the fifty-six overs which rain allowed, the last three wickets falling in 12.1 of the mandatory final twenty. Ellison's match figures of 10–104 were then supplemented in the concluding Test by 7–81. In a subsequent career cruelly deprived of the equivalent of two full seasons owing to injury, Ellison played four further Tests, gaining only eight more wickets at 46.80.

His successes at Edgbaston and the Oval owed everything to controlled, late swing. It is a mysterious art, so harshly dependent on rhythm and action that even minute, imperceptible changes – almost invariably associated with injury – can disturb it. When the quality swing bowler fires, victory in a series will often follow. Yet it is true to say that few, if any, of the great Test bowlers have based prolonged success primarily, or even substantially, on swing alone. Those, like Alderman or Kapil Dev, who have found that, for example, the wrist is no longer quite behind the ball, that the front arm has opened out, or that the bowling arm has fractionally dropped, have necessarily developed a wider armoury and a different mentality to maintain their effectiveness. Sadly, through half of the next six summers, Ellison (then twenty-five) found his development blighted by fitness problems.

The decline of Tim Robinson's career was less stark, although on the Caribbean tour his record (72 runs in eight innings) was to be disastrous. Robinson's formative years in county cricket had been on green Trent Bridge pitches of pronounced but even bounce. Excited by such conditions, opposing seamers would often bowl too short. Like Randall, he developed a technique against pace which in these circumstances was cleverly effective. Moving back so far that, from square-leg, it seemed certain he would tread on his wicket, he was in fact stepping outside leg stump. He was thus able, given bounce which could be accurately gauged and pace on to the bat, to play highly successful cuts and slashes. Against spin, too, this made him a disconcerting opponent.

Against the fastest Test bowlers on what were to prove badly uneven pitches, however, his method became very vulnerable. Moreover, even had he wished to adjust, always a dubious proposition in mid-series, net facilities on the 1985–86 tour were decidedly inadequate. The fact remained that Robinson's Test temperament had twice been outstanding in excellent series before the Caribbean. There was every reason to expect a return to runs in the following England summer. But, in marked contrast to Gooch's later treatment of Atherton, for example, Robinson was omitted from the side for a year.

When, at the end of the summer, an editorial in one of the cricket magazines anticipated Gower's next challenge with the words, 'If West Indies win the series by more than the odd Test, it will be a surprise', the thought seemed by no means outrageously sanguine. Ashes victories are heady indeed.

WEST INDIES v ENGLAND, 1985–86

Average England total: 202 *Average West Indies total: 417*

Date	**Venue**	**Result**	**Caps per Eng. Player**
21–23 Feb	Kingston	*West Indies* by 10 wickets	31.36
7–12 Mar	Port-of-Spain	*West Indies* by 7 wickets	33.64
21–25 Mar	Bridgetown	*West Indies* by an innings and 30 runs	35.64
3–5 April	Port-of-Spain	*West Indies* by 10 wickets	33.45
11–16 April	St John's	*West Indies* by 240 runs	36.36

Tour party: D. I. Gower (captain), I. T. Botham, P. R. Downton (wicket-keeper), P. H. Edmonds, R. M. Ellison, J. E. Emburey, N. A. Foster, B. N. French (wicket-keeper), M. W. Gatting, G. A. Gooch, A. J. Lamb, R. T. Robinson, D. M. Smith, L. B. Taylor, J. G. Thomas, P. Willey; A. S. Brown (manager). (Because of injury, W. M. Slack was added to the party later.)

Selectors: P. B. H. May (chairman), A. V. Bedser, P. J. Sharpe, A. C. Smith.

For all the evidence offered by the series against India and Australia, selection for the Caribbean tour party implied a return to aspects of the old thinking. Though Foster had bowled well in two of the three preparatory matches before the Kingston Test, it was soon apparent that, at least initially, the attack would be based on Greg Thomas, Botham, Ellison and a specialist spinner (Emburey or Edmonds) with the support of Willey. In that this entailed a spearhead role for both the uncapped, twenty-five-year-old Glamorgan fast bowler, Thomas, and Botham himself – with the probability that each would be expensive – it placed a familiar and unrealistic burden, and one that perhaps was not altogether fair, on the remainder to stem fast scoring.

The choice of the fiery Thomas, and that of the Worcestershire batsman, David Smith, appeared to indicate that the selectors were again embracing the needlessly adventurous option. Thomas was likely, on occasion, to strike rhythm and thereby generate real pace, but in general he was prone to looseness. Smith was correctly seen in the mould of Willey, the one batsman for whom the West Indians had unqualified admiration as a fighter with a good reputation against fast bowling. But he remained an unknown Test quantity where Broad, Fowler or Tavaré, for example, had fought well at this level in the past. All these batsmen had been excluded from the B tour of Sri Lanka, where conditions could hardly have been more dissimilar, which ended as the first Test began. England had expressly announced that should a replacement be required – always likely since, to permit a superfluous second spinner, only two openers amongst six specialist batsmen went to the Caribbean – he would be drafted from the understudy party. In the event another uncapped batsman, Wilf Slack, was flown in after playing well in Sri Lanka, though not as well as either Chris Smith or Bill Athey.

If Thomas and David Smith had the potential to be hailed as inspired choices, the suspicion lingered that England were pursuing quick, miracle answers rather than considering, carefully and logically, what the series would demand. Dilley, now absent from the ranks for two years, had not, it is true, had a spectacular season. Dissatisfied at Kent, whose cumbersome committee structure might legitimately be likened to England's amateur régime, he had taken thirty-two wickets at 33.59 in 1985. But he had made five overseas tours and his haul equated closely with Thomas's (thirty-nine at 31.8). The same faith in innovation governed the selection of support bowlers. Ellison had to be taken (and indeed achieved 5–78 in the first Test), but the medium pace of Les Taylor was preferred to the experience of either Cowans (seventy-three wickets at 22.95 in 1985) or Allott (fifty-eight at 22.89).

An attack of Dilley, Foster, Ellison, Emburey or Edmonds (supplemented by Willey) and a judiciously employed Botham would have represented a quite radically different philosophy. Given the actual personnel adopted, though, the key problem again centred on the necessarily central role assigned to Botham. Against Australia, firm handling, a need to reassert himself and the 'insult' of bowling in short spells or as first change had made Botham a valuable element in a rounded attack. If he was now to become one of only four specialist bowlers, with Thomas alongside him, then palpably Gower would be required to use him with discretion and strength of purpose. The problem caused by this basic error in selection would have to be confronted on the field, or England's bowling efforts would once more tend to drift.

For Gower, alas, such abstruse tactical issues must all too rapidly have appeared the least of his worries. Within fifteen days of the start of the series, three successive totals under 180 effectively ensured he would be 2–0 down with three Tests to play. In these games more than any other in the decade, England gave a firm impression, once the batting rudder had been loosened, of casting in the towel. It is therefore all the more imperative to stress the magnitude of the ordeal involved, not only in withstanding the West Indies attack, but in doing so on pitches so poor that England tendered an official complaint. Moreover, the side could know neither that Gatting would suffer a broken nose in the tour's third week immediately before the first Test nor that Robinson would fail so completely. In such circumstances, after the swift loss of two Tests, it would have been an immense task for any captain to restore a will to resist. As it was, rather than insist forcibly that they should be copied, Gower proved unable to do more than display his own standards in four courageous innings.

England's average total in that series (202) provides in some ways the most accurate index of the team's decline and rise. In the other West Indies series the sequence reads: 287 (1980), 259 (1980–81),

233 (1984), 214 (1988), 273 (1989–90), 273 (1991). Given that Gooch failed, Lamb had his third relatively poor series in succession, Botham failed badly, even Willey's resolve began to wane and Robinson could hardly find a run, it is unreasonable to think that the side might have fought to the last. Yet there is about this collective disaster a flavour of the resignation associated with the last days of Willis.

It can be unreservedly accepted that no side at this time was genuinely in a position to compete with West Indies. But where England lost to them in fourteen out of fifteen Tests between 1984 and 1988, other countries emerged with rather greater self-respect. During the decade under review Australia lost 3–0, 3–1 and 3–1; New Zealand managed to draw two out of four Caribbean Tests and held West Indies 1–1 at home; India succumbed 2–0 and 3–0 (in four Tests) away and 3–0 (in six Tests) in India; Pakistan achieved 1–1 in two three-Test series home and away. On that basis it is fair, if unkind considering the enormity of the challenge, to find but one more indicator that something in the state of English cricket was peculiarly unsound. That any itemisation of the faults determining this entails a repetition of features apparent for at least three years is disconcerting enough. More alarming still is the sense that, in comparison with 1984, the loss of cohesion was even more pronounced.

On only four occasions, in fact, were England even momentarily on something approaching level terms. In the second Test they reached 190–3 in their second innings (still 33 behind) before crashing to 214–8, whereupon the pluck of Ellison (36) and Thomas (31 not out) put earlier efforts to shame. In the next Test, responding to 418, England advanced to 126–1 but then fell for 189 and, following on, 199. The fourth Test saw the West Indies reply in the balance at 249–7 (49 ahead) before a recovery to 312 and the dismissal of England in thirty-eight overs. And in the final Test, with a good Antigua pitch upon which West Indies made 474, England had 127–0 before conceding a first-innings lead of 164 and losing by 240 runs. The pattern, however formidable the opposing attack and however under-prepared the pitches, was that of failure to achieve consistently the dignity of at least a fifth day's play.

Almost every batsman had his moment of great character but nobody, with the exception of the captain, resisted the subconscious excuse this may have provided for subsequent lapses. Were there not evidence of a more resilient attitude in other countries and in later England sides under Gooch (and indeed under Gatting), one would hesitate to call this a failing. In fact, the mood of the side, as early even as Bridgetown, was painfully consistent with what had long been gestating. Had the England selectors not dismissed Gatting two years later and ushered back disarray, the 1985–86 tour might conceivably have marked the culmination of a sorry process. Certainly it seemed to bring the low point of Botham's career. Harried yet again by the news media, he made 2 and 1 in the second Test and, as West Indies replied to 176, bowled five short-pitched overs to Greenidge which conceded 39 runs. Granted just 9.4 overs in the match, he returned 1–68. In the next Test, he came in with England following on and the rest day twenty minutes distant. Making 21 off thirty-two balls, he fell trying to dispatch the last delivery of the day. The fact that the irresponsibility of the rest of his top-order colleagues was equally culpable could not diminish the sense of an almost tragic descent. For his detractors, this was cause for gloating. But it was surely rather more profound than that.

Small things can say much. In marked contrast to that of India a year before, England's catching in this series was poor (Thomas being a particular sufferer) and the fielding generally was shoddy. This was less an additional shortcoming than a manifestation of the problem itself. In short, a side which loses self-belief, and fails to concentrate on a set strategy, is a side which will drop catches. In the circumstances, this made it doubly unfortunate that Gower and Willis, a more than odd choice as assistant-manager given that he remained so close to the nucleus of the side, should fail to give a more public lead.

After the calamity of the third Test, it was decided that nets would be optional. To defend Gower, his feeling would undoubtedly have been that, in the context of extreme duress and low morale, relaxation might achieve as much as a display of hard work. In the end, though, this was a misconception and one with which Willis, the personification of a very different outlook, would almost certainly have been unhappy. A touring side needs to practice as a unit, not for the sake of public relations but to establish in its own collective mind that it is a self-respecting professional group. The tone conveyed by an 'optional' attitude to practice, when a side is after all performing very poorly, is assimilated as much by the team as by the outside world. It again said much of the rather strange conception of talent which had begun to dominate the game – an attitude which the West Indians, for all the ability at their disposal, notably failed to share.

With England cricket once more in disgrace and Gower a Test away from dismissal, it is ironic, to say the least, how unlikely appeared the character whom circumstance would nominate as saviour. There was indeed a danger that Gooch might withdraw to his tent for the duration. Naïvely bewildered that his continuing references in print to the first 'rebel' tour should prompt West Indian hostility, and troubled through the following two seasons by his first spell leading Essex, Gooch seemed a man beset with doubt. He was to decline the invitation to tour Australia in 1986–87 and then miss the next summer's series before opting to visit Pakistan, rather perversely, in preference to New Zealand. It is quite without point to speculate on Gooch's frame of mind at the end of the Caribbean tour but, certainly, nobody would have felt the inadequacy of England's showing more acutely than he. It is equally clear that the conclusions he reached, when preparing for England's return to West Indies in 1990, elevated work and dedication far beyond intuition or flair.

This was a long way hence. In the light of new failure, England first began to think of permanent team management. Ray Illingworth, by no means an establishment figure, responded to early soundings by letting it be known he would take on the task, but only if given unfettered responsibility to implement wide-ranging plans of his own. Problems could be tackled, but only with some rearrangement of the present structure. To this, consent was unforthcoming; further scenes had still to be played of an as yet unimagined rancour.

5
Gatting and Power Cricket: 1986 to 1988

In many senses Mike Gatting, more than any other cricketer of his generation, might be said to exemplify the kind of play which has become characteristic of the modern county game. Most usually described by professionals as 'power cricket', it typically denotes a combative, even bludgeoning, attitude and style which, materially, is reliant upon the heavy bat and, in outlook, regards spinners as mere slow bowlers and county seamers, by and large, as candidates for assault and battery. It might alternatively be termed the 'subdue and dominate' approach to batting, and has evolved in response to a number of different factors: Championship cricket played over three days on flat pitches with reward, not for the draw, but for victory and through bonus points alone; a consequent prevalence of 'declaration' matches; balls which retain their hardness far longer than in the past; a familiarity with the limits of the possible in speed of scoring gained through long experience of one-day cricket.

In the two years of Gatting's period, however, the theme assumed rather more profound dimensions. In the last analysis, the notion of power – where it actually lies and who should best exercise it in the interests of a successful national team – is the central issue behind the decline of England Test cricket. Gatting came to the job from a background at Middlesex which is unique in the domestic game. There he had inherited from the efforts of Brearley an unfettered responsibility for the side's playing fortunes which no other county captain enjoys to quite the same degree. The subsequent path of his England captaincy seemed to lead unerringly towards conflict.

It is not the case that Gatting sought a conscious challenge to those in authority; and, in retrospect, the way in which events, on and off the field, brought matters to a head was regrettable because the real issues of Test organisation became obscured. Yet if the amateur basis to selection and management, with its echoes of a game built on patronage and privilege, was to be overcome, some confrontation, in the end, was probably necessary. Gatting fell; but so, too, did the old order. After two summers of near-total disarray, a new structure, granting effective day-to-day control to the England captain and manager, was conceded. Whether this has simply postponed an even more decisive clash – between cricket as an entertainment for commercial exploitation and cricket as a sport with a coherent history and identity – remains to be seen.

Aspects of modern cricket's relationship to various forms of power arose again and again in the last twenty months of Gatting's international career. It was not only that his approach typified a belligerent contemporary attitude towards both captaincy and batting. In his conflict with umpires in Pakistan he unknowingly found himself highlighting the largely unacknowledged role of cricket as an element in national prestige. On the surface, at least, his downfall was the most telling illustration yet of the potency of the popular press and of its desire to deal in scandal. The fact that those theoretically in power in the game chose to bow to such journalism, moreover, offered further evidence that cricket's sense of purpose was alarmingly confused. Five months later, after this had been confirmed by abject indecision over Gatting's replacement, Peter May, the chairman of the selectors, resigned. The source of power in the game remained ambiguous, however. When the new regime of Dexter and Stewart sought to reinstate Gatting the following (1989) summer, Ossie Wheatley, the chairman of the TCCB's cricket committee, exercised a prerogative of veto on behalf of the Board. And some ten weeks after that, outside money, the last of cricket's modern influences, made its entrance to carry Gatting and several of his team-mates off to South Africa in a final, practical, vote of no confidence in the leadership of the English game.

The concentration of these issues, with Gatting as their focus, through so short a space of time seems now to have had a quite historic, purgative effect on England Test cricket. With a new captain, Gooch, at last granted the freedom to plan and build on something approaching his own, rational terms, 1989 appears to have been a critical year. The question arises whether Gatting might have effected a similar recovery. Had Gatting not been deposed, would 1986, the date of his accession to the captaincy, have represented a similar turning point? The key examination of the advances Gatting had made would have been in the 1988 West Indies series. Since he was dismissed after drawing the first Test of that contest, any alternative outcome must remain one of cricket's great imponderables. From the evidence of his two years in charge, it seems unlikely that Gatting would have taken England quite so far forward as Gooch has done.

Gatting's approach was certainly far more in the mould of Gooch than of Gower. He did not look to flair and exuberance alone to carry the day. Nor, at risk of caricaturing England's attitude in the mid-1980s, did he subscribe to the belief that, thanks to talent, things would always come right on the night. Like Gooch, he based England's game essentially on commitment and effort. At the same time, he brought a highly pugnacious quality to leadership which, in contrast to Gooch's more quiet and subtle presence, emphasised aggression and indomitability. This sometimes lent a rather one-dimensional feel to his captaincy. There was a suggestion, too, that Gatting was very good at leading strong sides but that he was not particularly sensitive in responding to teams which lacked his own level of self-belief and ability.

Gatting grew up in the combative, hard and worldly-wise atmosphere of Middlesex teams which seemed to play excellent cricket almost instinctively. It was a manner distinctly different from the more relaxed, equable outlook of Essex, for example. When in charge of a decidedly weaker Middlesex squad in 1991, Gatting did not noticeably advance some of the younger cricketers under him, tending to overawe, perhaps, and intimidate. While this gave him the strength of character to insist on the best from Gower and Botham – and indeed to drop Lamb, when out of runs, for the only extended period in his career – England sides seemed to remain one final, conclusive element short of realising genuinely formidable Test stature. After a rather lengthy settling-in period in 1986, with a team still demoralised by events in the Caribbean, Gatting's sides undoubtedly improved and seemed continually to promise a great deal. But, arguably, the crucial grasp of when a game stands in the balance and must decisively be captured was never quite achieved. It is not coincidental that, though each of the five series after his first against India was evenly contested, only one was won.

Gatting took appreciably longer than Gooch to decide which were the cricketers in whom he might try to nurture the requisite Test qualities. His dogmatic, possibly even blinkered, assessment of colleagues in this regard was not always an advantage. There is an extent to which the aggressive approach can become deliberately confrontational, and players are allowed to believe that the Test attitude is about no more than standing up for yourself and challenging the opposition. It was Gatting's particular misfortune perhaps that his unyielding stubbornness, so often a prime ingredient of Test success, expressed itself in a period when players lacked all faith in their ability to influence officialdom and, thereby, the direction of the England game. The combination of extreme disenchantment and a deep sense of powerlessness can produce unsavoury results. There were times on the New Zealand tour of 1987–88, in the aftermath of infamous events in Pakistan eight weeks earlier, when the side was guilty of an attitude to authority, and to the cricket world in general, which was merely negative. There was a sense not of addressing the real issues in the English game but of sniping from the sidelines.

It is difficult, however, to see how matters might have been otherwise. The problems over umpiring in Pakistan, for example, could certainly have been anticipated, but players without trust in, or respect for, the game's hierarchy had little reason to believe that diplomatic lobbying in advance would make any difference. Certainly no formal mechanism for consultation or discussion existed. The incident in Faisalabad between Gatting and Shakoor Rana involved, at face value, an abusive exchange over allegations of cheating. All in the tour party were unequivocal in support of their captain's conduct and would remain so today. Yet far bigger issues lay beneath the surface; there was much more to the depth of discontent which emerged than dissatisfaction with the behaviour of one official.

At the very least, there was anger that a tour of Pakistan had been arranged without consideration of the problems it was likely to bring. Beyond that there was resentment that, in response to the impasse which resulted, no clear evidence of a readiness, at some stage, to face the issue was forthcoming. And in this something was felt to be all too symptomatic. The intensity of the bitterness which enveloped the England camp owed everything to grievances which had developed through perhaps the five years in which English cricket had seemed simply to drift. And given that the players were moved to take the unprecedented step, in breach of their tour contracts, of issuing a statement critical of the TCCB, it seems, in retrospect, that their greatest error was in failing to express themselves more fully.

In view of the character of the man, it now seems altogether unsurprising that it should prove to be Gatting who eventually precipitated an overdue examination of the game's leadership. Such prospects could hardly have been in his mind when taking over the captaincy from Gower after defeat in the first Test of the 1986 India series. In selection, Gatting's first decision was to recognise Dilley, at last, as the key England bowler. Where Dilley had gained just nineteen caps at various times over the preceding six and a half years, Gatting now played him in seventeen of his twenty-three Tests as captain, the six absences being due to injury. At least initially, he was less sure about Foster. Though Foster toured Australia in 1986–87, he did not appear in a Test, and it was not until the following summer that the Dilley/Foster pairing was established for, as it seemed, the foreseeable future.

To a degree, this delay in ascribing a central role to Foster (then aged twenty-four) reflected widespread excitement over the potential of Phillip DeFreitas, four years his junior. DeFreitas was immediately earmarked for the new ball in Australia and it could not have been known that a certain immaturity would prevent him fulfilling hopes for almost five years. Significantly, despite having retained the Ashes, Gatting did adjust his plans very quickly. Indecision also mirrored the fact that, like captains before him, Gatting for some time fell into the error – compounded or not by his fellow-selectors – of believing that Test success is achieved by the constant ringing of changes. Before recognising the benefits of continuity and faith in judgment, he employed twenty-one players in his first five Tests. By 1987, in contrast, he was sufficiently assured to resist panic changes to the team which lost the crucial Leeds Test by an innings.

Gatting also took time to come to grips with the fact that leading England was in no sense as easy as leading an experienced and hard-bitten Middlesex side. Used to a unit which could be relied upon to accomplish the basics with professional calm, there were times in his first Tests against India and New Zealand when Gatting seemed to lack either tactical control or an overall plan. Indeed, at no stage did he seem to bring to a series, or even a given match, the kind of forethought which Gooch would typically exhibit. From those games, however, he did learn the need for a settled team, knit together by a common and pronounced sense of endeavour. Whether this attitude was quite rounded enough is perhaps doubtful; Gatting's teams gave a growing impression of potential achievement without ever attaining the fullest awareness of when and how a game or series might be won and lost. County cricket is not the best of environments for such awareness to be inculcated; even later teams, under Gooch, took some time to achieve control.

The player who before any other, and from Gatting's first Test in charge, gives perhaps the clearest indication of the new captain's thinking and attitude is Bill Athey. Athey had made no England appearance since April 1981 when, at the age of twenty-three, he had joined the party in the Caribbean during the opening series of the decade under discussion. Like Dilley, he now played regularly under Gatting, appearing nineteen times and did so despite only modest success as well as favourable early performances from rivals such as Moxon. Fiercely committed on the field of play and highly patriotic off it, Athey brought an outlook, both on life and on the game, very similar to Gatting's. If Athey was no more gifted than other contenders, he was a superb fielder and clearly brought attributes to the psychology of the team with which Gatting identified closely. Moreover, he was to ally flexibility to application, to the extent that he batted in each of the top six positions save number four. In this, his value to Gatting might be compared to that of Randall to Willis or Alec Stewart to Gooch, though his make-up was hardly similar.

The other consistent element in Gatting's selection policy was an expansion of Gower's invariable desire for spin. Having watched Emburey and Edmonds operate so effectively throughout his formative Middlesex years, Gatting perceived spin as essentially a means to keep things tight, but also to win Tests on helpful pitches. Though he occasionally over-attacked, Gatting employed spinners more tellingly than almost any captain in county cricket and in seventeen of his twenty-three Tests as captain, he included two. There is every likelihood that he would have continued to do so had he retained the captaincy, despite Edmonds's retirement in 1987.

Latterly, his, and indeed England's, general reliance on Emburey as a stock-bowling all-rounder who found it difficult to switch from one-day norms of containment lent a decided novelty to the conception of the attack's balance. For the most part this innovation worked well, though, and, certainly for Gatting, the latitude which Emburey's tireless accuracy provided was essential to the manipulation of the attack. The emphasis on spin also perhaps influenced Gatting and the selectors in their immediate decision to replace Downton as wicket-keeper with the superior specialist skills of Bruce French.

ENGLAND v INDIA, 1986

Average England total: 221 *Average India total: 310*

Date	**Venue**	**Result**	**Caps per Eng. Player**
5–10 June	Lord's	*India* by 5 wickets	34.18
19–23 June	Headingley	*India* by 279 runs	22.36
3–8 July	Edgbaston	Drawn	26.55

D. I. Gower (captain for the first Test), M. W. Gatting (captain for the second and third Tests), C. W. J. Athey, M. R. Benson, G. R. Dilley, P. R. Downton (wicket-keeper), P. H. Edmonds, R. M. Ellison, J. E. Emburey, N. A. Foster, B. N. French (wicket-keeper), G. A. Gooch, A. J. Lamb, J. K. Lever, D. R. Pringle, N. V. Radford, R. T. Robinson, W. N. Slack, C. L. Smith.

Selectors: P. B. H. May (chairman), P. J. Sharpe, A. C. Smith, F. J. Titmus.

Following defeat in only one of the previous six home series, England crowds had to a degree been shielded from the recurrent loss of direction and self-belief which for some years had been overtaking the Test side abroad. If that was so, then illusion was about to be shattered with a vengeance. Four successive summers would now pass in failure and, between September 1985 and July 1990, only Sri Lanka (once) would be beaten at home. Yet for Gatting, 1986 was the only season which could be thought of as a disaster, and even that summer contained signs of renewal. By the following year, a sense of at least potential restitution had evidently returned before England effectively shot themselves in the foot by sacking Gatting and inviting the unabated dismay of 1988 and 1989.

Given the level of demoralisation which remained after England's batting efforts in the Caribbean, and the fact that Gatting, taking over after defeat at Lord's, could not immediately galvanise the upper order, there is a temptation now, uncharitable perhaps to India, to write off this series as an anomaly. The formidable strength of the tourists' batting order, exemplified by an undefeated century from Vengsarkar at Leeds which was amongst the most masterly seen in England during the decade, would always have been very difficult to overcome cheaply. Ordinarily, it might have been expected that the series would be decided by one conclusive Test alone – Headingley, in theory – and that familiarity with the conditions there would just favour England. In fact, owing to a level of underperformance with the bat which, like the abysmal fielding in West Indies, indicated almost stupefied resignation, England were probably saved from 3–0 defeat only by rain.

Though at the time there were criticisms of the bowling – Dilley, for example, gaining his first cap since March 1984, conceded 4.29 runs per over in the opening Test – the key lay with England's average total of just 221 against a gentle attack in which Chetan Sharma, Roger Binny and Maninder Singh took forty wickets between them at 18.45. Ironically, the captain, Kapil Dev, found only ten wickets at 30.60 and scored a mere 81 runs in the series. Time and again, England succumbed to medium-pacers who in Championship cricket would have posed less of a threat than at least half the contemporary new-ball partnerships. Chetan Sharma had innings returns of 5–64 in the first Test and 6–58 in the third, while Binny's match-winning 5–40 at Leeds was supported by 3–18 from a former Test bowler, Madan Lal, drafted in from the Central Lancashire League.

Much was made of the England batsmen's apparent inability to play a seaming ball as a technical legacy of one-day cricket, a conclusion perennially revived through the following seasons and one we will return to in discussing Alderman's successes of 1989. Here, however, the absence of straight bats, a tentativeness about getting well forward and an attraction to playing round the pad betokened not intrinsic defensive frailties, but a complete loss of confidence and purpose. The England batsmen whom Gatting found himself leading had in this series descended into a state of near-bemusement.

They were not assisted, certainly, by doubts over selection and

Gatting's early failure to address what we have identified as some of the key problems attending England's decline. Most relevantly, the incumbent established opener, Gooch, was accompanied by no fewer than five different partners in the six Tests of the summer. Ability alone will not suffice at Test level and it is ultimately necessary to create a batting order with the requisite qualities of character, inner strength and performance under pressure to ensure consistent competitiveness. This takes time, however. For one who had himself suffered from a lack of long-term endorsement and moral support, it is all the more curious, perhaps, that Gatting needed a summer to rid himself of the English passion, in the face of home defeat, for constant, counter-productive change.

Where Gooch established from the outset that it is not only manifestly unjust but also short-sighted to reach decisions on the evidence of less than a series at least, Gatting, at first, sought instant confirmation of the attitudes of mind he desired. Similarly the pace trios for the season comprised nine separate bowlers, so that the seam attack was never the same from one Test to the next.

One of those bowlers, John Lever, a 'rebel' tourist who had last played in December 1981, was specifically recalled at the age of thirty-seven to harness the conditions at Leeds. For all the enormous pressure it would undoubtedly place on Lever, this was in principal, an entirely defensible idea, especially since England were 1–0 down. It reflected again, though, Gatting's initial acceptance of another of the dominant tenets in English thinking, the bias towards easy solutions and one-off answers.

On the surface, Gatting vacillated over whether to bat himself at three, four or five. In fact, his unselfish changes of position accommodated both a firm sense of Gower as a number four batsman and a refusal to replace the out-of-form Lamb with another middle-order player for the sake of the formal balance of his side. Only on the 1987–88 tours, when Gower was absent, did Gatting take his place at four, while the sound policy decision was made that three openers of proven temperament would serve England better than an inexperienced or inadequately talented middle-order specialist. Though this denied Gatting the number three role for which he was admirably suited, it represented the kind of accurate assessment of England's resources which for too long had been disregarded.

By the third Test, his second in charge, Gatting gave the first indication that he might begin to overcome a crippling tendency towards inconsistency in batting which for some years had most notably let England down. Admittedly owing a colossal debt to his own undefeated 183, England reached 390 in the first innings and, though this was then followed by only 235, each of the specialists passed 25. When rain wrecked the finish, India needed 62 to win with five wickets standing. Gatting's definitive captain's innings confirmed that, like Gooch after him, he would very much lead by example. Where this had failed for Gower in West Indies, Gatting was both forthright and forceful enough to insist that others should attempt to follow. Yet the suspicion lingers that Gatting would always retain a greater difficulty than Gooch in understanding those who did not think like himself.

ENGLAND v NEW ZEALAND, 1986

Average England total: 360 *Average New Zealand total: 343*

Date	Venue	Result	Caps per Eng. Player
24–29 July	Lord's	Drawn	27.18
7–12 Aug	Trent Bridge	*New Zealand* by 8 wickets	27.18
21–26 Aug	The Oval	Drawn	39.91

M. W. Gatting (captain), C. W. J. Athey, I. T. Botham, G. R. Dilley, P. H. Edmonds, J. E. Emburey, N. A. Foster, B. N. French (wicket-keeper), G. A. Gooch, D. I. Gower, A. J. Lamb, M. D. Moxon, D. R. Pringle, N. V. Radford, G. C. Small, J. G. Thomas, P. Willey.

Selectors: P. B. H. May (chairman), P. J. Sharpe, A. C. Smith, F. J. Titmus.

If the first signs of batting recovery had been evident towards the end of the India series, they disappeared again in the decisive second Test of the New Zealand encounter which followed. This was all the more a pity, in that much of the cricket which England played against New Zealand was very good, giving an authentic cause, as it proved, for restrained optimism. But at Trent Bridge, where the visitors gained their first-ever victory in England, things went badly astray: two familiar batting failures were accompanied by a critical period of perhaps two and a half hours on the third day when

England lost all semblance of grip in the field and, in consequence, surrendered not only the match but the series.

The first Test had been an even game which neither side would probably have won, even without the loss of more than half the fourth day, though England might well have been able to put pressure on New Zealand by the close. The game established the tone for much of the cricket: one of closely matched sides which, eschewing spectacular scoring-rates, simply stalked each other, awaiting the one opportunity to secure an abbreviated series. And, in that this attitude arguably represented the crux of appropriate tactics for the context, England's thinking was reassuringly sound. All in the top order, save the captain, made responsible contributions and the attack fought well. For this reason, though Willey had been brought in only after Pringle was injured, it seems all the more strange that England needlessly altered their approach for the next Test by both omitting the extra batsman and dropping Foster and Radford. This provided Small with his début and, when Dilley withdrew, Greg Thomas with his only Test appearance in England.

After four home Tests without success, the pressure to win had once more prompted the superficially bold move. It may be conceded that when the best bowler in the world takes ten wickets, as Hadlee then did in Nottingham, his second home, there is a good chance a side will lose. Yet England allowed a promising first-innings position to slip (they totalled 256 from 170–3, none of the key batsmen making a big innings and Gower falling for his characteristic 71) while New Zealand recovered to 413 from 144–5. Whatever it may have promised, the high-risk strategy made both occurrences more likely in fact.

New Zealand's fight-back on the third day effectively decided the series. Beginning at 211–5, they were carried by Gray and Hadlee to 278–6 by lunch. Shortly after the interval, on 326–8, their lead was still a manageable 70 runs. At this stage, however, Bracewell – *en route* to the one century of a Test career whose sixty innings took him past 50 only five times – was joined by Derek Stirling to add 65 for the ninth wicket. England's old failing of letting the vital period escape, even when, in general, playing commendably professional cricket, had reappeared. If this was a fault by now almost ingrained, it could hardly be overcome by continuous changes of personnel, which made lack of cohesion all but inevitable. A side develops its ability to retain control at key junctures, after all, only when bound by a shared awareness and confidence. Moreover, though Gatting's tactical decisions were not the most astute at Nottingham, a settled team abide by an almost intuitive grasp of the game which has seen them through difficulty in the past.

We need to draw a distinction here between a novice side on tour, where a player's place is far less under threat, and such a side at home. In England's case, with a team always unclear about its future and, at that time, assembled for only the five days of a match, the requirement to do well was incalculably greater and susceptibility to pressure accordingly more intense. Where Gower's squad in India responded positively to a challenge, inexperience and fear in a three-man fast attack at Nottingham, which together had only twenty caps, produced uncertainty and inhibition.

Nor was this exclusive to the bowlers. After only seventy-five minutes play had been possible on the Monday, England started the last day 93 behind at 64–3. Effectively, seventy overs of batting would save the game. As it was, England fell the vital 40 or 50 runs short of holding the line. In this further example of their inability to perform at critical times, we see not only the results of fielding a new side under a new captain, but the culmination of previous years of drift. It would be harsh to expect that, at this stage, Gatting could so have welded his unit to produce the added element of, say, 50 key runs at the right moment. In time he did forge most of the features of a good Test team. Whether he quite completed the task is more debatable. It is important to note again that the moments when England had fallen short were not necessarily those involving the bid for the kill; rather, they concerned intervals earlier in play.

To Gatting's credit, much of England's cricket in the final Test not only went well, but also indicated how events would unfold in Australia. Gatting and Gower played with determination. The all-round team effort which Gatting now drew from his side was a taste of things to come in the winter and Botham, back after a two-month ban following his Sunday-paper revelation that he had once tried cannabis, was handled intelligently. Since nearly two-thirds of the match was lost to rain, speculation is largely pointless but, on the basis that New Zealand would have needed around 450 to be safe in their second innings, England had evidently obtained the initiative.

By now, two factors of significance to the Ashes tour, the one circumstantial the other relating to Gatting's character, had already come together. Circumstantially, each of Lamb, Gower and Botham had found the recent past disturbing. Lamb had scored few runs during the last two years and, illustrating that nobody was immune to demotion, was dropped after Gatting's first Test in charge. Gower had already lost the captaincy and if he failed to make consistent contributions, so the example of Lamb indicated, he might also lose his place. Botham's ban and then immediate injury, after his wretched tour of West Indies, had cost him all but one of the home Tests. Beyond that, Gatting, even after five matches, was very evidently a demanding captain – too demanding, perhaps, in his learning phase of 1986. To survive, a player would require far more apparent commitment to a cause than had been called for under Willis or Gower. If this could by no means account on its own for the forthcoming success in Australia, it was certainly not without relevance.

AUSTRALIA v ENGLAND, 1986–87

Average England total: 381 *Average Australia total: 338*

Date	**Venue**	**Result**	**Caps per Eng. Player**
14–19 Nov	Brisbane	*England* by 7 wickets	35.36
28 Nov–3 Dec	Perth	Drawn	36.36
12–16 Dec	Adelaide	Drawn	29.45
26–28 Dec	Melbourne	*England* by an innings and 14 runs	36.18
10–15 Jan	Sydney	*Australia* by 55 runs	39.09

Tour party: M. W. Gatting (captain), C. W. J. Athey, I. T. Botham, B. C. Broad, P. A. J. DeFreitas, G. R. Dilley, P. H. Edmonds, J. E. Emburey, N. A. Foster, B. N. French (wicket-keeper), D. I. Gower, A. J. Lamb, C. J. Richards (wicket-keeper), W. N. Slack, G. C. Small, J. J. Whitaker; P. M. Lush (tour manager), M. J. Stewart (team manager).

Selectors: P. B. H. May (chairman), P. J. Sharpe, A. C. Smith, F. J. Titmus.

It is perhaps worth re-emphasising the point that, tempting – and assuredly less perplexing – though it is to view the history of a cricket team as a continuum, its actual development is not so comfortably linear. Progress is always subject to varying surfaces and conditions and to the ever-changing levels of advance achieved by different opponents. In that sense a side's emotional and psychological make-up cannot really be known until it has passed, successful and intact, through some two or three, preferably difficult, series. The emergent team which England now beat 2–1 to retain the Ashes was, like that of fifteen months earlier, still very far from being a vintage Australian side. Alderman's ban continued, McDermott had lost his way, Merv Hughes lacked a settled attack to relate to, and the twenty-three-year-old Bruce Reid was, in effect, the only serious bowling threat. That said, the victory gained by a happy and settled England tour party, of which only thirteen players appeared in the Tests, was not simply excellent, but depended on possibly the greatest range of individual contributions in any series during the decade. This is an important point, because if a side's match-winning players realise their talent at the most only periodically, then the key is for the captain to get the best from the other players under him.

The first Test was won by several batting offerings, but crucially by a genuinely weighty Test innings from Botham (138 as opposed, perhaps, to 60 or 70) which made the difference between Australia being forced to follow on and their escaping to fight for a draw. On the bowling front, first Dilley, with 5–68, and then Emburey, with 5–80, made this advantage tell. Moreover, the attack was conceived as a unit. While Dilley would always be the spearhead, Botham was used in the Brisbane Test first as third change and then with the new ball. This he retained at Perth before bowling second and first change in the fourth Test and first and third in Sydney (Adelaide had been missed through injury). In short, Gatting became the first captain, since Botham's loss of his wicket-taking edge, with the strength of mind and tactical grasp to employ him as part of a plan which did not automatically reserve for him a leading role.

In the second Test, every batsman, save Lamb and Botham, had cause for satisfaction in a total of 592–8 declared and Dilley again bowled well. Context is all in cricket: with such a cushion of runs behind him after almost two days' batting, Gatting had exactly the right opportunity to indulge Botham and ask him to find wickets irrespective of cost. That this approach was unsuccessful did not detract from the merit in these circumstances of entrusting him with the new ball. In Adelaide, where Australia batted first on the customary perfect pitch, a further facet of the England game found Emburey and Edmonds bowling 98 overs at 2.56 an over which meant that, though only five Australian wickets were lost, they needed two days for 514 runs. Having thereby made the task of gaining the draw appreciably less forbidding, England again batted well with only Lamb and the débutant Whitaker failing. The sense again was of each player fulfilling his part and of the side, in consequence, acting in concert.

The greatest advertisement for the frame of mind Gatting had now instilled came in Melbourne where, with a result always likely and England still only 1–0 up, Dilley was unable to take the field in the critical game. Gaining the advantage of winning the toss and putting Australia in, Gatting saw his replacement for Dilley, Gladstone Small, take 5–48 in his third Test. Even more notable than this, perhaps, was that Botham, used in a calculated back-up capacity, followed his captain's plans to return 5–41. Influenced by a rib injury, Botham had been prevailed upon to offer support bowling off a short run. The rethink delayed for four years had at last been undertaken and was to be continued against Pakistan the following summer.

To the dismay of Australia's followers, both Small and, more so, Botham were assisted by some decidedly rash batting from a side too anxious to display its self-belief. If this was poignantly a case of England turning the tables, it spoke highly of the squad mentality Gatting had begun to build. Test cricket is all about the imposition of a team's collective will, a subtle process in which aggression plays only a part. Where England in the past had betrayed the insecurity and lack of cohesion which results from failure to find an identity, the same was now true of an Australian side still in its formative years. Yet Border's fate, need it be reiterated, was rather different from Gatting's.

Even in the defeat at Sydney, most of the England players had a good match, with the key exception of the openers. For once denied a start, the side just failed to gain a draw, though fighting qualities were again refreshingly apparent in recoveries from 142–6 to 275 and from 102–5 to the 264 which took England to within an over of saving an enthralling match. Chris Broad, taking first strike and to a degree the batting star of the series, had, like Robinson against India and the 1985 Australians, provided consistent foundations. Using his height to get on top of the rising ball, he patiently allied the faster and more even bounce of Australian pitches to his particular strengths in the cut and the flick behind square off his body. This, and the fact that all his six Test centuries (three in this series) came overseas, has led some to imply that his essentially back-foot method (arguably a great asset in an opener) would never be so suitable in English conditions. Nothing in county cricket confirms this and his greedy, even bloody-minded, Test temperament argues that Broad's loss to 'rebel' cricket has been one of the few of lasting significance.

At risk of labouring the point, it also seems relevant that in the one Test lost, Gower started the third day by driving a half-volley to extra-cover, thus falling for 72; and Botham went first ball in the second innings to leave England 102–5. Concentration understandably wavers when a series has already been won, but such dismissals looked back to earlier years, more than to the future Gatting was trying to secure. Interestingly it was the same Gower, of course, who, four years later, scored two centuries in an Ashes series and finished second only to his captain in the averages, but was nevertheless discarded by Gooch for precisely such flashes of inappropriate cricket. This has given rise to the argument that, unlike Gatting and the 'best' captains (the Brearleys and Illingworths), Gooch is not disposed to create within his ranks an allegedly ideal blend of determination and flair.

The terms of such a debate tend to be altogether too simplistic. Not only was Gooch, with his eyes set on the decade ahead, now dealing with Gower in his mid-thirties, he was also looking at an appreciably less sound player technically. While no captain could ever have staked money on Gower scoring the hundred which saves a Test, his mercurial quality had become more pronounced. Test cricket concerns contexts not aggregates. Errancy in a senior player is rebuked, not only because it risks surrendering key situations but because the lead it offers to others can detract from their own potential for runs. Since such a view had been so totally overwhelmed in the 1980s, Gooch was conceivably all the more determined to mark an irrevocable break. Moreover, the parody of Gooch as one surrounded by sober and characterless cricketers is contradicted by Robin Smith, who crucially tempers his 'flair' with a disgust at losing his wicket, and DeFreitas, who has been firmly led to realise his talent.

The argument is anyway somewhat otiose. While Gatting clearly – and to good effect – showed faith in Gower in Australia, it is foolish to conclude that this would always have been so. In the following series against Pakistan, Gower failed (his eight innings bringing 236 runs) and then chose not to tour in the winter. We cannot know what would next have transpired, for Gatting was dismissed. His response to the continuing failure of Lamb, however, is arguably instructive. At this stage of his international career, Lamb seemed in some danger of losing his sense of purpose in playing the professional game. To the end of the Ashes series, during which nine innings achieved just 144 runs, Lamb had appeared in all but three of the fifty-four Tests completed since his England eligibility was established. After the great summer of 1984, when he recorded four Test centuries – three, phenomenally, against West Indies – twenty-four games had realised 930 runs at 25.80. Without the 1984–85 India tour, where his batting was comparatively unproductive in fact, his recent record was leaner still: 689 at 23.12 in nineteen Tests through two years.

Given this chronology, and the inherent limitations of Lamb's outlook at the time, it seems fair to conclude that in the deflation following his achievement against the West Indian attack, he rather lost motivation. Lamb's game was a very simple one, his attitude and his batting – because of, rather than despite, technical deficiencies – being ironically best suited to the clear, though for most wholly daunting, challenge of West Indian pace. It was not really until Lamb gained the captaincy of Northamptonshire, a fresh stimulus he keenly desired and from which his appetite has benefited appreciably, that he confronted aspects of a team game little considered hitherto.

Interestingly, where a common love of life had given Lamb a special affinity with Gower, his relationship with Gatting was always rather more uneasy. Very similar in their fighting response to cricket, they did not share the same instinctive desire to display this at all times. More to the point, in terms of Gatting's continued team-building, Lamb was not only now dropped for seventeen months, almost unthinkable previously, he was also excluded from the next winter's tours. In that Gower had opted to miss those trips also, Lamb's middle-order experience gained strong advocates: Gatting's decision, despite this, to take other batsmen reinforced the firm impression that nobody was now indispensable and that new players would be offered a fair chance.

The other failure of this series, Phillip DeFreitas, offers an example, perhaps, of even more thematic significance. Taken with unreasonably high expectations as the most recent surprise package, he fell away markedly as the tour progressed and was left out by the final Test. It is probably only with hindsight that we can term Gatting's failure to bring in Small or Foster by at least the third Test as his one clear mistake of the series. More relevantly, when Small was injured for the first half of the 1987 summer, Foster did indeed become the main choice. For the next four years DeFreitas rather seemed to go backwards, developing something of the insouciance and imperviousness to advice which Botham had displayed. Indeed in his cultivation of indifference he appeared, unconsciously or not, to be following both the persona Botham himself sometimes projected and the image which the age had placed upon him. More than any other cricketer of the new, Gooch era, perhaps, DeFreitas once seemed to have all the worst potential for believing that occasional spectacular displays will suffice at Test level. In that sense there was a real danger that, influenced by one-day spectacle and the media's desire to transform sport into show business, he would become the latest expression of his time.

If DeFreitas bridges the divide between a decade which did not consistently demand that players performed to their potential and a rather more rigorous regime, he also shows perhaps that Gooch is not quite the dour, lacklustre, method cricketer as some would portray him. For that, most of the credit must lie, of course, with DeFreitas himself. In that he came to heed the demands of his captain and manager to bowl with the concentration which could fulfil his talent, two elements seem vital. First, that having initially opted for 'rebel' cricket and then withdrawn, DeFreitas brought an unavoidable clarity to his future perspectives. Second, that by gaining only a late chance to participate in the next Ashes tour following injury to Small and Lewis, he was made aware that ability alone would be unacceptable. Four months later, against West Indies, DeFreitas looked as good as any medium-fast bowler in the world. We have learned by now, perhaps, not to indulge optimism too soon: dull Tests, flat pitches and less inspiring cricket may yet see DeFreitas return to petulance. It is profoundly to be hoped, however, that in his cricket we have witnessed most graphically the transition from one era to another.

Defeat in the Sydney Test, which DeFreitas missed, tended also to obscure the fact that Emburey, with career-best international figures of 7–78 on the one pitch which turned, had again played his integral part in the bowling unit. But it is a matter of fact that this was the one series under Gatting in which he gained a significant haul of wickets. Indeed, the fixed position of Emburey in England sides throughout this period, and the precise role he performed, provides one of the more intriguing tactical curiosities of the decade.

Between his two 'rebel' excursions (June 1985 to August 1989), Emburey appeared in thirty-eight of the forty-four Tests played. In that time, he took eighty-two wickets at 41.61, thirty-seven of them in the two Ashes series. But during the final two years and eighteen Tests of his near-permanent tenure, he gained only twenty-three wickets at exactly 64 runs each. Two other statistics are required to explain his value to the side. Over the four years, his remarkable degree of economy is shown by the fact he conceded on average just 2.20 runs per over; only in the 1988 encounter with West Indies, and then effectively in two innings alone, did batsmen successfully attack him. Moreover, his batting, improving all the while in efficacy if eccentric to the last, brought him 26.60 runs an innings in that same period. By the latter stages of his international career, it is difficult not to conceive of Emburey as a highly individual all-rounder who batted in the late middle-order and provided specialist stock bowling.

A strategy of containment involving only one man in alliance with expensive strike bowlers will not succeed. Under Gatting the norm was for two spinners to bowl in tandem. But, if at least two of the remaining three seamers in, say, even a four-man attack are not particularly profligate, there may be a case for the man who holds the ground for long periods as the thrust bowlers recuperate. While it is true that, to win a Test, a side will have to take all twenty wickets, the question of how best to take those wickets will rightly involve compromise over the actual resources available. It is doubtful that England were entirely conscious of the strategy to which they had become committed during Emburey's wicketless years. Whether or not they were aware, it prefaced a change in self-perception from a side which seeks forever to dominate and a side, such as New Zealand, who wait for the right opportunity to make their series-winning move. In Australia, certainly, Gatting's maturing feel for watchfulness ahead of the gamble worked well: Emburey bowled almost thirty per cent of England's overs in the series and Dilley, Small and Botham responded at key times.

Moreover, it is clearly not the case that Emburey was content with his increasing inability to take wickets, even when pitches offered slow turn. Brought up under Titmus, a highly effective but essentially straightforward bowler, Emburey was to a degree a victim of his great success in one-day cricket, where he would often be employed in even the final overs of an innings. The economy he achieved by bowling quick attempted yorkers with a strong arm at leg stump was, for the most part, precisely what was so valued by England. On those few occasions when a Test pitch proved helpful, he had difficulty in adjusting his approach, still bowling to too full a length at leg and middle. His failure to make breakthroughs in Lahore a year later, for example, so frustrated him that eventually he began attempting a different delivery to a different field with almost every ball he bowled.

For the most part, given the scarcity of turning pitches, this was not a particular problem. And, by circumstance or design, his role became part of an imperceptibly changing emphasis in England's cricket. While this shift may help explain how the side lost only four times in twenty-two matches after Gatting's first Test in charge, it may, in part, also account for the fact that they won just twice in that period. In the light of what preceded and followed Gatting, however, this was hardly a sign of negativity; rather, it represented a slow, perhaps over-slow, return to realism.

A final question is whether or not there would have been a place for the then ever-present Emburey in Gooch's plans, had he not disqualified himself by joining the 1989 'rebel' team to South Africa. In the England context, Gooch's own predominant emphasis on 'percentage' cricket has tended for the most part to insist upon seamers bowling to common and consistent levels of accuracy. It is, moreover, highly unlikely he would play two spinners and, at present, Tufnell seems most secure. If Emburey were to play under Gooch, one would anticipate a slight re-examination of how he should bowl and, in line with the planning and preparation so characteristic of Gooch's leadership, one would expect him to be given clear ideas to work with. But like so many of the questions which flow from Gatting's time as captain, the matter remains irresolvable, lost in the chaos ahead.

ENGLAND v PAKISTAN, 1987

Average England total: 328 *Average Pakistan total: 410*

Date	**Venue**	**Result**	**Caps per Eng. Player**
4–9 June	Old Trafford	Drawn	34.91
18–23 June	Lord's	Drawn	38.64
2–6 July	Headingley	*Pakistan* by an innings and 18 runs	35.45
23–28 July	Edgbaston	Drawn	40.45
6–11 Aug	The Oval	Drawn	40.09

M. W. Gatting (captain), C. W. J. Athey, I. T. Botham, B. C. Broad, D. J. Capel, P. A. J. DeFreitas, G. R. Dilley, P. H. Edmonds, J. E. Emburey, N. H. Fairbrother, N. A. Foster, B. N. French (wicket-keeper), D. I. Gower, M. D. Moxon, C. J. Richards (wicket-keeper), R. T. Robinson.

Selectors: P. B. H. May (chairman), P. J. Sharpe, M. J. Stewart, F. J. Titmus.

The summer of 1987 produced what was, in many ways, a very odd season. After the Pakistanis had been accorded their first full series in England for twenty-five years, rain, which permitted less than forty per cent of the total playing time in the first two Tests, effectively restored business as usual and made it a three-match contest. Moreover, with a predictably bat-oriented pitch slumbering in wait at the Oval, Headingley, the venue for the third Test, would probably now determine – if not the series itself – then at least who could not lose. Leeds has produced a result in every Test staged in the period under review; by 1987, it had seen England lose three of the previous four Tests, including Gatting's first in charge a year earlier. By 1991, when Gooch's monumental century and DeFreitas's eight wickets were to have such a historic bearing on the West Indies series, the statistic had become yet more discouraging: six defeats in seven games, of which the 1987 fixture was to be one.

The size of Pakistan's victory suggests that they were worthy winners of the series. Yet it is fair to say that, but for the loss of two hours on the second day and, more critically as it proved, precious minutes to bad light on the final afternoon, England would immediately have squared things in Birmingham. There, against all expectations, Pakistan were bowled out for 205, from 80–1, on the last day. The stoppage changed a target of 124 in twenty-one overs to one of 124 in eighteen, a decisive distinction. This, and the fact that England had appreciably the better of such play as was possible before Headingley, suggests that 1–1 might indeed have been a more accurate reflection of the cricket. It is worth noting that without Pakistan's highest-ever Test total, 708, at the Oval, the average scores in the series would have been England 328, Pakistan 325.

That said, England did fall at the key hurdle and, genuinely Test-calibre though the majority of their cricket was in the summer, they again offered the sense of a side approaching fruition but short, perhaps, of the right mettle at the right time. England reached Leeds after a fine fielding display, with the wickets shared again in the first Test, and with another good all-round batting performance, in which Robinson's hundred was outstanding. They had also batted well at Lord's, where the weather had prevented them from taking the field. These auguries, and the repeated application and calm of the batsmen in Australia, made failure on the first morning at Leeds all the more disappointingly reminiscent of the past.

Given the much-condemned proliferation at this time of medium-pacers who gained ill-deserved assistance from green pitches, and the experience of home batsmen in dealing with such conditions, it may be wondered why Headingley did not offer an in-built advantage. Unquestionably players allowed their knowledge of Leeds to induce a negative and fearful state of mind, rather than a determination to succeed. Batsmen were to a degree psychologically beaten before they took the field and bowlers felt an inordinate pressure to perform. Lacking the time for preparation later won by Gooch and Stewart, England were nevertheless clearly aware of the game's significance, in that they batted down to the débutant Capel at seven. It could not be known that Botham would be injured and unable to bowl and that, therefore, Capel would become the fourth member of a four-man attack. And while it can be argued that failure to restrict Pakistan's reply to less than 353 – on a surface whose par was perhaps 225 – was significant, the telling problem was with the bat.

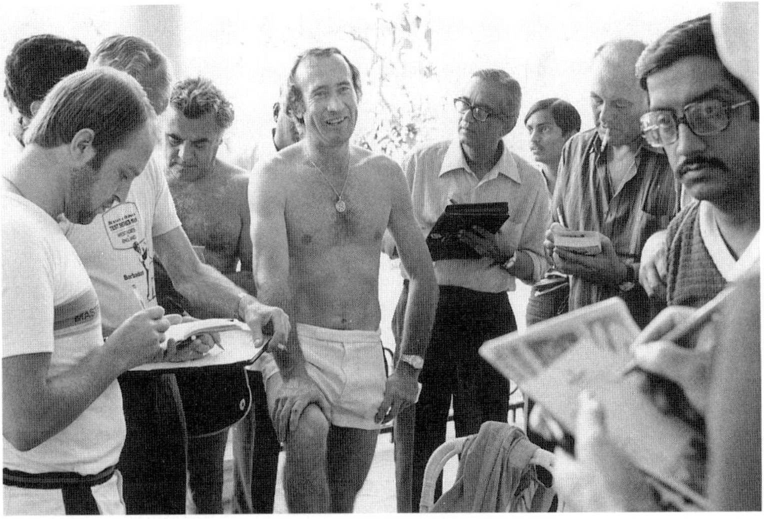

1. November, 1981. Keith Fletcher answers the modern media's relentless demand for quotes during the first Test against India in Bombay. Defeat in that match effectively settled the outcome of Fletcher's one series in charge.

2. August, 1983. Bob Willis, with Bob Taylor close behind, leads out England at Trent Bridge for the Test which decided the New Zealand series in England's favour. Behind him are, *left to right*, Lamb, Chris Smith, Cowans, Gower, Botham, Tavaré and Gatting. Nick Cook, who has escaped the photographer, did more than anyone to win the last two Tests and, thereby, the series.

3. August, 1984. Gower evades a Marshall bouncer during the Oval Test in which West Indies completed their spectacular series win. This was the first of Gower's five series as captain.

4. September, 1985. Gower's third series brought a deceptive triumph over the Australians, largely determined by the success of Richard Ellison, congratulated here by Botham and Gatting.

5. August, 1986. Botham claimed his record-breaking 356th Test wicket when umpire David Shepherd gave Jeff Crowe (New Zealand) out lbw in the Oval Test. *From left to right*, Emburey, Gooch, Gatting, French and Wright (New Zealand) await Shepherd's decision.

6. December, 1986. England celebrate the retention of the Ashes after the fourth Test in Melbourne. *From left to right*, Edmonds, Foster, Micky Stewart (obscured), Small, DeFreitas, Botham (obscured), Whitaker, Laurie Brown (physio), Slack, Athey, French, Lamb, Richards, Dilley, Broad and Gatting.

7. December, 1987. The infamous incident at Faisalabad in which umpire Shakoor Rana and captain Mike Gatting disputed the legitimacy of a fielding change. But far more lay beneath the surface.

8. (*top left*) January, 1988.
Chris Broad strikes his stumps after being bowled by Steve Waugh during the Bicentennial Test in Sydney. Broad, despite his eccentricities, was one of England's few genuine losses to 'rebel' cricket.

9. (*top right*) June, 1988.
Gatting contemplates his future on the balcony at Trent Bridge. Responding to newspaper reports which they claimed not to believe, the selectors relieved Gatting of his captaincy the following week.

10. (*right*) June, 1988.
DeFreitas's wicket is acclaimed by Downton, Gatting and Gooch in the Trent Bridge Test against West Indies. DeFreitas was one of several young England cricketers of the 1980s who took some time to mature.

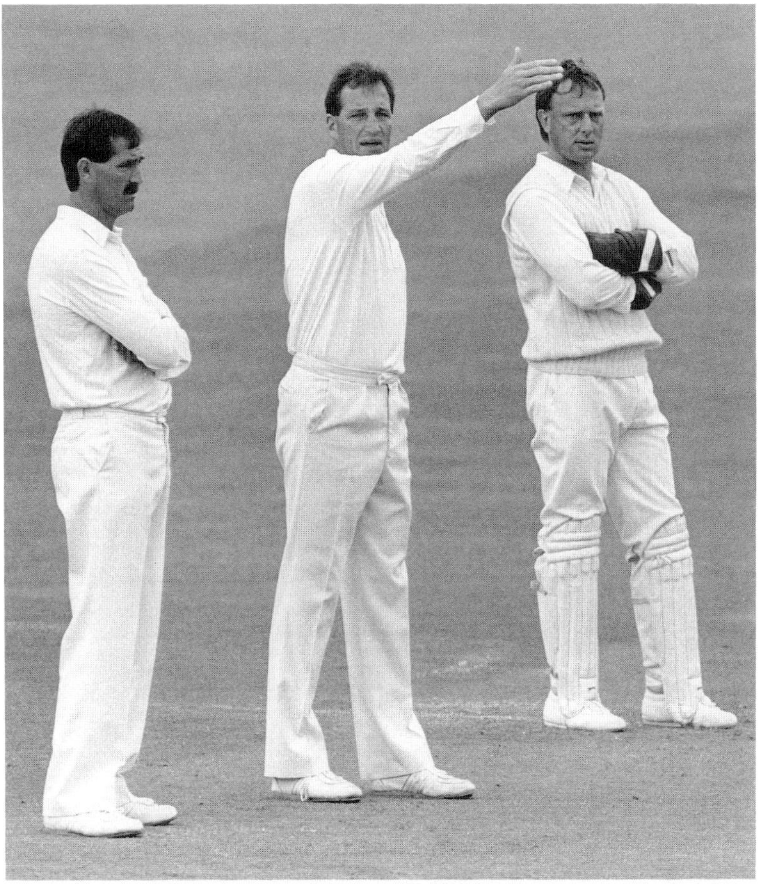

11. June, 1988. Emburey directs the field in the first of his two Tests as captain in the disastrous series against West Indies. The expressions of Gooch and Downton say much about the state of England's cricket at that time.

12. July, 1988. Chris Cowdrey was even less fortunate than Emburey, his reign lasting only the length of the Leeds Test. Watched by Jack Richards, Cowdrey is bowled by Walsh's off-cutter for 5 in the second innings, having failed to score in the first.

13. June, 1989. Kim Barnett about to be caught by Boon off Hughes during the disastrous Ashes series. Of the 'rebels' still banned from the England side, it is conceivable that Barnett might not only return to Test cricket but also gain the England captaincy.

14. February, 1990. England, now under the captaincy of Graham Gooch, gain their historic victory over West Indies in Jamaica. Here Devon Malcolm – a much criticized choice as spearhead – bowls Vivian Richards.

15. April, 1990. West Indies fight back to level the series in Barbados. Lamb (*centre*), in the first of three Tests as stand-in captain for the injured Gooch, briefs (*left to right*) DeFreitas, Larkins (obscured), Small, Russell, Stewart, Hussain (obscured), Malcolm, Bailey, Robin Smith (obscured) and Capel.

16. (*above*) February, 1991: Lamb and Robin Smith, the key South African-born England players of the era, consider Smith's 50 in the final Test at Perth.

17. (*below*) August, 1991: Conclusive evidence of England's resurgence? Alec Stewart, another much criticized Gooch selection, takes a catch off Tufnell's bowling to dismiss Viv Richards at the Oval. The capture of Richards's wicket was the critical factor in England's victory over West Indies in that match.

18. (*right*) August, 1991: Further into Tufnell's match-winning spell at the Oval, Patterson is dismissed for 2 and a West Indies follow-on appeared inevitable.

19 & 20.
Neil Foster (*left*) and Graham Dilley, fast bowlers of substantial achievement who appeared in only eight Tests together before defecting to South Africa. Muddle over a replacement for Willis, and over the role of Botham, was a key problem in England's strategy during the 1980s.

Having won an ideal toss to lose, all of England's five specialist batsmen were out within the first hour, the result, in the main, of indecision and fear of the pitch rather than of the pitch itself. From such a position (31–5), precipitated by a chilling recurrence of past flaws in attitude, prospects of recovery were minimal. Thus, though much was made of Dilley's ability to find only one wicket in support of Foster's superb 8–107, England had conceded the series in an hour of self-doubt. The temptation to contrast this with their performance four years later is again strong but, in respect specifically of Headingley, somewhat misleading. The Leeds match in 1991, one of two climacterics, it seemed, in the restoration of English pride, saw no fewer than twenty-five of the forty completed innings finish in single figures. If that rightly confirms Gooch's 154 not out – more than twice the next-highest score, Richards's 73 – as an innings of true, historic greatness, it argues as well for the continuing unacceptability of Leeds as a Test venue.

Moreover, in the light of a repeated tendency to succumb after set-backs through the previous three years and more, it is notable that England's cause in 1987 was certainly not simply abandoned. At Leeds, Botham, coming in next, fought hard and Capel, possessing an exemplary textbook technique and, in his first Test, less intimidated by previous experience of the ground, made one of only four fifties in the game. Foster produced a performance with the ball the equal of Imran's. Far more pertinently, in the next match, England all but reversed things by inducing a collapse when Pakistan were virtually home. Not only did they come back from defeat, they did so with a quality of team cricket associated with the best professional units, a fact unfairly overshadowed at the time by their ultimate inability to reach 124 from eighteen overs.

As in Australia, several factors came together at Edgbaston. On a good pitch, with a score at one stage of 284–3, Dilley's 5–92 prevented Pakistan from exceeding 439. Undeterred by that total, England's openers, Broad and Robinson, played a proper role, everybody sought to make a contribution, and a lead of 82 was gained. From shortly after lunch on the final day, Pakistan, then 2 runs behind, were reduced from 80–1 to 205 by Foster's well-supported 4–59. The target England consequently faced would probably be achieved more than fifty per cent of the time in the Championship. Gatting, offering no excuses, said after the game that his side should have won. Certainly the bitterness of failing to square the series was the more intense for the fact that England, who finished fifteen runs short at 109–7, had earlier been 72–3.

Yet the chances of scoring at 6.88 per over against two bowlers of the unbroken pace of Imran Khan and Wasim Akram, pitching short and wide in a Test match – where the norms of one-day play are quite immaterial – would always be less than even. The point which was perhaps lost, in the exasperation of a draw consistent only, it seemed, with recent frustration, was that few England elevens of the past five years would, by all-round efforts, have worked their way to such a position in the first place. Final winning touches were still absent, but grounds for hope had now been sustained through two series. Perversely, they were evident again at the Oval, even in the context of a massive Pakistan score, in England's refusal to capitulate when the series was clearly lost.

In appearing at the Oval, Foster, now twenty-five, played in a full series for the one and only time during the fifteen completed in his international career. The fact seems astonishing still. Appropriately, perhaps, injury prevented him bowling more than twelve overs in the Pakistani 708, for injury, undoubtedly, had a great deal to do with this. Vagary of selection, however, had more, and even by the following summer, Foster was again being omitted. In this series, also, England had two main fast bowlers (Dilley, fourteen wickets at 27.71, and Foster, fifteen at 22.60), who, for the first time since Botham and Willis in 1982, were not only effective but seemed earmarked for the key roles of the medium-term future. But for injury to each in turn, Gatting would, almost certainly have sought to consolidate this pairing into his established strike-force during the winter.

And it is worth adding that, to this day, the sense of a settled, largely permanent, attacking core which can lead the way for England through some three or four years remains disturbingly elusive. So prevalent is injury among England seamers that even the plans of Gooch, with his pursuit of continuity in the face of criticism, have been repeatedly disrupted. This has most obviously been true of Fraser, the prospective hub of the bowling but out with back and hip injuries, for at least a year, with an average after eleven Tests of 26.70. In that 1987 was the only year in ten when England's attack seemed – prematurely as it proved – to have about it the makings of competent stability lies one of the keys to decline. With batting problems now at least identified, despite Headingley, this was also, perhaps, the prime source of hope.

Qualified hope it certainly remained, for in the final Test England found themselves following on 476 runs behind. Dilley's figures of 6–154 on a perfect batting pitch represented manful Test bowling and led, again, by their captain's 150 not out, England were 315–4 when the match was saved. The disparity between Qadir's match figures of 10–211 in ninety-eight overs of leg-spin and the 0–240 in ninety-three from Emburey and Edmonds between them was certainly disconcerting – even prophetically so – but, in the conditions, not entirely inexplicable. Had the spinners gained between them the four or five wickets they might have expected, it is doubtful that the outcome would have been other than a draw. Demonstrably, England's resources of attacking spin were inferior here, just as, man for man, Pakistan's side in the series was, on paper, clearly the better. The point, however, was that England were now repeatedly making the best use of their talent.

This was perhaps most significantly true of Botham. Although it was not known at the time, this game effectively marked Botham's departure from the long-term international stage. Choosing not to tour and destined, nine months later, to discover his need for major spinal surgery, Botham played in only six of the next forty-three Tests. Given the nature of the Oval pitch, and the depletion of England's attack, it is wholly unreasonable to read meaning into his figures. Yet his match contribution in this unacknowledged farewell seems to have an irresistible aptness. On the one hand, his 52 overs for 217 runs at 4.00 an over cost more than had ever been conceded by an England bowler. On the other hand, and in total contrast, his undefeated 51 – which, with unimpeachable responsibility, supported his captain's successful bid to save the game – occupied 250 minutes, the lengthiest Test fifty he ever recorded. If, with whatever poetic licence, the one statistic recalled his oldest failing, the other indicated perhaps what might have been had sensitive leadership undertaken to turn his sights unfailingly towards appropriate cricket. It was a considerable feat that Gatting should have achieved this, both against Pakistan and in Australia.

PAKISTAN v ENGLAND, 1987–88

Average England total: 234 *Average Pakistan total: 318*

Date	Venue	Result	Caps per Eng. Player
25–28 Nov	Lahore	*Pakistan* by an innings and 87 runs	24.45
7–12 Dec	Faisalabad	Drawn	25.36
16–21 Dec	Karachi	Drawn	25.18

Tour party: M. W. Gatting (captain), C. W. J. Athey, B. C. Broad, D. J. Capel, N. G. B. Cook, P. A. J. DeFreitas, G. R. Dilley, J. E. Emburey, N. H. Fairbrother, N. A. Foster, B. N. French (wicket-keeper), G. A. Gooch, E. E. Hemmings, P. W. Jarvis, R. T. Robinson, R. C. Russell (wicket-keeper); P. M. Lush (tour manager), M. J. Stewart (team manager).

Selectors: P. B. H. May (chairman), F. J. Sharpe, M. J. Stewart, F. J. Titmus.

Between the first one-day international of 21 May 1987 and the end of this tour's third Test in Karachi, the players of England and Pakistan, whose relationship was not the most amicable, found themselves scheduled to meet on forty-eight of a possible 192 playing days. For the seven members of the England side involved in most of this, effectively one day in four of their cricketing lives through seven months of 1987 thus entailed a match against Pakistan. Additionally, the Pakistanis, during their tour of England just completed, had twice objected to umpires – David Constant and Ken Palmer – who were nevertheless appointed to stand in two Test matches each. Unreasonably or not, both facts would be seen by England players as symptomatic of the lack of foresight and awareness endemic in the management of the national game at the time.

Both also served as a prelude to events in Lahore and Faisalabad. If, alerted not only by this but by the memory of previous visits to Pakistan, agreement had been sought over a protocol for the tour, a predictable problem with umpiring might have been resolved in advance. Such an agreement would necessarily have entailed the right to refuse certain officials – a right England had just denied Pakistan – and, conceivably, to insist on neutral umpires. Logically and practically, it would follow that each controlling Board, both English and Pakistani, would in future have an equal licence to exercise such prerogatives. With the clarity of hindsight it is only too apparent that, if the subsequent discord was to have been avoided, England had either to address this issue or decline to tour. As it was, the question was ignored – if posed at all.

And indeed it was precisely such an example of inaction, even abdication, which, for the players, was at the heart of what transpired. It is impossible to understand the depth of bitterness in the England camp without appreciating the extent to which it went beyond discontent over umpiring. That the position in which they found themselves should ever have been allowed to develop seemed but one more illustration of a general refusal in English cricket to take responsibility for the game's direction. In that this perspective failed to emerge, the players were largely at fault. In retrospect, matters could certainly have been handled more rationally. The statement put out at the height of the crisis in Faisalabad could have been more carefully and cogently worded, its scope altogether more full. Ill-digested and confused grievances, mounting over the seasons, should have been articulated much earlier, rather than brought out on the field.

The crux of the argument, undoubtedly, was the issue of power: professional cricketers had never gained, or pursued with any great vigour, realistic representation within the organisation of the English game. This estrangement is clear enough in the earlier of the tour's two main incidents. The opening Test's first innings had seen three England batsmen given out wrongly, in the opinion of the team, and two others dubiously. Nick Cook's diary recorded: 'The new boys, Capel, Russell and Fairbrother, just couldn't believe what they were seeing and the majority of the players are resigned to the fact that it's simply not worth playing cricket in these circumstances.' How, then, should the side act? 'Resignation' here is in some ways the problem. As in so much else, nothing had been done in the past to resolve the matter or, more accurately, to oblige others in authority to resolve the matter. What happened, of course, was that a player, Broad, brought things to a head in the second innings by remonstrating, for a full minute, with the umpire who had deemed him caught behind.

The obvious unwritten premise upon which any two sporting teams take the field is that, with regard to the arbitration of the law, they will start on a precisely equal footing. They may be victims of error at some stage but they must not be subject to systematic bias. Cricket's own hallowed premise that the umpire's decision is final is in the end tenable only if this first principle is observed without discrimination. This does not mean that a particular player can take it upon himself to defy the codes of the game, even in order to highlight the fact that a more fundamental precept is being breached. It means either that the side should not be asked to take the field in the first place, or that it should make its position known to the world. For, whatever contractual obligation the team had signed to remain silent, Broad's action, and specifically the fact that he received only a token reprimand, offered the very loudest of statements. In retrospect, it was far from the most honourable statement the team might have made. Isolated and fearful of recrimination, they allowed resentment to fester. It was accepted that Qadir had bowled magnificently in the Test and that therefore England would probably have lost anyway. This should have been said at the time in preface to a reasoned and public complaint. For twelve days later, words were indeed released, inadequate though they were.

The precise sequence of events behind the incident between Gatting and umpire Shakoor Rana, as perceived by the players, was as follows. At the end of the second day's play, with Pakistan at 106–5 (186 behind), England were attempting to ensure that the last six deliveries went to the No. 7 batsman, Aamer Malik, by denying his partner, Salim Malik, a single. Before Hemmings had started to bowl the fourth ball of his over, and after informing Salim Malik of his intention to do so, Gatting moved Capel into a single-saving position from deep-square-leg. This was not only not furtive, it was a quite orthodox tactical alteration, and Capel had ceased moving prior to Hemmings beginning his run-up. Only when he was into his run-up did the umpire intervene. Let it be said that, however provocative this appeared, Shakoor Rana undoubtedly acted within the letter of the law which decrees, 'The umpires are the sole judges of fair and unfair play'. He was, though, immediately heard by at least two fielders to accuse Gatting, in the most abusive language, of being a cheat. Gatting responded with equal ardour.

It was not until next morning that it became known, through suggestions in the local press, that, without an apology, Shakoor Rana might refuse to stand. England arrived at the ground to find no preparations being made for play and the umpire's stance was shortly confirmed. Stalemate ensued. Gatting would issue an apology only if Shakoor Rana reciprocated; the umpire found this unacceptable. Following the loss of a third day's play in which various efforts were made by the tour manager, Peter Lush, to settle the impasse, Gatting received a TCCB instruction to give way. This was on the rest day, almost forty-eight hours after the incident. His team-mates, outraged by the Board's decision and the evasion it was taken to represent, remained adamant that he should not concede. The question was discussed until a quarter past one on the morning of the game's eventual restart. Only when Gatting insisted did the players agree to resume. In doing so, they released their public statement which referred to the Board's own reasoning: 'We are unanimous in the view that the . . . "wider interests of the game" . . . had been completely ignored by the Board of Control for Cricket in Pakistan . . . The incident was sad for cricket but the solution forced upon us is even sadder.'

The above version of events has been set down as necessary background, although on its own it is misleadingly incomplete. Faisalabad has been lodged in history as a debate about an umpire who may or may not have called the England captain a 'cheat' – and embellished this observation with invective – and an England captain who either replied in kind or, as the umpire insisted, initiated the exchange. The players did themselves an injustice by allowing this alone to become the issue. The real sources of their intensifying anger were avoided or insufficiently understood. Since they took the unprecedented step of declaring their position, it now seems mistaken that it was not far more embracing. At the very least they should have dared to speak the ideas everywhere disallowed: partisanship, chauvinism, dishonesty indeed. More than that there was the state of English cricket itself.

The 'wider interests' line adopted by the establishment went further, for the players, than the specific prospect of breakdown in relations with Pakistan cricket which, presumably, it implied. Evidently it went further also for the Foreign Office, and indeed Downing Street, whose intervention, sources confirm, in a period where the façade was of politics and sport not mixing, stressed the danger to commercial and political concerns. To the TCCB, 'wider interests' seemed to denote a horror of anything which might link cricket with sensational press headlines. It meant reacting to Botham's admission that he had once smoked cannabis, but not to the mismanagement which undermined England's ability to compete. It would mean the sacking of Gatting when he became linked with a newspaper rumour of inappropriate behaviour, but not an examination of the problems facing the domestic game. The divide, in short, certainly as it was perceived, was between those trying to tackle the question of how to win again and those who sidestepped that central issue by fixing eyes on the media rather than the field. For so long the concern had been with the image of English cricket, and thus its marketability, rather than with the substance of those playing problems which prevented success. Looking back, it was an outlook typical of the 1980s: ignore the product but package it sweetly.

If such was the undercurrent to the emotion which surfaced, however, there is no doubt that the players could have acted more intelligently to ensure a fuller interpretation of events. Certainly, whatever their fears over future careers, the statement should more adequately have suggested some of the complexity involved. Best of all, this more comprehensive statement could have been issued, a formal apology made (evidently lacking in conviction) and further play could then have been attempted. Given the match-situation, the abandonment of the third day's play, and the additional loss of three and a half hours to rain on the fourth day, prevented England achieving a position from which, at the very least, they might have required Pakistan to bat through the final day to save the game.

Moreover, the team should probably not have accepted, however grudgingly, the £1000 per player offered, without the TCCB's authority, by the chairman, Raman Subba Row, during the third Test. Since this was a week after Faisalabad, and came as a complete surprise ('We were all dumbfounded', Cook's diary records), it had no bearing on the resolution of the incident. The players, some quite insulted, 'didn't ask for it and certainly didn't expect it.' But it was naïve in the extreme not to foresee how this might be construed: that cricketers stand on their dignity only until they are financially induced to do otherwise.

Nor, let it be said, was Gatting's side free from sin hereafter. The captain's conduct, and the behaviour he appeared to condone in his team, did much to detract both from the individual argument implied – the impossibility of playing in Pakistan – and the wider challenge to England's organisation and priorities which his approach manifested. A month later, Broad was to strike his stumps in puerile self-reproach after being bowled off his body in Sydney. Though fined, he was not publicly reprimanded by Gatting. Three weeks after that, Dilley loudly expressed violent frustration in Christchurch, the kind of antic so deprecated in Pakistan sides, and Gatting made it clear that he resented the ensuing punishment.

Indeed, the team is remembered still in New Zealand for a sour, surly and rather inglorious demeanour. The irascibility the players displayed seemed to imply that to play hard you must act boorishly. It is difficult to avoid the conclusion that the side, after Faisalabad, were expressing a discontent with the direction of English cricket which it was not prepared, or able, to articulate more effectively and openly. Such posturing could only be seen as irresponsible: if there were complaints to be made, then a more intelligent challenge to cricket's ills should have been instigated. That no such possibility of redress seemed remotely feasible reflected little credit on anyone.

It is with some relief, after these matters, that one returns again to the cricket. Yet, now as then, the actual play which the series featured seems altogether secondary. Given the nature of the tour, it was difficult for all concerned to view the matches with quite the seriousness demanded by Tests. This was all the more unfortunate in Lahore particularly where, if umpiring error had been less prominent, an excellent and potentially very close game would probably have resulted. On a pitch of slow turn suited to Abdul Qadir (more than eighty-five per cent of Pakistan's overs were completed by spinners), he bowled quite exceptionally well in returning the best innings analysis – 9–56 – ever achieved against England. In the conditions, with a par of perhaps 220 or so, reasonable figures for the finger-spinner might have been, say, 5–70. That being so, Pakistan would in all likelihood have won, with or without the benefit of several disputed decisions. For England there might have been encouragement in the continuing, rediscovered readiness of the tail to fight for dignity (restoring the opening innings from 94–8 to 175), if the first hours of the game had not so radically upset confidence in the umpiring.

Ironically, there was further evidence in Faisalabad of the elements of solid team cricket. Foundations were carefully laid,

Gatting provided the required acceleration even against spin and Foster's 4–42, backed up well, dismissed Pakistan for 191 when eventually their reply resumed on the fourth day. Gatting's 79, an innings rich in latent significance, provided one of the few examples in Qadir's career of sixty-seven Tests, certainly in Pakistan, of successful assault on his deliveries. This dispersed the close field early and indicated that, however disturbed the side was about events in Lahore, it retained a grasp of what would be needed for victory. For this to be achieved, Qadir, who was always anxious about bowling to Gatting, would have to be denied the initiative. It is worth noting, in final reference to Faisalabad, that in this Test England came considerably closer than most sides of the last two decades to beating Pakistan at home, a feat accomplished just three times (on each occasion by West Indies) since 1970.

Although progress was always so slow on the pitch at Karachi that realistically the draw was almost inevitable, after playing correct and measured cricket in the previous Test, England lost their only chance of squaring the series by batting abjectly on winning the toss. They needed enough runs to enable at least some pressure to be applied. But, as at Leeds, the top order succumbed lamely and, from 85–6, England, recalling the Oval this time, enlisted the conditions well to gain the draw. In both innings they were rallied by Emburey, first to 294 in support of Capel's 98 and then from 115–5 to 258–9 in support of Gooch. Without this, England would probably have allowed their lack of concentration, however understandable at this stage, to produce an unworthy defeat.

The selection of different parties for the World Cup in India and Pakistan, for the Pakistan tour which immediately followed it, and for the Australia and New Zealand trip upon which, after Christmas at home, England now embarked, had been made at one meeting. In general, decisions were in keeping with the philosophy Gatting had begun to evolve, with the choice of Fairbrother, for example, selected ahead of Lamb. The only slight oddities involved the absence of Gladstone Small, the use of two off-spinners in New Zealand and of three different wicket-keepers in all.

This last, selecting separate deputies for French – Russell in Pakistan where spin would predominate, Richards in Australasia where extra batting might be needed – had a limited logic to it, but

AUSTRALIA v ENGLAND, 1988 (the Bicentennial Test)

Date	Venue	Result	Caps per Eng. Player
29 Jan–2 Feb	Sydney	Drawn	23.45

NEW ZEALAND v ENGLAND, 1987–88

Average England total: 305 *Average New Zealand total: 395*

Date	Venue	Result	Caps per Eng. Player
12–17 Feb	Christchurch	Drawn	22.45
25–29 Feb	Auckland	Drawn	21.09
3–7 Mar	Wellington	Drawn	23.00

Tour party: M. W. Gatting (captain), C. W. J. Athey, B. C. Broad, D. J. Capel, P. A. J. DeFreitas, G. R. Dilley, J. E. Emburey, N. H. Fairbrother, N. A. Foster, B. N. French (wicket-keeper), E. E. Hemmings, P. W. Jarvis, M. D. Moxon, N. V. Radford, C. J. Richards (wicket-keeper), R. T. Robinson; P. M. Lush (tour manager), M. J. Stewart (team manager).

Selectors: P. B. H. May (chairman), P. J. Sharpe, M. J. Stewart, F. J. Titmus.

smacked heavily of the kind of committee compromise which could only increase anxieties. And while Small had missed half the 1987 season for Warwickshire through injury, taking only thirty-four wickets at 31.38, he had enjoyed notable success in Australia the previous year and was chosen for the World Cup. Paul Jarvis was preferred to Small on the theory that his raw, youthful pace, if employed at all, would be used in short bursts on generally dull pitches. But when Nick Cook (as replacement for the retired Edmonds) gave way after the Pakistan leg, Neal Radford came into the squad. This gave England their two off- spinners and six seamers for a tour involving Sydney, where turn was likely, and Tests on the dead surfaces of Auckland and Wellington, where variation would be an asset. The thinking here was no doubt partly influenced by the scheduling of five one-day internationals, but again it is possible to detect caution, perhaps over-caution by now.

Radford's county performances in this period were extraordinarily impressive, and it may be wondered why the third cap which he gained in Auckland was to be his last. Not only had he taken 109 wickets in the 1987 season but, through the five summers from 1985 to 1989, he gained 423 Championship successes at 23.43. The invariable professional dictum here would be that you cannot argue with his record. But, bowling on often green New Road pitches within the context of a powerful and balanced Worcestershire attack, Radford required a considerable number of overs to achieve significant analyses. His strike-rate, even in these years, was one wicket every seven and a half overs, those overs conceding, on average, 3.11 runs each. Through a career this might well be considered incisive. But, given the aggregate of wickets taken, it did not represent genuine attack bowling.

Such statistics reflect perhaps the full length and straight line he would typically bowl, a combination likely to gain late-middle-order county wickets but not usually Test match success. On flatter international pitches, the most probing fast-medium bowling is more often just short of a length, as exemplified recently by Foster, Fraser and, latterly, DeFreitas. Where even a swinging half-volley will have effect in the county game, good Test batsmen, getting that six inches or so further forward on true surfaces, will more readily counter, or indeed drive, bowlers like Radford or Agnew. This is not to say that both men would forever have failed to adjust – again, the fact they gained only three Tests each can hardly be considered fair.

Arguably, Radford's Test in Auckland provided the last of two final instances under Gatting of the side not quite pressing advantage far enough. In neither case could victory have been expected and criticism is a matter of degree, no more. The one-off Test in Sydney, commemorating Australia's bicentenary, had first replayed the other theme of Gatting's captaincy. Contributions down the length of the order took England to 425 and wickets were then shared to force the follow-on. Given the state of mind after Pakistan, this said much about the resilient unity Gatting had built. Less satisfactory was the ease with which Australia escaped, England claiming only two second-innings wickets in 135 overs. Albeit with the impediment of far slower turn than the ground often provides, Emburey's and Hemmings's joint figures of 1–205 from ninety overs here would have disappointed them more than the spinners' performances at the Oval the previous August. Not only was turn, though limited, more marked at Sydney, the Australians are in no sense as skilful at playing spin as the Pakistanis.

The circumstances of every game are unique. But, in however attenuated a form, a new pattern is again just visible of England sides as good at the rearguard action and – with spectacular exceptions – at the careful first innings, yet not so well-equipped to kill. The Championship, where so much of the cricket is meaningless and contrived, does not encourage discrimination over precisely when and how to attack. On this tour, let it be said, the theme was no more than hinted at. Certainly a general criticism at the time of the side in New Zealand – that it lacked spark and vitality – mistook the typical blandness of pitches there for soullessness in the team.

In fact England did better than most touring squads. New Zealand's home record of never losing a series in the twelve seasons between 1979 and 1991 was certainly a tribute to the admirable character of the side, but it also reflected the pitches upon which home Tests were played. As in 1983–84, but with a notably better response from England, Christchurch offered the one genuine chance of a result. Indeed the details of the match seem incontrovertibly to argue for an England victory, had five hours not been lost to rain. The second-wicket pair this time laid the excellent, patient base. Broad and Robinson, who for four years now had been opening for Nottinghamshire, illustrated the soundness of Gatting's three-opener policy in a stand of 168: the next-highest partnership, of thirty-four completed in the match, was to be 56.

Dilley returned 6–38 to restrict New Zealand to 168 and give England a first-innings lead of 151. In a convincing exorcism of his Leeds performance in similar conditions, Dilley had been complemented by the now customary professionalism of the bowling unit as a whole. In short, the cricket was thorough. By the close of the match, though the pitch was now playing altogether more calmly, New Zealand were 130–4 in their second innings, 173 behind. Given that, Broad and Robinson apart, the game's average partnership was of 18 runs, the missing two sessions on the fourth day very probably denied England a series victory.

On the most turgid of Eden Park surfaces in the second Test, England's reply to New Zealand's 301 was not completed until the fourth day. Even in these conditions, Dilley again bowled with maturity to find 5–60 in twenty-eight overs. Batting a second time, New Zealand were unexpectedly reduced to 154–5 overnight and carried a lead of 132 into the final day. Effectively, then, England needed to take the final five wickets in three hours at most if they were to force a victory which nobody could have anticipated. That they failed in these circumstances, with New Zealand batting, as usual, down to the wicket-keeper, Ian Smith, at nine, provided what in some senses was the archetypal conclusion to a Test match in New Zealand. For that reason, Emburey's second-innings figures, 57–24–91–1, startling though they certainly are on paper, reveal more about Auckland than England's caution. Nevertheless, this was now the third time in less than a year that wickets had eluded Emburey.

Mercifully, rain washed away the last two days of a final Test moving steadfastly to the mandatory Wellington draw – 695 runs had been yielded at this stage for the loss of eight wickets, each a cause for rejoicing. By the qualified criteria of a game whose statistics permit nothing to be deduced with certainty, England deserved to win this series and would have done so but for rain on the South Island. This was no doubt of little consolation to Gatting. His final series in charge ended with the first phase of rehabilitation long over but no conclusive evidence of a second move forward. And the allotted two-year span which the decade seemed bound to grant England captains was now up. His successors broke the mould.

6

Summers of Disarray: 1988 and 1989

ENGLAND v WEST INDIES and SRI LANKA, 1988

Average England total: 214 *Average West Indies total: 377*

Date	Venue	Result	Caps per Eng. player
2–7 June	Trent Bridge	Drawn	40.55
16–21 June	Lord's	*West Indies* by 134 runs	35.64
30 June–5 July	Old Trafford	*West Indies* by an innings and 134 runs	39.91
21–26 July	Headingley	*West Indies* by 10 wickets	30.72
4–8 Aug	The Oval	*West Indies* by 8 wickets	13.36
25–30 Aug	Lord's	*England* by 7 wickets	23.64

M. W. Gatting (captain for the first Test), J. E. Emburey (captain for the second and third Tests), C. S. Cowdrey (captain for the fourth Test), G. A. Gooch (captain for the fifth Test and v Sri Lanka), C. W. J. Athey, R. J. Bailey, K. J. Barnett, B. C. Broad, D. J. Capel, J. H. Childs, T. S. Curtis, P. A. J. DeFreitas, G. R. Dilley, P. R. Downton (wicket-keeper), N. A. Foster, D. I. Gower, P. W. Jarvis, A. J. Lamb, D. V. Lawrence, M. P. Maynard, M. D. Moxon, P. J. Newport, D. W. Pringle, C. J. Richards (wicket-keeper), R. T. Robinson, R. C. Russell (wicket- keeper), G. C. Small, R. A. Smith.

Selectors: P. B. H. May (chairman), P. J. Sharpe, M. J. Stewart, P. J. Titmus.

After the disappointment which had visited English cricket for varying periods through the previous five years, one could be forgiven the feeling in 1988 that no new development, however unpleasant, could come as a shock. In fact, turmoil on a hitherto unknown scale was about to ensue, for 1988 brought selection decisions so devoid of any apparent rationale that they defied explanation; the winter tour was then cancelled – raising the prospect of long-term division in the international game – following the Indian government's objections to the South African connections of several England players; and in August 1989, opting for cash before Test cricket, sixteen players withdrew to form a second 'rebel' party, which perhaps ninety per cent of their colleagues might have joined had they been asked.

Peter May resigned on 25 November 1988 to be replaced in February 1989 by a new chairman, Ted Dexter, presiding over a new selection régime – even as, ironically, the initial soundings for this latest 'rebel' tour were clandestinely made. The immediate signs however, promised little change: Gooch, the captain nominated for the abandoned Indian visit, was now superseded in a retrograde return to Gower and twenty-one different players appeared in the first four Tests of 1989. This seemed merely to endorse the indulgence of the summer before. Five separate captains had now seen England through seven Test matches: Gatting (first), Emburey (second and third), Chris Cowdrey (fourth) and Gooch (fifth) in the West Indies series; Gooch again versus Sri Lanka, and now Gower was to be in charge against the Australians.

The 1988 season had also involved the selection of twenty-three players against West Indies, twenty-eight in all or, indeed, thirty if the squad chosen for India is included. It was a process better conveyed by remembering alterations match-to-match: the Manchester side showed four changes from the first defeat at Lord's, the next had seven, the fifth Test had five and by the time, a fortnight later, the Sri Lankans were played, seven more changes were made, no fewer than four players gaining a first cap. More than indecision, this was chaos.

Ironically, the nucleus of the potential attack was as effective as any put out against West Indies in the decade. Dilley took fifteen wickets at 26.86, Pringle eleven at 29.63 and Foster nine at 27.77. If, in theory, the West Indian batting was weaker than of late (five of their eight specialists were on their first England tour), the only significant alteration to a settled top order was Logie for Gomes and he, in fact, did better than anyone. With Pringle, in the absence of

Botham, offering consistently dependable support for the first time (he conceded 2.73 per over through the series, mainly as fourth seamer), and Dilley and Foster as his first-choice spearhead, Gatting had hopes of a sound front-line.

Against expectations, the weakness proved to be with Emburey, for so long the core of Gatting's bowling plans. Emburey, concerned about the role he had come to assume, and fearful of being pigeonholed as a one-day spinner, found his anxiety increased by the ferocity of Vivian Richards. Whether by tactical design or because the mood was with him, Richards was chiefly responsible for Emburey being savaged in the first two of only three extended bowls he had before losing both his place and the captaincy in the final two Tests. 'Rebel' allegiances meant he would gain only four further caps. But it says much of Emburey that, like Boycott and Amiss in an earlier era, he departed to reassess his game in his mid-thirties, where those of lesser strength of character might have been damaged irreparably.

Clearly Emburey continued to figure prominently in such strategic plans as Gatting had developed for the summer. It is apparent, even from his one Test in charge, that he was moving towards the emphasis on depth of batting and tight bowling, upon which Gooch later built his tactics against West Indies. Lamb, with his unique record of resistance, was reinstated. Downton came back after two years and Pringle, still viewed as the archetypal home seamer, was asked to bowl steady second change.

At Trent Bridge, batting first, England suffered a recurrence of the worrying tendency to collapse. They fell from 125–0 to 186–5 – Gatting out to the reticence against inswing which periodically seemed to affect him in times of tension – and from 223–5 to 245. Though over a day was lost to rain, and Marshall broke down midway through England's rearguard defence, the ease with which England survived, after being left to bat about a hundred overs to save the game, offered heart for the future. Gooch, playing the kind of innings soon to become his signature, faced 303 balls in making 146 and Gower, after his winter off, remained with him responsibly while 161 were added for the third wicket.

The realism of England's approach – and of Gatting's captaincy, indeed, compared with two summers earlier – was seen in England's determination to restrict the West Indian speed of scoring on the fourth day. West Indies, starting at 264–4 in their reply, were soon 334–7, an advantage already, however, of 89 and with Marshall and Ambrose now together. Such positions are of high tactical interest. In these circumstances, a West Indies lead of anything more than perhaps 60 runs made victory for England wholly improbable. Moreover, there comes a point when it can be counter-productive to bowl opponents out swiftly, as New Zealand were to confirm at Edgbaston two years later. Though England clearly did not bowl in avoidance of wickets, Gatting resisted the superficial appeal of excessive attack and the 184 runs added that day, before West Indies declared at 448–9, required fifty-six overs. Had they been dismissed by lunch, thirty overs earlier, for, say, 350 (a lead of 105), England's chances of the draw would have been reduced by perhaps ten per cent, a small but possibly significant margin against West Indies.

Given the preference of the period for effect rather than reason, it is perhaps not surprising that Gatting's tactical judgement in this instance was widely criticised. A rather more serious manifestation of the outlook followed immediately and deprived him of the captaincy. Newspaper stories had appeared during the Trent Bridge Test alleging a liaison between Gatting and a barmaid at the team's hotel. With an illogical response all too prevalent in this summer, England's selection committee first offered a public acceptance of Gatting's denial of events and then dismissed him anyway for 'improper behaviour'. At face value, this could mean only that being awake after midnight was a moral offence. In reality, it would seem, the decision owed rather more to the Pakistan tour and to the conflict of power it had highlighted. It is worth recording that the cricket public, in deference to whose sensibility authority now claimed to act, offered its own comment on affairs during the three Middlesex away matches which followed the ruling. In turn, at Tunbridge Wells – of all places – Basingstoke and Luton, Gatting was warmly applauded to the middle by sympathetic, and evidently unaffronted, crowds.

Even if we concede the justice of what was to prove a permanent debarment from office, palpably the obligation of the selectors was to appoint a replacement to serve at least until the end of the summer and probably for the winter tour as well. The options were presumably Emburey himself; Gooch, still two months away from taking back the Essex captaincy he had only that season relinquished; Lamb, out for the previous three series; Gower, dismissed two years before; or somebody from outside the team like Barnett, Graveney or, as it proved (with ignominious brevity), Chris Cowdrey.

In the light of the unseemly and indefensible muddle into which the selectors fell trying to resolve a problem of their own making, it would perhaps be inaccurate to dignify the process by terming it a debate. Nor is it easy to give serious consideration to deliberations whose results, to the growing dismay of cricketers, became almost ludicrous. While in the circumstances, the choice of Emburey, for example, perhaps had most to commend it, the decision, seven weeks later, to opt after all for Gooch questioned the initial decision. Moreover, the uncharacteristic grace shown to Kim Barnett – for whom a place against Sri Lanka was reserved after injury had prevented his début in the fifth Test, despite the performance of the stand-in, Bailey – suggested he might be the long-term candidate. Speculation, in short, filled a vacuum left by an apparent departure from coherence.

Still some three months before the full extent of disarray became clear, Emburey began the first Test of what was taken to be the latest reign of captaincy. On a difficult pitch, in overcast conditions, West Indies won the toss, batted and gained a first-innings lead of 44. The key to a game, which tail support for Lamb's century would extend to the final afternoon, was not so much West Indies ability to score 397, but to make 338 at 3.75 an over on the third day. Dilley took 9–128 in the match, Small 4–64 in the first innings and Jarvis 4–107 in the second, but only Dilley and Pringle could prevent rapid runs. After his 2–95 in sixteen overs at Nottingham, Emburey now conceded 0–62 in fifteen in the second innings. He was hindered by inexcusable confusion over Foster's fitness for five-day cricket which, though he appeared throughout for Essex, prevented him playing both at Lord's and at Old Trafford.

There, in the third Test, despite the efforts of the previous two years to tackle the critical weakness of England cricket in the decade – the lack of batting resolve against the best attacks – the side proved incapable of withstanding the doubt and lack of purpose in which the England game was again immersed. Gatting, returning to the ranks for a single further Test that summer, confessed afterwards that he found it quite impossible to bring the right frame of mind to his task. While he was losing the conviction he had repeatedly attempted to engender, the same was visibly true of the batting in general. During the first series of the decade under review, England had fought, in the Caribbean, to enlist the aid of bad weather in the search for a draw. With well over half the Manchester match washed out, even minimally improved application could have saved this game. But, resigned to defeat after declining to 61–5 on winning the toss, England lasted but 60.2 overs in the first innings and 42.4 in the second: it was as though the period since 1984 had never occurred.

Selection for Old Trafford, where, in the Championship, the ball will often achieve slow turn, had promised a further test of the overstated theory that West Indies are vulnerable to spin. As was frequently the case in England, however, with the showcase preparation of Test surfaces negating county norms, neither Emburey, who opened the bowling, nor the débutant John Childs, gained any appreciable assistance. Moreover, the poverty of England's showing meant that West Indies had to bat for no more than a few overs on the final two days. The theory had derived from difficulties experienced against Hirwani and Qadir in the past and seemed to be confirmed the following January when Border's occasional slow left-arm brought him eleven wickets in Sydney. Certainly, the West Indians lack a familiarity with spin at home, and an indisciplined desire to dominate too soon can undo them on genuinely turning pitches. The impression of submission is then misleadingly magnified by the inability of their own bowlers, for once, to reply in kind.

The rarity of such occasions, though, should alert us to the theory's limitations. It is not usually the case that even tight spin bowling will, in itself, induce error. Formidable power-batting skills on flat Test pitches will permit the same liberties to be taken against spin as are visited upon seam. Put under unusual pressure, both by the situation in the series and by the overall tightness which Gooch's attack was consciously entreated to maintain, West Indies batsmen perished one by one, in 1991, to the excellent, combative bowling of Tufnell. It should not be forgotten that, performing with equal technical merit in the second innings, he took 1–150. The question, in short, on typical Test surfaces, is which three and even four bowlers, one or two of whom may happen to be spinners, will best sustain accuracy against intimidating batsmen. There have been no easy solutions against West Indies.

It was just such a last throw of the miracle-cure card, so favoured ahead of planning and forethought, which the selectors now offered for Headingley. Two months earlier, Chris Cowdrey, by no honest appraisal a Test player, had resurrected his Kent side – fleetingly it proved – by stressing competitive enthusiasm and tigerish fielding. Aware that the problem was one of attitude, England accordingly appointed the would-be inspirational leader. Such specious reasoning missed two points: that the attitude problem had most to do with the folly of selection in the first place, and that it is grossly unfair to expect any real change in the course of a single match.

With some irony, and much hard-headed sense for Leeds in fact, the side assembled was possibly the least overtly attacking of any in the decade. Effectively seven specialist batsmen (Cowdrey was to bowl only two of the eighty-one overs in the West Indies innings) were augmented by Jack Richards at eight and Pringle at nine. Yet if even experienced, well-knit teams had succumbed to West Indies in the past, it would have been remarkable for a side without motivation or an established identity to resist now. Until the late afternoon of the fourth day, against all odds, it seemed the gamble might succeed. At 80–1 in their second innings, England led by 6 runs. The remaining nine wickets were then swept aside for the addition of 58, and the series had been lost.

For a man whose side had done better than the selectors had any real right to expect, Cowdrey's subsequent treatment was shameful. Officially, the captaincy passed to Gooch for the final Test because Cowdrey had injured his foot. That Gooch then retained the job despite Cowdrey's return to fitness was as much a surprise to Gooch as to the erstwhile captain himself. In fact, Cowdrey learned that he led England no longer only when the team announced for the Sri Lanka Test did not include his name. The fact that England had played relatively well under Gooch could in no sense justify this farce. To argue or criticise was hardly now appropriate; only incredulity seemed to belong.

Admittedly, due in the main to the presence of three Essex colleagues in the attack, England's first performance under Gooch offered glimpses of the team game to come. The inexperienced trio of Curtis, Bailey and Robin Smith fought hard in the first innings;

one bowler, Foster, with 5–64, provided the thrust which others backed up well; and Gooch himself, in a remarkable innings of 422 minutes for 84, tried to provide the best of examples. It is impossible to know if West Indies, left to find 225 for victory would have fared less comfortably had Gooch not left the field after seven deliveries of their pursuit, having dislocated a finger in an attempt to catch Haynes. Even in this there is a familiar, if more disconcerting, ring to his opening match in charge.

The last and most bizarre aspect of this unreal summer awaited the concluding Test against Sri Lanka. Robinson, Barnett, Russell, Lawrence and Newport, the last four uncapped and all five destined to be selected for India, were brought in for what could only be the easier pickings of playing the weakest side in the world. Those who had been selected to withstand the punishment of West Indian pace – Curtis, Moxon, Athey, Broad, Capel and DeFreitas, for example – were thus denied a reward they had earned and with it the chance of a place on tour. It is quite impossible to explain how DeFreitas, Pringle, Capel, Small and Jarvis were considered worthier bowlers than Newport and Lawrence to take on West Indian batsmen, yet all four now made way for débutants who denied them tour selection. This is an argument not about the undoubted abilities of these players, but about elementary fairness and probity. In that both qualities had for so long been transient, it was fitting perhaps, as the end drew near, that they had been disavowed altogether.

Following Peter May's resignation, Ted Dexter, the new chairman of selectors, became the first post-holder to receive a salary for his responsibilities. Indeed, selection now passed into wholly professional hands with Dexter joined by the England manager (Stewart) and the England captain in a new, more streamlined regime. This, at least, was the theory. In fact, Dexter and Stewart's very first decision, to re-appoint Gatting as captain, was immediately overruled by Ossie Wheatley on behalf of the TCCB, invoking a power of veto which was not to be made public until some months later. Thus, Gower returned to the helm as the compromise candidate only to find that the core of his side was about to follow Gatting's lead in defecting to South Africa.

ENGLAND v AUSTRALIA, 1989

Average England total: 274 *Average Australia total: 579*

Date	Venue	Result	Caps per Eng. Player
8–13 June	Leeds	*Australia* by 210 runs	29.09
22–27 June	Lord's	*Australia* by 6 wickets	36.91
6–11 July	Edgbaston	Drawn	38.00
27 July–1 Aug	Old Trafford	*Australia* by 9 wickets	38.09
10–14 Aug	Trent Bridge	*Australia* by an innings and 180 runs	23.45
24–29 Aug	The Oval	Drawn	22.82

D. I. Gower (captain), M. A. Atherton, K. J. Barnett, I. T. Botham, B. C. Broad, D. J. Capel, N. G. B. Cook, T. S. Curtis, P. A. J. DeFreitas, G. R. Dilley, J. E. Emburey, N. A. Foster, A. R. C. Fraser, M. W. Gatting, G. A. Gooch, E. E. Hemmings, A. P. Igglesden, P. W. Jarvis, A. J. Lamb, D. E. Malcolm, M. D. Moxon, P. J. Newport, D. R. Pringle, R. T. Robinson, R. C. Russell (wicket-keeper), G. C. Small, R. A. Smith, J. P. Stephenson, C. J. Tavaré.

Selectors: E. R. Dexter (chairman), M. J. Stewart, D. I. Gower (captain).

It is fair to say that the pitches for the 1989 Australia series were amongst the best, if not *the* best, for home Tests in the entire decade. Given the positions often achieved, the surfaces played on and the innings which individual England batsmen were repeatedly able to offer, a strong argument can be made that each of the first four Tests could and should have been drawn. This is less easy to maintain by the fifth Test in that defeat was by an innings with almost four sessions remaining. By that stage, however, the Ashes had been lost, removing the initiative, and, more relevantly, the 'rebel' defections had been announced, throwing a novice side into even more confusion than usual. Man for man there was not a great deal between the sides at the start of the summer. If the difference was, therefore, one of approach, a question of organising similar abilities such that a team's sum proves greater than its parts, frames of reference were now further dislocated by the imminent 'rebel' tour.

If for no other reason than that it is easier to foster the right attitude in a side by excluding those who will disappear in mid-series, it is strange that no efforts were made to establish the detail of the forthcoming tour. Of the twenty-one players employed through the first four Tests, after all, eight were to absent themselves.

Contact had been made with possible recruits – representing a wide section of the English game – since February of that year, initially on behalf of what might be termed a sports impresario and later for the then South African Cricket Union itself. If specific signatories had not been identified, recruitment was essentially an open secret and one of which some in the hierarchy of the game were unquestionably aware. That no attempt was made to pre-empt developments, most obviously, perhaps, by announcing future plans and new financial incentives for contracted players, says much about the merely day-by-day mentality of those in charge of English cricket. It illustrates also, perhaps, that, though changes of personnel had now been made, a wider alertness to the game's crisis had not yet been realised. Only in the aftermath of this series did county authorities begin to awake from their parochialism and from the apparent belief that the national game could be a matter of local indifference.

At the playing level, split allegiances and endemic uncertainty manifested themselves once more in the repeated failure of the top order. There were times, indeed, when the words 'lbw bowled Alderman' seemed more like an epitaph for English Test cricket than a phrase on a scorecard. Batting in Tests is a hard matter, calling for sustained concentration and, in the best-spirited sides, a positive desire not to let team-mates down. The consistent playing errors detected by observers, and invariably termed technical defects, owed most to the loss of these attributes. Clearly, three-day Championship cricket (even more influentially than one-day games) does place an emphasis on technically flawed play, to innovate quick scoring in matches which are unlikely to reach a finish without artifice. Since no points are gained for the draw, it is vital for the batsman to cultivate those skills of improvisation which, in the main, bring leg-side runs. Though this may have a natural tendency to encourage bad technical habits, it is bad mental habits which are critical. In short, a batsman must enter a Test match thinking in a quite specific way.

The point is that Gooch's team did not, months later, suddenly discover the lost arts of orthodox batsmanship, much though preparation at Lilleshall, for example, placed emphasis on proper play. Rather, they developed the mental strength and discrimination to perceive which shots were appropriate when; they learned, that is, to carry Test attitudes into Test matches and leave

Championship thinking behind. For good batsmen, there is no necessary connection between errors at Test level and the modification to technique so often dictated by three-day cricket. The critical ability is to make adjustments and that, in turn, is facilitated by a dressing-room which attentively monitors match requirements and insists upon high standards. A game is engaged as a collective, not confronted in isolation. In this series, where discipline and strength of commitment were undermined once more by uncertainty and the continuing absence of team identity, sloppiness took over. The real problem was not identified: it lay not with technique in itself, but with the lack of a common resolve to adapt and apply technique.

The success which Alderman gained, for example, with swing allied to unflagging persistence and accuracy, was less an exposure of faulty mechanics than an exploitation of doubt. Many of the wickets he gained with the new ball were indeed the result of fine deliveries but, as an all-round strike bowler, he was less formidable than in 1981, especially on the pitches which prevailed. Alderman's three seasons in county cricket brought him 249 dismissals at 21.35, figures which might suggest one of the finest performers in English conditions of the last twenty years. Undoubtedly he was a formidable opponent, but much of his cricket then was on green pitches and, for two of his summers, he operated within excellent, balanced attacks. More to the point, the combination of controlled, though limited, variation with unerring straightness at medium pace has a virtue at county level, where batsmen must press on, which should not be so decisive in Tests. In 1985, Alderman would have been invaluable to the Australians in preventing the kind of momentum that carried England surging through the series. Then, as in this summer, twenty-five dismissals in six Tests, enviable enough in itself, would perhaps have reflected his true threat: forty-one at 17.36 in 1989 was in part a measure of English indeterminacy.

We have already discussed the outlook which had prevailed in 1980s Test cricket and which perhaps exerted an influence again here. The emphasis on dominating, 'inspirational' batting, even in inappropriate contexts – as opposed to a balance between aggression and long, grafted innings – naturally embraced both technical looseness and over-ambition. The previous home Ashes series had provided its apotheosis. Now that the approach proved vulnerable, technical weakness became the theme. If such weaknesses were indeed ingrained in the fabric of the domestic game, Gooch would not have been able to effect recovery so swiftly. More than structural change, such as the limited shift to four-day games, it is the attitude which Gooch inculcated, and the faith his team-mates have in selection, which has altered the Test mood.

The mood encountered when Nick Cook joined the 1989 team, 2–0 down at the half-way point, was of resigned aimlessness. The dressing-room lacked confidence, commitment or any spark of creativity; entering it, his diary records, was 'like walking into a morgue'. In absolute contrast, the Australians, with their settled team, were buoyant and purposeful, alive to established batting and bowling policies. It did not help, obviously, that, on the last day of the Test, certain of the side would make public their 'rebel' involvement. If their disenchantment was specific – and expressed, for example, in a refusal to sign the bats being circulated, as usual, for autographs – it was not markedly at odds with the general spirit in which the team passed the final two summers of the decade.

The essence of team consciousness, and the prime ingredient which can bring individual talents towards collective fulfilment, is perhaps a deep desire not to let team-mates down. For the most part this requires familiarity with fellow-players and common funds of experience. Yet so atomised had England become that John Stephenson, playing in his one and – to date – only Test, spent five days at the Oval during which, he confessed, barely a word was spoken to him. In the same game, David Capel, also making his single appearance of the summer and equally at a loss to sense the side's direction, played down several innocuous bouncers from Alderman which, in a county match, he would instinctively have hooked with contempt. The most relaxed but committed of sides will offer well-meant admonition, even healthy sarcasm, to anyone falling short with the ball or in the field, thereby keeping everyone to a common task; by this stage, England dealt in mutual commiseration alone, sharing not enthusiasm but inertia.

It was a state of mind produced by another series of alarming under-achievement, notably in the top order. Expecting the usual low-scoring game, England had entered the Leeds Test with six batsmen and four seamers. The key to failure, on what, against the odds, proved to be the first of the summer's easy pitches, was less the looseness of the bowling than the inability of the batsmen to survive eighty-three overs for the draw in a match where the previous twenty wickets had cost 57 runs each. If it was inexcusable to be bowled out in fifty-five overs, it was even more culpable to score at almost 3.5 an over in doing so. Gower's own dismissal, as he attempted an airy glance after the leg-trap had been baited – a lapse of concentration the Australians would recall and exploit again eighteen months later – indicated the false priorities which can assail a team motivated by, at best, personal pride rather than group obligations.

Precisely the same inappropriate response was offered at Lord's where, batting first, England made 286 at 3.29 per over. Entertaining this may have been, but the unarguable arithmetic of Test cricket on good surfaces dictates a first-innings target of at least 350 to 400, the Lord's par for that game. Each of England's first nine batsmen, save Gatting and Emburey who both fell for nought, reached double figures: but nobody exceeded Russell's undefeated 64. Allowing Australia to recover from 265–6 to 528, England were again committed to the defensive search for a draw which, with one and a half hours lost to rain on the final day, would have been achieved by perhaps just twenty further overs of batting in the match. The fourth-day performances of Gower, applying himself with character to record a century, and Robin Smith – admirable in themselves – simply increased the sense of frustration that England had needlessly conceded the game. If this implies criticism of Gower for failing to rally his side, it should be recalled that the Lord's team contained only four players who would not, five weeks later, announce their defection. Following the demoralisation of the previous summer, it is hardly surprising, then, that the batting lacked discipline.

Despite the loss of ten hours in the third Test, England just managed to reach their modest requirement of 225 to save the follow-on with nine wickets down and more than two sessions remaining. Botham, back for his first Test in twenty-three months, added the crucial 96 runs with Russell for the sixth wicket which took England to Old Trafford knowing that failure would surrender the Ashes. The game proved to be a personal triumph once more for the two men, Robin Smith and 'Jack' Russell, who best exemplified the attitude which was at last to re-emerge under Gooch. With England again falling about twenty overs short of sufficient crease-occupation to prevent defeat, it also provided the clearest illustration of the absolute difference in approach between the sides.

Smith and Russell, who at the start of the summer had just four caps between them, were the only England players in the series single-minded enough to resist the infection of a side without point. Both brought a certain sense of culmination to Test cricket: Smith as one who had departed South Africa with precisely this goal, Russell as one forever fearful that doubts over his batting would deny him a fitting stage for his skills. For others who lacked their reserves of innate strength, the absence of group congratulation, or even concern, was deeply debilitating.

Smith, whose first hundred, most significantly, was a big one, and Russell, unbowed in the second innings with 128 not out, combined with Emburey's 64 to supply two-thirds of England's runs from the bat. Only two other innings, of the twenty completed, realised more than 30. Australia, however, in nine contributions from top-order batsmen, had only one failure (Boon's 12) and two lengthy foundations (80 from Border in fully 266 balls, 85 from Taylor in 180), which enabled Jones and Steve Waugh to attack. In short, with the professional virtues once associated with England, Australia had a group of individuals fulfilling specific tasks and roles. Marsh and Taylor provided solid opening runs; Boon, himself once an opener, and Border formed the adaptable early middle order; Jones and Waugh, the aggressive late middle order. Added to this were, in the main, straight, honest bowlers who stuck steadfastly to a plan and accordingly gained rewards well beyond their ability. England in this series, riven with intrigue and disrupted both by injuries and capricious selection, offered only a more inappropriate variant of the same game, based on would-be dominant batting, that they had pursued for much of the decade.

On the few occasions when this had worked in the past, England had been too readily applauded. Those who celebrated the success of the approach in 1985, against inexperienced and less methodical Australian bowlers, had cause for a rethink in 1989. With the exception of Gatting's sides, which many had dubbed lacking in colour or excitement, England teams, in essence, had played to much the same plan since Botham resurrected the 1981 Ashes series. Given that strong and aware direction had subsequently been lacking, a triumphant success produced a perversely harmful legacy.

To a certain degree, the same methods now castigated as feckless had been welcomed in 1985. What was missing might be termed discrimination, a quality peculiarly alien to the era. The age placed instant entertainment before painstaking appraisal; the media preferred instant judgement, as strident as it was superficial, to considered reflection. Few, at either county or national level, were disposed to look beneath the surface.

With the Ashes gone and the side at its lowest ebb in the decade –if not ever – public sympathy at Trent Bridge was, ironically, almost tangible. For certain players, at least, there was an impression that the air had been cleared and that a sense of gravity might, if nothing else, provide an appropriate new starting point. Not that anything materially changed. Indeed, with the Australian juggernaut seemingly obeying its own laws of motion by now, England went to their heaviest Ashes defeat at home. Faced with scoring 403 to save the follow-on, it was with a certain inevitability that Curtis, Moxon and Atherton, effectively strangers to one another, fell while the first 14 runs were scored. Atherton, at least, selected after only twenty-three appearances for Lancashire, provided a prophetic obduracy at the second attempt. But Moxon, the victim of a superb Alderman delivery, found himself demoted to five so that, in the summer's final illustration of day-by-day, purely reactive thinking, Gower, as a left-hander, could counter Alderman's movement with the new ball. Now bowled by one that kept very low, Moxon was summarily dropped after his one Test of the series. Such features were hardly novel, and were viewed more in sorrow than in anger. Something would surely have to change.

At the end of a wretched season heavy with the weight – one way or the other – of finality, England at least drew the Oval Test after Border delayed his second-innings declaration. The fact that Cook and Small, with 73 for the ninth wicket, saved the follow-on perhaps tells us something about the pitch. But this was by no means the first time in the summer that the tail, on easy surfaces and admittedly relieved of pressure by the very failure of specialist batsmen, had scored a high percentage of the runs. That England had lost 4–0, in a series where even two results might have been surprising, was an entirely apt end to the decade. Interestingly, Gooch had not the slightest idea at this stage that he would become the next captain; indeed, he was not even confident of selection for

West Indies. The climate in which he took over – of numbness, even dishonour – was all. Yielded a freedom, however indefinite, no modern captain has enjoyed, he was probably more aware of what must *not* be done than of any precise path of recovery. Of his chances of success, the professional game was as sceptical as the world at large. But he carried a degree of benevolence rare indeed in the era; a certain seriousness had perhaps interposed.

7
The Turn of the Tide? Gooch/Stewart: 1990 to 1991

Shortly before his departure for West Indies in 1990, Rob Bailey returned from one of England's practice sessions sporting a black eye. Asked what had happened to him, he revealed that the tour's selected seamers had been simulating Caribbean conditions by pitching short from a distance of eighteen yards. This was an innovation discussed a few months earlier during Gooch's first, brief overseas engagement, the very happy Nehru Cup trip to India. It confirmed not only that preparation had been given a welcome new emphasis but, as significantly, that the suggestions of players were now being listened to and implemented.

This element of preparation has proved perhaps the most distinctive emblem of Gooch's period. From the same training sessions emerged, for example, the repeated insistence on basic accuracy in Test fast bowling – the endlessly stressed idea of concentrating, to quote Micky Stewart's watchword, on that 'channel of uncertainty' around the batsman's off stump. More than this, Stewart would offer long-contemplated thoughts both on the opposition and on the conditions to be expected in a given series. Where all past England sides had valued team talks, these necessarily lacked the depth of close, intelligent analysis now pursued. Though Gooch's own determination and rigour clearly became vital, his captaincy was not, then, built on exhortation or example alone but on foresight and deliberation. Typically, he would recognise the key strengths of an opponent but then highlight the wider, superior abilities which, if applied unwaveringly, would enable England to compete.

From comments which Gooch has occasionally attracted, there is something about this conscientious, very rational approach, invariably caricatured as artisan or plodding, which seems to offend

English myths of leadership. At first sight it certainly seems at odds with the character of Essex sides. Relative to their county opponents, Essex enjoy a markedly greater advantage than England can hope to presume internationally. They have interpreted Championship cricket to demand a batting depth which can find volumes of rapidly scored runs, so that perhaps only four specialist bowlers gain wide freedom to attack. This, however, is based on reserves of confidence which it took Brian Taylor and Fletcher years to establish. Gooch's first England priority was to achieve precisely this confidence. He was consequently more tolerant and patient than with his highly self-assured county; provided evident commitment and effort were forthcoming, he would certainly allow for mistakes.

There is an element of the Essex philosophy in England's play against sides perceived to be weak in bowling but strong in batting, and ultimately, no doubt, the ideal would be to bring the same dominating outlook to bear in all games. As the side has evolved, however, it has sought varied tactics appropriate to different opponents and conditions. Consistent strategic points have been the desire for six genuine batsmen and the use of an accurate, and thus constantly demanding, four-man attack – initially all-pace but, since the 1989–90 West Indies series, invariably involving a spinner. In the three Tests where the need to win has been all, Gooch's compromise has been to play Alec Stewart as wicket-keeper and thereby create the space for a fifth bowler. Moreover, his desire has been for batsmen of a certain calibre rather than of a given role, a preference most notable in the frequent absence of a recognised opener.

The lack of such a specialist has remained, perhaps, the one grey area in Gooch's approach. Having observed the turmoil over openers through most of his career, and the effect this had on England, Gooch has retained absolute determination to have the right man as partner. He first chose the thirty-seven-year-old Larkins to do the job in West Indies and, when he was injured, replaced him with the twenty-two-year-old Atherton, who bats three for Lancashire and had never even opened for Cambridge. In the further absence of Atherton, Alec Stewart was then pressed into service. The lack of continued experience at county level inevitably means that both batsmen have been prevented from assimilating the specific tricks of the most difficult and critical of batting trades.

Nevertheless, Gooch has persisted with a policy which, logically, can only mean that his manufactured openers are thought more likely to score Test runs than eligible, specialist alternatives.

Two points are important here. First, whether one agrees with it or not, Gooch has shown the strength of mind to act upon his own assessment and avoid the vacillation and discontinuity so damaging in the past. Second, like nearly all of his – much criticised – moves into heterodoxy, it has for the most part worked. Larkins, his one, widely derided, chosen specialist, was a success in West Indies, if less so in Australia. Atherton, though destined to fail completely against the 1991 West Indians, passed 50 eight times in his eleven innings of the 1990 summer. Stewart, following four commendable opener's innings after Gooch was injured in the Caribbean two years earlier, immediately made two centuries against New Zealand in 1991–92.

Despite, or even possibly because of, initial unhappiness with the Essex captaincy, Gooch's largely misunderstood relationship with his individual players has shown considerable sensitivity. A captain, we have suggested, is often all the better for having known hardship of his own. Always working carefully at his game and alive to incipient technical problems, Gooch was more alert than most to the effect of leadership on his batting. In addition to the pressure of succeeding the revered Keith Fletcher for what proved to be Essex's only disappointing season in modern times, he was at this stage deeply unsure of his attitude to England's Test cricket. Crucially, though, after some three months of reflection in which lessons were perhaps absorbed, Gooch did come back to the captaincy and with a positive enthusiasm for his task. As with most aspects of play in his career, his leadership has shown continuous improvement; it is improbable, for example, that introspection would again detract from his ability, were he to be confronted by another period of poor form.

The parody has emerged in some quarters of Gooch and Stewart issuing severe encyclicals on attitude and effort which players disobey at their peril. While, whatever a player's talent, there is undoubtedly an insistence upon fitness and wholehearted fielding, attempts to curb creative individuality are made only when it is manifestly harmful to the side's agreed goal. Gooch will outline his general ambitions for a match, and what, in principle, this might imply, but he will allow players to pursue these ends in their own way. He would not, for example, try to tell Tufnell how to bowl, nor would he seek to stifle an aggression which is integral to the make-up of his cricket. Where younger players – Tufnell himself and DeFreitas – have failed to commit themselves either consistently or to all aspects of their game, they have been dropped. But it is hardly true that Gooch offers no second chances or that, as in the past, demotion is left unexplained. Indeed, it is characteristic of the contemporary set-up that, with certain exceptions, actions have been justified to players and requirements fully laid out.

A more profound concern has been that an excessive reliance on Gooch's powers of encouragement, support and persuasion has prevented players developing their own feel for the minute shifts of initiative in Test cricket. On those occasions when the captain has been injured, the effect on the side has been disturbing. This owes much, however, to the absence of Gooch's authority and presence as a batsman, a loss as encouraging to opponents as it is disconcerting to the team. In the field, the side has only rarely lost control. What did recur – if mainly, and quite catastrophically, on the Ashes tour alone – was that deep-seated modern susceptibility to the batting collapse.

We shall discuss this key feature at further length later. But it is worth saying here that there is only a certain extent to which a captain can convey the implications of batting situations in Tests. The mounting impetus of collapse, and the growing pressure exerted by eleven aware opponents acting as one, is, by definition, experienced only by the individual batsman in isolation. His ability to resist depends very much on a confidence gained from witnessing survival in the past, a fact which places great responsibility on senior batsmen. In the long haul back from failure and demoralisation, the first concern in the Caribbean had been to restore the side's sense of a right to take the field. Having overcome an inferiority complex and gained three victories on the strength of sizeable, well-worked first-innings leads, the next phase in the psychological evolution of the side was to prove it could win even from potentially losing situations. This degree of self-belief had now been achieved by the Australian unit and was effectively what separated the sides. For England, first, but by no means conclusive, steps towards such maturity still awaited the following summer.

In selection, Gooch's policy, only rarely forsaken, has been to allow at least three games for a player to establish his presence. Since there is but the finest of distinctions between intrinsic limitations of ability or temperament and those induced by the Test ordeal itself, even this most welcome improvement is arguably inadequate. Given that early failure has not overwhelmed a player's self-esteem, a full series might be more fair. For the most part, though, apparently unlucky players, like Nasser Hussain or Hugh Morris, are now aware of the management's thinking and can remain confident they have at least not been discounted.

A final element in Gooch's outlook, and one which has also attracted a strangely English mistrust – all the more odd for the decade's record of injury – is a strong emphasis on fitness. This rests on the idea, most forcefully espoused in modern cricket by Dennis Lillee, that sharpness in body is closely allied to alertness of mind. Again, it is a belief more personal than prescriptive. Gooch himself gains undoubted benefit from his devotion to training but, at the pre-play team level, only fielding and catching practice, rather than group stretching exercises, for example, is mandatory. Part of the focus here is on forging group morale. And indisputably, an accentuation of group allegiance and obligation has been at the heart of the new régime's identity, to the disquiet of the more romantically inclined. Such uneasiness misses the point: of itself, cricket, even modern Test cricket, can only be an examination of the individual. Yet it is an examination with a measurable outcome in team success or failure. By that inescapable standard, England had for too long fallen short.

England's performance in the Caribbean, gaining defeat with true honour in a contest which, but for rain, would certainly have been halved, came as a profound, uplifting surprise, and it would be upstaged sixteen months later by the side's finest series achievement since Illingworth regained the Ashes in 1970–71. Victory in Kingston was perhaps the single most unexpected success since April 1974, when Denness' team won in Trinidad, thanks to Boycott's batting and the spin bowling of Tony Greig.

Any idea that this achievement was devalued by a marked decline in West Indian power bears little examination. Their batting was as good, on paper, as ever before. That it failed to do itself justice – or was prevented from doing so by the execution of England's bowling plan – is altogether a separate discussion. Moreover, the impression that the fast-bowling unit was not quite as lethal as of old owes most to a general improvement in pitches. Injury dictated a permutation of only three of the first-choice quartet (Marshall, Bishop, Ambrose and Walsh) in any given Test but Ezra Moseley, one of the replacements, proved as threatening as anyone. And if injury is the issue, England unquestionably suffered far more from the loss of Fraser and Gooch for the last two Tests. The real point is that, in common with most of the cricket world, West Indies could not believe the transformation in will and application which had been effected.

WEST INDIES v ENGLAND, 1989–90

Average England total: 273 *Average West Indies total: 294*

Date	Venue	Result	Caps per Eng. Player
24 Feb–1 Mar	Kingston	*England* by 9 wickets	16.64
10–15 Mar	Georgetown	Abandoned	
23–28 Mar	Port-of-Spain	Drawn	17.64
5–10 April	Bridgetown	*West Indies* by 164 runs	12.64
12–16 April	St John's	*West Indies* by an innings and 32 runs	13.64

G. A. Gooch (captain for the first, second and third Tests), A. J. Lamb (captain for the fourth and fifth Tests), R. J. Bailey, D. J. Capel, P. A. J. DeFreitas, R. M. Ellcock, A. R. C. Fraser, E. E. Hemmings, N. Hussain, W. Larkins, C. C. Lewis, D. E. Malcolm, K. T. Medlycott, R. C. Russell (wicket-keeper), G. C. Small, R. A. Smith, A. J. Stewart; M. J. Stewart (team manager).

Selectors: E. R. Dexter (chairman), M. J. Stewart, G. A. Gooch (captain).

The initial composition of the tour party envisaged a potential spearhead of either Devon Malcolm or the twenty-four year-old Ricardo Ellcock, a largely unknown quantity whose thirty-two wickets for Middlesex the previous summer had come at only 19.21 but cost 3.37 per over. As back-up, the desire for genuine batting depth rather than the dubious compromise of 'bits-and-pieces' cricketers made Capel's bowling a vital component. Fraser would also be a certain starter with Small, DeFreitas or Hemmings to complete the attack.

It is important to stress here that a more modest strategy of containment alone would have been better served by the inclusion of Cowans, Allott or Munton. Gooch's plan did not involve the traditional concern to balance between strike bowling and containment, but demanded that the two modes should go together. This was not only highly ambitious; it meant that Gooch and Stewart first took upon themselves the hard work of preparing the attack and second that they backed their own ability to achieve results. Ellcock, as it proved, was immediately injured. But the fact that two such expensive fast bowlers in county cricket, Malcolm and Capel, successfully fulfilled requirements for two of the four Tests was a tribute not only to the bowlers themselves but to Gooch's preparation, encouragement and motivation.

Equally, the ability of opener Larkins, one of the circuit's most exhilarating strokemakers, to remain at the crease for 100 overs while scoring 46 and 54 in the first two Tests played, was to many almost astounding. These were no vague hunches: success was the outcome of a carefully conceived and developed idea. Malcolm became the first in the long line of 'surprise weapons' to gain real success since Cowans in 1982–83. But for the rain, his 10–137 in Trinidad would have won the match and, at the least, drawn the series.

The one evident error in selection, taking a second spinner in lieu of an extra batsman who, given the probability of injury, was always likely to be needed, bowed perhaps to more traditional wisdom. As it was, the Guyana Test was abandoned without a ball bowled, but even there the use of two spinners would have been highly doubtful. The choice of Medlycott at least confirmed an admirable return to specialism, most apparent, perhaps, in the use of Russell ahead of more orthodox wicket-keeper/batsmen such as Blakey, Hegg or Steve Marsh.

The dual features of Gooch's strategy have already been hinted at: a four-man fast attack with unfailing off-stump accuracy as its prime, shared characteristic; a batting line-up strong in specialists but made aware of the paramount need to survive for as long as possible to the last man. To a degree this embraced long-established Test principles. More specifically, it was designed to counter the bases of West Indian supremacy – incisive attack bowling which had to be blunted and fast scoring which had to be stemmed. The latter was throughout undertaken by an exclusively pace attack: for England to pass through four consecutive Tests in each of which four nominated seamers completed every over bowled, a policy criticised after the event, almost certainly remains unique.

If carried out to the letter, England's plan seemed realistically to promise that for long periods of a game they would retain the chance of a draw. To return having lost, say, 2–0 would have been more than acceptable to cricket followers. At the outset, the main emphasis was almost certainly on containment – any winning opening would have been viewed as a bonus. The Jamaica pitch, however, proved to be slow, West Indian batting in the face of the plan was confused, the fielding, under threat of embarrassment, was poor and the bowling, inexpertly handled, was often inappropriate. Victory was gained both by the all-round tightness of England's attack and by a 172–run stand from Lamb and Smith in England's reply to 164. It was significant that each of the top six reached double figures, and Russell made 26 with the tail, to deny the kind of morale-breaking collapse so often inflicted by West Indies. As pertinently, Lamb's contribution was 132 in six hours, rather than a more exciting but less telling 102, say, in four.

Following the Georgetown wash-out, the third Test was all but won by much the same methods allied, this time, to a key strike bowler's thrust from Malcolm which, in four balls, altered the West Indian second innings from 100–1 (a lead of 11) to 100–4. The final wicket was taken within the first fifteen minutes of the last day and, needing 151, England reached lunch at 73–1, though Gooch had retired hurt for, as it proved, the rest of the series. At this stage, rain fell for two hours. Thereafter, Haynes, standing in for the absent Richards, so orchestrated West Indian time-wasting that only seventeen of the outstanding thirty overs were bowled, despite an additional hour's play beyond the scheduled close. Though the umpires should undoubtedly have intervened here, England's tactics in a similar situation, if more subtle, would certainly have attempted the same ends.

The strategy had worked, then, for two Tests and was almost sustained long enough to draw the penultimate match. Thanks again to Lamb and Robin Smith, England remained in contention until halfway through the third day when, at 268–3 in the first innings, they were 178 behind. Though the game then became a fight for the draw, a last-day stand between Russell, who batted five hours, and Smith carried England to the new-ball burst from

Ambrose which won the Test with enough daylight remaining for perhaps seventeen overs. Here the inexperienced England side met their long-awaited and seemingly inevitable nemesis as Ambrose, moving to the best figures (8–45) ever recorded in West Indies-England Tests, removed Russell (55), Hussain (0), Capel (6), DeFreitas (0) and Malcolm (4). The significant point was not that the terminal collapse had now materialised, but that it should do so just once in the series and against genuinely great bowling. There would be altogether greater cause for concern the next winter when disintegration under pressure became commonplace, a tendency which arguably would not have proved so prevalent had England gained the critical extra assurance of saving this game and with it the series.

Only in the final match was the traditional pattern versus West Indies restored, and even here England made 260 at the first attempt, all seven batsmen reaching double figures, five passing 25 and three of these, as it proved, either already carrying broken bones or sustaining them in the process. At Kingston, West Indies had been restricted to 2.56 and 3.31 per over, in Trinidad 3.05 and 2.83. Only then did the familiar norms reappear: 3.66 and 3.92 in Barbados, 3.69 in Antigua. For their part, England's six completed innings averaged 269 at 2.75. What is an advantage – fast scoring – to West Indies, in that it provides pace bowlers with the freedom to operate at their own tempo, will usually be a disadvantage to England. Unless aggregate match scores consistently exceed 550, for fifteen years against West Indies a near-impossibility for all sides, insufficient time is used up and opposing bowlers remain fresh and repeatedly enthused by success.

The resurgence of West Indian speed of scoring was crucial in the fourth Test, where England came so close to saving the game. Post-match wisdom accordingly decried the all-pace policy, arguing that, with Fraser now injured, Hemmings, who had taken 5–77 against Barbados a week before, should have come in. As it was, DeFreitas, Fraser's replacement, bowled more tightly than anyone in the last two Tests, Small performed excellently and neither Malcolm nor Capel, who now proved expensive, could possibly have been dropped after their earlier success. Interestingly, it was Vivian Richards, arriving at the crease with West Indies 108–3 in the opening innings of this Test, who now deliberately and successfully assaulted Devon Malcolm – not without risk. Hitherto Malcolm had taken 15–263. At Bridgetown his combined figures were 0–188 in a total of only forty-three overs. Given that, in the context of the overall series defeat, the key breakdown in the containment strategy was here, this event seems as decisive as any.

Since Test cricket between sides who have successfully and responsibly realised comparable ability becomes less a contest of talent than of competing wills, it is worth contrasting Richards's downfall against Tufnell in 1991 at the Oval. Attempting to regain the initiative which, if held for even thirty minutes, would have saved the follow-on and the match, he sought to drive and was caught behind. In the best-fought series, every incident can be seen as critical. This 'error', however, which made the difference between succumbing to pressure and turning it back to the opponent, meant that England drew the series, 2–2, rather than losing, as in 1989–90, 2–1. In terms of the difference to England's competitive self-esteem, the distinction may prove incalculable.

If ever a tour provided heroic failure, it was to West Indies in 1990. The drama, recalling epics of the Golden Age, was probably all the more intense for the ultimate re-imposition of West Indian dominance through violent pace and breathtaking strokeplay. England had presumed to flout expectation on the basis of a rational, well-prepared plan which, but for a storm, would have brought at least a draw. Some went further and attempted to rewrite events as a morality play: virtue denied by infamy. Gooch's side insistently refused so glib a view. If West Indian tactics in the third Test did not quite elicit admiration, there was a sense that the hardness of which they spoke, cynically or not, was just the kind of attitude England wished to recover.

In predicting England's development in the coming summer, it was clear that judgment could again be based on cricketing criteria. Having noted the care and intelligence of Gooch's preparations for the Caribbean and the effect this had had in the first two Tests, one no longer felt obliged to anticipate the shocks so characteristic of the panic and indecision of England's past leadership. Yet, even now, it is worth noting that Gooch would not be confirmed as captain for the India series until after the second New Zealand Test.

ENGLAND v NEW ZEALAND, 1990

Average England total: 359 *Average New Zealand total: 289*

Date	Venue	Result	Caps per Eng. Player
7–12 June	Trent Bridge	Drawn	19.91
21–26 June	Lord's	Drawn	20.91
5–10 July	Edgbaston	*England* by 114 runs	20.36

G. A. Gooch (captain), M. A. Atherton, P. A. J. DeFreitas, N. H. Fairbrother, E. E. Hemmings, A. J. Lamb, C. C. Lewis, D. E. Malcolm, R. C. Russell (wicket-keeper), G. C. Small, R. A. Smith, A. J. Stewart.

Selectors: E. R. Dexter (chairman), M. J. Stewart, G. A. Gooch (captain).

With Larkins breaking his finger in early May and Fraser still unfit, England brought Atherton and Hemmings in for the summer. Only Capel was replaced, effectively by Fairbrother, who himself gave way after the New Zealand games to John Morris. Alec Stewart, who also scored few runs in this series, made room for the return of Gower. Though Lewis made his début at Edgbaston in place of the hamstrung DeFreitas, England's attack still comprised only those who had toured West Indies, until Neil Williams was surprisingly included for the last Test of the season. The fact that DeFreitas's injury did not prevent him appearing for Lancashire two days later may have had a bearing on his non-selection either against India or for the Australian tour. The Ashes party, however, contained just two new bowlers, Tufnell and Martin Bicknell; thus continuity had now been maintained through four series.

The slight change in emphasis to a six-man batting component accompanied by four specialist bowlers reflected both the side's growing confidence and, more particularly, the weakness of opposing attacks. The choice of a spinner might also be seen as a marginal reassessment but, for the most part, was equally dictated by changed circumstances. Playing in England, the spinner, Hemmings, was considered essential. On a turning pitch at Birmingham, he did as much as anyone to secure the series victory over New Zealand; on fast pitches against the flamboyant Indians he bowled more containingly, conceding 2.7 runs per over to an Indian norm of 3.6. Were Gooch to tour West Indies again, the high quality of Tufnell would certainly influence his thinking; without such an excellent spinner, his option would probably remain for seam alone.

All such strategic considerations proved largely academic in the opening two Tests of the summer. During the first three days of both matches, rain prevented significant progress: little more than five and a half hours' play was possible at Trent Bridge and forty per cent of playing time was lost at Lord's. Even when England were 45–3 replying to New Zealand's 208 in the first Test, so little time remained that defeat was never a realistic prospect. For that reason, the tail's fine performance in support of Atherton's 151, which carried England from 168–5 to a declaration at 345–9, lacked a genuinely taxing context. But it offered the first of several signs over the summer that, with the right attitude inculcated, there need not be a liability in a lower order beginning with Russell at seven.

At Lord's, given the play lost, New Zealand were unable to score quickly enough in reply to 334 to put pressure on England. Hemmings's thirty overs for 67 runs on a sluggish pitch and another Malcolm burst of three wickets in four deliveries which, despite the surface, reduced New Zealand from 278–1 to 285–5, meant that an overall total of 462–9 declared came at 2.93 per over. Even this owed most to a run-a-ball 86 from, as he had now become, Sir Richard Hadlee, the first bowler to be knighted, he suggested, since Francis Drake. Perhaps overdoing the caution which had served New Zealand so admirably through the 1980s, John Wright failed to declare either when Hadlee fell forty minutes before the close of the fourth day (408–6, a lead of 74) or overnight (440–8, 106 ahead). If he had conceded that the chance of bowling out England a second time in the conditions was minimal, the last day proved him correct. Needing to bat for about seventy overs to be safe, England finished on 272–4.

Justifiably enough, Wright's insertion of England at Edgbaston, in what turned out to be the deciding Test, was also a defensive move. If New Zealand should prove unable to win, they would at least be best placed, in theory, to gain the draw. It is all the more ironic that this in part backfired because of superb strike bowling from Hadlee on the penultimate day of the series. England led by 186 on first innings with two days left. From 87–1 they were then dismissed for 158, some forty minutes before tea (Atherton, with 70, was eighth out), which left New Zealand to score 345 at little more than 2.53 an over. One of the sides, in consequence, would almost certainly now win and, given the pitch, the odds favoured England. Hadlee departed Test cricket with a thirty-sixth five-wicket haul which was, it seemed, probably not quite effective enough to bring victory but, perversely, too effective for his side's own good. Had England continued to a declaration, New Zealand would probably have had an hour to an hour and a half less time to bat. As it was, they were bowled out in just under ninety-two overs and the game ended, not in a tense finish, but with a comfortable England win.

For this, England could thank all of the lower order save Malcolm for the crucial runs which took 254–5 on the second morning to an imposing 435; Hemmings, who claimed the last six wickets for 58 runs as New Zealand succumbed to 249 from 161–3; and Malcolm, whose 5–46 secured eventual victory. At this point, Malcolm had gained thirty-four wickets at 24.88 in England's last seven Tests after a disappointing début eleven months earlier. In the next ten games, he would find only twenty-three at 49.27, before being dropped and then missing the 1991–92 New Zealand tour. The figures do not in fact convey how well he shouldered new responsibilities in Australia in 1990–91 as the one fast bowler to remain fit throughout. But they do perhaps indicate a heavy reliance on rhythm, in common with David Lawrence, his replacement as the spearhead, and, indeed, with many other strike bowlers. When things flow smoothly for Malcolm, his follow-through will carry him almost to the batsman's end; when less fluent, he will run on only three or four yards.

For Derbyshire, he has tended to play but one Championship game in two and to bowl for an average of no more than twenty-five overs per match. It has been suggested, therefore, that his more arduous England workload began, in the end, to reduce his competence. A more rigorous assessment might be that, in responding so laudably to Gooch's endorsement, the mental effort required by both Malcolm and Lawrence to realise a full, controlled ability at all times inevitably took its toll. Within a month of one another in early 1992, Malcolm celebrated his twenty-ninth birthday and Lawrence his twenty-eighth, shortly after which, tragically, Lawrence was badly injured in New Zealand. Before that injury, both could have carried unreserved hopes for a new-ball role in the

Test side for some three or four years to come. Where, after five series under Gooch, most other aspects of the attack had begun to assume, illusorily or not, a certain appearance of permanence, the cutting edge of the unit seemed rather more problematic. Now celebrating England's first series victory for three and a half years, this threat was not yet a concern for the captain.

ENGLAND v INDIA, 1990

Average England total: 717 *Average India total: 458*

Date	**Venue**	**Result**	**Caps per Eng. Player**
26–31 July	Lord's	*England* by 247 runs	29.00
9–14 Aug	Old Trafford	Drawn	30.00
23–28 Aug	The Oval	Drawn	30.73

G. A. Gooch (captain), M. A. Atherton, A. R. C. Fraser, D. I. Gower, E. E. Hemmings, A. J. Lamb, C. C. Lewis, D. E. Malcolm, J. E. Morris, R. C. Russell (wicket-keeper), R. A. Smith, N. F. Williams.

Selectors: E. R. Dexter (chairman), M. J. Stewart, G. A. Gooch (captain).

At Championship level, where pitches were prepared to new guidelines, the 1990 season will forever be remembered for record scoring-rates and record volumes of runs. With June rain at last giving way to sunshine, the same phenomenon now transferred to the Tests. In county cricket, the changes brought about such a one-sided tyranny of the bat that play was often of a stultifying tedium. The pitches did not teach the players how to perform in tense, high-pressure situations nor to fashion innings which, outside the familiar surrounds of a run-chase, could have a positive bearing on match results. Rather they provided dubious instruction in making runs under false pretences: if risk was avoided, centuries could prove almost inevitable. This possibly had some relevance to repeated failure with the bat at key times in Australia two months later.

In the series against India, the run spree enjoyed by both teams offered high entertainment. Entertainment in the form of scintillating strokeplay is not always synonymous with Test success. And a contest replete with boundaries was rather short of the more cerebral fascination associated with watching two sides manoeuvre for advantage. The series saw India score runs at 3.59 per over and overall partnerships average well in excess of 50, so that, statistically, a typical day's play at the start of an innings might promise a closing score of 323–4 and a final total of 572. Such figures suggest that no side should lose. Or, more accurately perhaps, that defeat will owe at least as much to batting error as to bowling ability. This, in effect, proved precisely so: India, with inappropriate cricket, failed to bat through 100 overs to draw the first Test, while England successfully negotiated the 135 or so needed to survive at the Oval.

India's performance at Lord's was remarkable. How often can a side have contributed 678 runs to a match in which the third innings does not begin until the second hour of the fourth day and yet still lose by 247? By the close, the pitch, just beginning to break up, was certainly offering greater assistance to bowlers than hitherto, which meant that, in successive Tests, England had benefited from a defensive insertion. Yet the condition of the pitch could not begin to justify India's dismissal in sixty-two overs in their second innings given that, of the previous twenty-two innings, nine players had passed 50, six had continued to 100 and one of these, Gooch with 333 from 485 balls, made the sixth-highest total in Test history.

In pursuit of 472 to win in a little more than 100 overs, India's aggressive batting was reminiscent of England's in the past, five men reaching 27 but no one emerging from the 30s. Such facts, in a midsummer dominated by figures, make their own point: India, starting their second series under Azharuddin, were guilty of exactly the kind of ill-conceived tactics from which Gooch was seeking to free England. In this, he was wonderfully supported by Fraser, who had at last returned to the side after his injury in West Indies. His match analysis of 8–143 at Lord's indicated a success gained through control so complete that, where the remaining bowlers conceded 4.60 an over, Fraser restricted India to 2.33.

Also back in the side, after almost a year away, was David Gower, presumably preferred to Ramprakash, who was to make the A tour to Sri Lanka but miss selection for Australia. Gower's success was less immediate. Indeed, a tally of 134 runs in five innings would hardly have guaranteed a place in the tour party until, at the last opportunity, he made the responsible, undefeated 157 in six hours, which helped ensure that the final Test at the Oval was saved and the series won. It was perhaps a fateful performance. The decision to omit Gower from the West Indies squad had given the earliest and most clear indication of Gooch's outlook. Despite a Championship average for Hampshire at this stage of 42, wholly unexceptional in a season overflowing with runs, Gower was offered the chance to show that the implications of this decision had been drawn. His approach in Australia suggested otherwise.

The second Test came very close to replicating the pattern of the first. After scores of 519, 432 and 320–4 declared (the loss of an important few overs perhaps denied Gooch the chance to close at the end of the fourth day), India were set 408 in eighty-eight overs. Again indisciplined batting, as much as good bowling from Hemmings, found India declining to 183–6 with almost half this allotment remaining. But this time India survived, Tendulkar batting out the overs with Prabhakar.

In a final match which recalled England's rearguard defence against Pakistan at the same venue three years before, the Oval again provided England's sternest examination of the summer. It was preceded by perhaps the one selection decision during Gooch's captaincy which seemed to refer back to the illogical oddities of earlier times. While Neil Williams, a late replacement for Lewis but named in the selected twelve for the Oval, had a consistent enough Middlesex record to merit a cap, three other bowlers would go to Australia ahead of him. DeFreitas and Small were having indifferent seasons, but Martin Bicknell's fifty-two Championship wickets at 26.75 prior to the Test compared favourably with Williams's forty-five at 30.62. Bicknell, moreover, would have been on home soil. A choice which subsequent selections made inexplicable was all the stranger for the fact that, in the last Test of the season, good analyses would probably have taken Williams on tour.

As it was, all the bowlers toiled to little effect while India moved to a declaration at 606–9. Following what, at this stage, was a rare recurrence of the middle-order slump (Gower 8, Morris 7, Lamb 7), England approached the mid-point of the match on 139–5. In a series decided by a difference in determination between the two sides, the fight-back now began. Gooch, playing an attritional game which contrasted significantly both to his own and the Indians' approach at Lord's, had made 85 of the 233 runs scored by the time he became the seventh batsman out. Equally important and, it now seemed, characteristic resistance from the tail then extended the innings towards lunch on the fourth day and an all-out total of 340. Following on, England would need to bat perhaps 135 overs to escape. As 80s from Gooch and Atherton helped to post 251 before the fall of the second wicket and Gower passed on to his century, this objective was effectively achieved by tea on the final day, with only three men down.

Gooch's side had fought magnificently in West Indies, held their nerve against New Zealand and displayed exactly the kind of fortitude at the Oval which India had lacked at the critical time. If this spoke of a growing mental toughness sufficient to defeat traditionally weaker foes once more, England would now face Australian opponents hardened by years of common adversity which they were dedicated to leaving behind.

AUSTRALIA v ENGLAND, 1990–91

Average England total: 269 *Average Australia total: 386*

Date	**Venue**	**Result**	**Caps per Eng. Player**
23–25 Nov	Brisbane	*Australia* by 10 wickets	25.64
26–30 Dec	Melbourne	*Australia* by 8 wickets	27.73
4–8 Jan	Sydney	Drawn	28.82
25–29 Jan	Adelaide	Drawn	34.09
1–5 Feb	Perth	*Australia* by 9 wickets	34.27

Tour party: G. A. Gooch (captain for the second, third, fourth and fifth Tests), A. J. Lamb (captain for the first Test), M. A. Atherton, M. P. Bicknell, A. R. C. Fraser, D. I. Gower, E. E. Hemmings, W. Larkins, C. C. Lewis, D. E. Malcolm, J. E. Morris, R. C. Russell (wicket-keeper), G. C. Small, R. A. Smith, A. J. Stewart (wicket-keeper), P. C. R. Tufnell; P. M. Lush (tour manager), M. J. Stewart (team manager). (Because of injuries, P. A. J. DeFreitas, H . Morris and P. J. Newport were added to the party later.)

Selectors: E. R. Dexter (chairman), M. J. Stewart, G. A. Gooch (captain).

It is important to be clear for just how long, in each individual Test of this series, England remained in positions of parity; often, indeed, they were favourites to win. This confirmed the impression before the tour that the two sides were of about equal ability. Yet Australia emerged as 3–0 victors, consistently able to regroup and fight back, most critically by inducing batting collapses. One of the key flaws of the past – and one which Gooch had apparently begun to leave behind – had not only resurfaced, then, but proved to be the decisive factor. Hence the deep sense of disillusion with which the side returned to England and, on Gooch's part, a feeling akin to despair.

It could be seen with hindsight that England's failure to hang on in Barbados, and thus at least draw the 1990 series, was vitally significant. Undoubtedly, and rightly, Gooch would have drawn attention to all the positive aspects of that tour rather than dwell upon the two Tests lost. Yet for all the rapid improvement over the last twelve months, what England had still not done – not, in effect, since Melbourne in 1982 – was win a match which for long periods had stood in the balance. Far less had they come back to take a game in which, at various stages, they seemed marginally more likely to be beaten. That Melbourne victory, moreover, had been gained in the context of a series which was lost. Not since 1981 had England sustained sufficient mental superiority over an opponent to prevail at the end of an even encounter.

The final test of a side has not, perhaps, been overcome until it has maintained poise and conviction through three or four series against assured opponents; until, in essence, it has repeatedly displayed the belief that, in the face of bad sessions and even bad days, it can still claw back victory. Gooch's three successes had been built upon substantial first innings and appreciable early advantages thereby gained. This was hardly a fault: dominance had been achieved by applying the basics of good Test cricket. Both his teams and Gatting's had fought back to draw, and, on occasion, to the verge of victory, but not to win. This is what Australia now did twice at the start of the tour, damaging England's self-respect in the process. The harm inflicted can be seen particularly in the appalling fielding which, reminiscent of the 1986 Caribbean tour, began to characterise England's play.

Examination of failure in this series in terms of how a side's identity develops – of how confidence grows and resilience is gained – suggests that a draw in Barbados the previous winter would have better equipped the team to handle the pressure it now faced. The fascinating process of collapse operates on at least three levels. The rapid fall of wickets puts increasing pressure on each new batsman coming to the wicket, thus producing an effect which is to a degree self-sustaining. And each instance of collapse is more likely to generate further repetitions, because as one side's anxiety intensifies, so the other's sense of command is enhanced. Much of this is dependent on the opponents' feel for the precise time to strike and their awareness of how to explore advantage to the full. Confronted with a side which had passed England's present stage of development some two years earlier, England tended to buckle and the Australians to triumph.

So much, perhaps, provides the primary element of context. We have already hinted at a more structural influence behind England's modern proneness to collapse – a predominantly three-day Championship which carries neither reward for the draw nor penalty for defeat. This means not only that late-middle-order batsmen lack time to play lengthy innings but, more important, that they are obliged to think aggressively. It is usually a disadvantage for those at six, seven and even eight to score slowly or to extend a Championship innings by prolonged resistance. County success, and the habits of mind it promotes, only occasionally involve the late-order fight to repair early damage.

Yet Gooch's teams so far had, for the most part, overcome this impediment. A specific problem in Australia was that, as in the summer, the tail started early, and were now facing an attack more ruthlessly disposed and able to exploit this. Either Russell or DeFreitas batted at seven throughout; numbers nine, ten and eleven were always, at best, only limited and twice Gladstone Small came in as high as eight. This made it particularly unfortunate that Robin Smith, so valued by Gooch for his ability to encourage and shepherd the tail, endured his one loss of form in six series to 1992. Injury, and the need to win the last two Tests, also meant that a similarly out-of-touch Stewart played in all matches, ultimately as wicket-keeper ahead of Russell. At no point, then, could Gooch field his first-choice side. The captain himself missed Brisbane, Lamb and Small the second Test (before which Lewis had returned home), Lamb and Fraser the third and Fraser the fifth. In contrast, Australia, by then 2–0 up, lost Alderman for Adelaide and Bruce Reid for Perth.

All of this, and especially the tendency to collapse, placed great responsibility upon the senior player, Gower, batting mainly at five, and considerable emphasis on the team retaining its unity of purpose. Gooch could accept failure and occasional underperformance, but would not tolerate any apparent lack of concern at defeat, or a repeated indulgence of inappropriate cricket. Most obviously, and most contentiously, his displeasure, given the circumstances, fell on Gower, despite two centuries and 407 runs. Whatever disagreement, in terms of apportioning blame, his interpretation of the Australian set-back excited, two points seem crucial. That Gooch was perceptive enough to realise the potential for regression which the side's new shortcomings threatened, and that he was strong-willed enough to address once more precisely those issues upon which further development seemed to depend. In that the following series saw such a stirring recovery of the best attributes of earlier matches, Gooch's conclusions, we might suggest, seemed immediately vindicated.

For all that they fell from 117–2 to 135–6 in difficult conditions at Brisbane, England gained a valuable first-innings lead after being put in to bat. Within an hour of the second-day's close – the match destined to last just a few minutes under three scheduled days – they were apparently comfortable at 42–1, 84 runs ahead. They then collapsed against Alderman's 6–47 to total 114 and lose, by ten wickets, a match which, twenty-four hours earlier, they were winning. The paltry contributions of succeeding batsmen can hardly be blamed on Gower. Yet it would not have passed unobserved that his was the second wicket to go in both declines, on each occasion to a loose stroke, when well set, in the over after his partner had fallen.

At tea on the fourth day of the second Test, with about 120 overs outstanding in the match, England, on 103–1, led by 149. Since a further hour and a half of batting would effectively secure them from defeat, the draw was probably now likely, although if either side were to win the odds, at this stage, stood at perhaps 65:35 in England's favour. Yet, succumbing this time to Reid's 7–51, they crashed to 150 all out and Australia moved to an eight-wicket victory with a session to spare. Again, the key question concerns the extent to which Gower could fairly be criticised. In the first innings, having scored exactly 100, he returned a catch to the bowler and became the fifth man to fall – at 274–5 – in England's passage to 352. Now he was out to Matthews for 0 when, as a left-hander, it was hoped he might counter the left-arm pace of Reid which, after Brisbane, had already been identified as the major danger. The answer turns, perhaps, on whether or not a captain has the right to ask different things of different players. The fact that others fail is arguably not in itself an excuse: the most experienced and talented batsmen may be required to attain standards altogether more stringent than those set for newcomers, a sentiment which, since Willis's Ashes tour of 1982–83, had not always been observed.

Notably, unlike some sides in the past, England did not now throw in the towel. Indeed, they made inspired bids at Sydney and Adelaide to emulate Australia's earlier recoveries: in both Tests, however, this represented a valiant attempt at the near-impossible rather than an outside assault on the barely conceivable. Replying to Australia's 518 in the third Test, Gooch was able, thanks in part to Gower's fine 123, to declare behind, an hour before the close of the fourth day, at 469–8. In the period to the seventh over after lunch next day, Australia fell to 166–7, 215 ahead. Even to be left an asking rate of 5 an over, England had perhaps just ten overs in which to get the last three wickets. With Rackemann surviving through twenty-one of these, the draw was ensured.

On the customary batsman's pitch at Adelaide, a début 138 of the highest calibre from Mark Waugh helped to carry Australia from 124–5 to 386. England's reply again moved in the opposite direction, 160–3 to 229. Watched by his crestfallen captain at the other end, Gower, the fourth man to depart, wafted the last delivery before lunch on the third day, a ball deliberately pitched well up on leg stump, to a deep backward-square-leg positioned precisely for that shot. Melodramatically, it might be deemed the stroke which ended Gower's long-term Test career. More prosaically, it was a final illustration of the one failure – to play to a context and the evident needs of a side – which Gooch would not countenance.

Before lunch on the fourth day, Australia were reduced to 130–5, a lead of 287. Again, realistically, England now had to find five wickets in a session to have an outside chance of winning. In fact, Australia reached a declaration which set England the target of 472 at 4.75. Amazingly, with England venturing to explore the limits of the feasible, this had become 184 at 6 an over when, twenty minutes after tea on the final day, Lamb's run-a-ball 53 was ended, Gower followed for 16 and Stewart fell for 9 to leave England abandoning dreams at 297–5.

Fittingly, two final collapses brought a third defeat in the last Test at Perth. It seems harsh indeed to fault the stand of 141 in 150 minutes between Lamb and Smith which took England to 191–2.

But it is legitimate to detect a return to old, enticing – and too often false – values in Lamb's dismissal during the first over after tea, pulling McDermott to mid-wicket as he tried to pick up too soon where he had left off. Contrary to the wiser policies he had himself observed in West Indies, Lamb thus fell for a glittering 91 from 122 balls, rather than the more circumspect 135 which could have made an appreciable difference at a prime time. Leaving Gower stranded on 28 not out, the last six batsmen contributed a combined total of 14 runs, McDermott – as the absent Reid had done, returning to the side in this series for the first time in two years – rather flattered by his 8–97.

England were still in an even position midway through the second day, however, when Australia, at 168–6, trailed by 76 runs. At this point Matthews, a colleague greatly valued by Border in Emburey's late role of a stock-bowling number seven, guided the tail to 307. As England approached lunch on the third day, 22 behind at 41–0, they nevertheless retained a realistic chance of victory. But, bowling better in this innings than at any stage in the season, Australia then reduced the tourists to 144–9 and, ultimately, to 182 all out, before winning by nine wickets in the second hour of the fourth day.

In summary, England had been in the better position to win the opening match for some two-thirds of its duration. Their advantage was even more marked three-quarters of the way into the following game. They then retained an outside chance of victory through eighty per cent of the third Test and sixty per cent of the fourth. At Perth, the odds were still about even after seventy-five per cent of play. Competing for well over half the distance, then, in each Test in turn, England nevertheless fell to a 3–0 defeat. Confessing to a certain shame at the deficiency in outlook and attitude he acknowledged this to denote, Gooch evidently had further refinements to undertake before the optimism of 1990 might be deemed well founded. It was with altogether less hope that the visit of the West Indies, four months hence, was now anticipated.

The opening Test of this series provided débuts for Graeme Hick and Mark Ramprakash. It also saw the return of Pringle in an all-rounder's role which, probably wrongly in retrospect, had been thought unnecessary in Australia but which was again deemed

ENGLAND v WEST INDIES and SRI LANKA, 1991

Average England total: 273 *Average West Indies total: 301*

Date	**Venue**	**Result**	**Caps per Eng. Player**
6–10 June	Headingley	*England* by 115 runs	25.36
20–24 June	Lord's	Drawn	26.36
4–9 July	Trent Bridge	*West Indies* by 9 wickets	25.64
25–28 July	Edgbaston	*West Indies* by 7 wickets	25.45
8–12 Aug	The Oval	*England* by 5 wickets	26.55
22–27 Aug	Lord's	*England* by 137 runs	28.09

G. A. Gooch (captain), M. A. Atherton, I. T. Botham, P. A. J. DeFreitas, G. A. Hick, R. K. Illingworth, A. J. Lamb, D. V. Lawrence, C. C. Lewis, D. E. Malcolm, H. Morris, D. R. Pringle, M. R. Ramprakash, R. C. Russell (wicket-keeper), R. A. Smith, A. J. Stewart (wicket-keeper), P. C. R. Tufnell, S. L. Watkin.

Selectors: E. R. Dexter (chairman), M. J. Stewart, G. A. Gooch (captain).

essential against West Indies. And when Lewis withdrew on the morning of play, Watkin, too, gained his first cap. By the Nottingham Test, Watkin had given way to another débutant, Richard Illingworth, while Malcolm's continued poor form eventually brought in Lawrence. In all, eighteen cricketers were to be employed in the season's six games, and the party then selected for New Zealand – albeit influenced by the subsequent demands of a World Cup – contained eight (of sixteen) who had not visited Australia, five of whom had never appeared under Gooch before this summer. The numbers were swollen by major injury problems, not only for Fraser but for Atherton now also. It remained significant that much was done to assist these two players and to assure them they were not forgotten.

From the outset, Gooch's captaincy had been notable for an element of careful adjustment guided by medium-term needs. If this was now accelerated by experiences in Australia, change, in the end, amounted to the departure of Gower, Larkins and Hemmings, all of whom would be over thirty-five by the start of Pakistan's 1992 tour. The one real exception to the refreshing new rule of loyalty was in the accession of Hick to the ranks immediately his England eligibility had been established. This was most obviously a disappointment to Hussain, perhaps. Yet Hick's record was not so much unusual as genuinely historic. Few batsmen indeed have maintained an average well in excess of 60.00 through even two or three seasons: Hick had done so while scoring over 15,000 runs.

His failure, despite the prodigious talent which this record unarguably attests, says much about the vast difference in outlook demanded by Test cricket. Technically, he was exposed by short-pitched bowling angled in to the body, a vulnerability which, despite extensive net practice, was still evident on the New Zealand tour in 1991–92. Such tactics had not consistently been encountered before on the slow pitches of Zimbabwe and New Road, Worcester. They found Hick strangely uncertain over whether to hook, to evade or, in a manner curiously reminiscent of bygone coaching manuals, to play the ball down. His will be a fascinating development to observe: ultimately, ability of this order should confirm itself more rapidly, given the sensitivity of a new era, than did, say, Gatting's or Gooch's.

Hick's failures, and abject Test seasons in 1991 for Lamb and Atherton, also tell us something about the continuing calibre of West Indies bowling in this series. It will be a travesty if, in later years, England's performance is seen in the light of major changes to the West Indies team made after the tour was over. Effectively, the visitors lacked only two players: Bishop, injured during the previous summer with Derbyshire, and Greenidge, forced to undergo a knee operation following the first one-day International. Far from beginning their transition, West Indies had just provided only the third instance in history of a side going unchanged through a five-match series. In that encounter, the same Australian team which, two months before, had beaten England 3–0, was itself defeated far more comfortably than a 2–1 margin suggests.

Though Patterson was to miss two games in the series, the attack – Bishop apart – was at full strength for both England victories. And, on paper, the ability of the batting, prior to the Headingley Test, seemed only marginally short of the 1988 side's – perhaps 200 runs short, over a full series, if we are to attempt a quantification. While such assessments cannot convey the specific importance of the break-up of Greenidge's great partnership with Haynes, West Indies undeniably started as the firmest of favourites. The failure of Richards to cover Greenidge's absence by moving himself to three was perhaps but one of several errors of captaincy over the summer.

At Leeds, replying to 198, West Indies were 54–1 when Simmons drove Watkin on the up and Ramprakash, at square-cover, flew to his right to take a superb catch, airborne and at full stretch. Two overs later, he swooped on the push with which the new batsman, Hooper, was attempting to get off the mark and threw down the stumps. Such things are not incidental; indeed, they are integral to the belief which a team develops. After an Australian tour notable for appalling fielding, the confidence shown by a débutant and the general demeanour of the side spoke well of the frame of mind Gooch had refashioned.

After they had gained a first-innings lead of 25, any score above 225 at the second attempt would, in the conditions, give England a better than even chance. Gooch responded with a quite colossal innings and shared two crucial partnerships, first with the débutant Ramprakash, who contributed 27 to a 78-run stand, and then with Pringle, who in his first appearance for twenty months made 27 in a seventh-wicket stand of 98. By lunch on the third day, England had reached 47–3, all the wickets falling to Ambrose. Oddly, he was withdrawn from the attack directly after the interval and, through to tea, the off-spin of Richards himself and Hooper accounted for eight of the thirty-two overs bowled. Despite repeated stoppages, Ambrose (6–52) was employed only within the framework of rotation characteristic of West Indian attacks, completing but twenty-six per cent of the overs in the innings.

To those key components of possible success against West Indies already mentioned – stifling the batsmen and withstanding the bowlers – might be added, then, a disruption of the crude tactics which have invariably proved so effective. And there is a fourth feature: creating the kind of anxiety which, whatever the talent of the batsmen, will force the types of error from which West Indian bowlers had themselves long profited. Not only was this critical in unsuccessful attempts at the Oval to get after Phil Tufnell, it had considerable significance on the final day at Leeds. At 77–2, West Indies needed 201 further runs for victory. Like England middle orders in the mid-1980s, Hooper, Richards and Logie gave slip catches attempting forcing shots off Watkin, and the side slumped to 88–5. For once, England had turned Leeds to their own advantage by bowling a tight line and waiting for the opposition to seek the indiscreet, inappropriate batting counter. It was almost ten years to the day since the great Botham/Willis resurgence on the same ground.

When Test cricket is at its tightest – and, because so closely fought, this series was one of the very best seen in England since the war – such small points are vital. Half of England's specialist batsmen, Hick, Lamb and Atherton, contributed the remarkable aggregate of just 242 runs at 10.52 in a total of twenty-three innings. On the batting side, victory was gained by Gooch's great, staunchly supported, innings on a bad pitch at Headingley and a series of well-wrought innings from all but one of the top eight which augmented Smith's century at the Oval. On one level, this argues for much caution in contemplating England's future. At the same time, it makes clear, perhaps, how minimal the difference is, when two good sides compete to the last, between drawing 2–2 and losing 3–0. It is precisely a question of making the smallest distinctions work in your favour rather than count against you. This England did as never so consummately since 1981.

Rain through almost all of the last two days at Lord's brought the draw which Smith's 148 not out, again crucially supported by the tail, had already made likely. Replying to 419, Smith was 13 – and England became 84–5 – when Gooch fell. The remaining five batsmen in the lower order stayed six hours, adding 116 to Smith's 135, with only Malcolm, out fourth ball, failing. In past contests, the limits of resistance in this situation might have been about 250, Smith perhaps just supported through to his hundred. Such pluck would have been applauded with deep relief. Typically, the continuing pattern would then have been for West Indies to gain a lead of 475 by tea on the fourth day and for England to make an unsuccessful attempt at batting 120 overs to save the match. Yet only in the third and fourth matches of this series did the relentless arithmetic of West Indies Tests dictate this usual, remorseless passage to defeat – and then only after England had retained the profound benefit of self-respect by dictating several unexpected shifts in the narrative.

It is important to re-emphasise that the team which confounded the old, clinical logic was neither more talented in top-order batting nor significantly stronger in the tail than the teams which lost fourteen of the fifteen Tests between the two sides in 1984, 1985–86 and 1988. And, though it is a subjective and difficult comparison to make, the pace quartet which they faced was probably only ten per cent less efficient than the most menacing units of the past. The difference, therefore, was mental and structural. The former, a desire to give everything for one's colleagues and the team, would have been impossible without the latter, the complete rethink of cricket's organisation and leadership.

When the past crowded back in, at Trent Bridge, it did so only after most of the first two days had remained even. England recovered again, from 228–8 to 300, with Smith (64 not out) this time accompanied for 112 minutes by the newcomers, Illingworth (13) and Lawrence (4). In reply, West Indies were first 45–3 and then 118–4 before Richards, Logie and Marshall carried them to a first-innings lead of 97. Surprisingly, for a side 1–0 up and with DeFreitas bowling so well, Gooch, though he dropped Malcolm, opted not for greater containment and further batting via Reeve, but for the attack bowling of Lawrence. Mainly, perhaps, because Illingworth did not prove as tight as expected, the Lawrence gamble seemed to leave England particularly exposed.

As it proved, it was not really the speed of West Indian scoring (397 at 3.35 per over) which was important anyway, but the first batting demise of the summer. Left two hours to negotiate on the third evening, with a need to reach lunch on the last day to be safe, England were reduced to 54–3 by the close. At the time, the session seemed all-important, the one which, at the halfway mark, would effectively turn the series and bring West Indies back to overall victory as in the Caribbean.

The impression is worth recalling, for faith in the resurgence of England did not at this stage outweigh the apparently rational, cricketing reasons why West Indies would still finish on top. The expectation at large was that England would certainly play to the best of their ability but that, with no dishonour whatever, this would simply not be enough. Given the widespread strength of this assessment, the point is that amongst the very few who still entertained genuine hopes were the players themselves. This was despite a rearguard action which, on this occasion, materialised too late at 115–8, only 18 runs on. The correctness of throwing the bat at this juncture (DeFreitas making 55 not out from 86 balls and Lawrence 34 from 38) showed that, to the end, England were trying to do the right thing, but only rain prevented defeat inside four days.

Assisted by a very poor Edgbaston pitch, the fourth Test was the one game in the series which, for West Indies, went very much to an intelligently executed plan – at least, until within ninety minutes of the close of the third of four days' play. Minus the injured Smith, England were inserted and then dismissed for 188. West Indies then went to 253–4 by the close of the second day, led by a superbly judged 103 not out from Richardson. England's initial fightback on the third day, built upon Lewis's 6–111, which restricted the final total to 292, was the preface, however, to two batting collapses on their part, first to 5–3 and then from 71–3, just before tea, to 144–8, a lead of 40 runs.

At this point Pringle, who in the end batted five hours and withstood 236 balls for his 45, was joined by Lewis to add 92 for the ninth wicket. In turn, Illingworth then provided support for a further hour before Lewis fell on 65. Needing 152 to win, on a pitch where 225 might have proved highly taxing, West Indies were suddenly reduced to 24–3 by DeFreitas. For about two hours, it seemed possible that England might again provoke alarm but Richards, with complete determination, made an undefeated 73.

Without the experience of having fought so successfully at Leeds and Lord's, it is impossible to believe that England would, by this stage, still have retained the will to contest every inch. More to the point, the fact that they resisted with such credit again here made the prospect of a second victory, to level the series at the Oval, all the more feasible to the side itself. Each of the last two Tests of the series, however, involved starring performances from players uninvolved in the opening two matches – Lewis, Tufnell and, to a degree, Lawrence. How is it that continuity is maintained?

It is once again important to stress the extent to which new players now felt themselves to be part of a clear, wider outlook in English cricket which did not consign them to the one-off role of media scapegoat. Evidence of this had again been confirmed by Gooch's refusal to bow to a press clamouring, even after two Tests, for the swift removal of Hick and Lamb. Beyond that, if we recall the dressing-room at Old Trafford for the fourth Test against the 1989 Australians, when England were 2–0 down, much of the answer may be seen. Even a newcomer to the scene, unless of a remarkable strength of character, will pick up a mood of despondency from those around him. Conversely, despite defeats, the present England team exuded a sense of hope and confidence to new arrivals; an immediate air of relaxed calm, even an air of relish, provided the encouragement to do well. And, to a degree, the genuine desire for a team-mate's success carries its own demands for requital.

Prior to the final Test, England explicitly announced that, in exceptional circumstances, they would field a 'high-risk' side. Effectively, this meant only that Stewart would come in as wicket-keeper to enable both Lawrence and Tufnell to play in a five-man attack. With Pringle injured, Botham gained his first cap for almost two years as fourth seamer and number seven batsman. Eschewing unnecessary attack, England achieved a well-worked 419 at 2.77 an over. On 158–3 in reply, West Indies appeared well placed, before lunch on the third day, to restrict any possible first-innings deficit to a manageable 75 or so, at most.

Suddenly, in a bizarre, even unruly, determination to assail Tufnell's second spell, six wickets fell from thirty-three of his slow left-arm deliveries either side of the interval – the last four, at no cost, in nine balls. Tufnell is the most promising spinner yet to have emerged from the era of covered pitches and his very aggression offers a palpable challenge. But the West Indies response was monumentally out of context, an undignified farewell, it seemed, from a side which had dominated the Test game for fifteen years and whose core was now departing. Yet in fact, this was the one time in that long period when the failure of such batting methods had made a material difference to the outcome of a series. Keeping their heads, England had gained control and with it the chance of a memorable victory.

This was by no means assured, however. Following on 243 behind midway through the match, West Indies needed to bat towards lunch on the fifth day, and to compile a score of around 450, to revive a significant chance either of drawing or of winning should England have to chase quick runs. Since, on the Oval pitch, this was clearly not beyond them, the innings became as testing an examination of England's advance as any in the series. More specifically, it provided an examination of the breadth of their attacking abilities and of their tactical flexibility for here, indisputably, was a case for aggression rather than success through containment.

Indeed, the West Indian batsmen were entirely content to allow Lawrence's four colleagues 107 overs between them at less than 2.5 runs each. Granted the licence to find wickets irrespective of expense, however, Lawrence's figures of 25.5–4–106–5 were, in the context, match-winning. Richardson and Richards had carried the score to 305–4, a lead of 62, when Lawrence, who had earlier removed Haynes, had Richards caught trying to drive and removed Dujon with a bouncer. At the end of the fourth day which, due to bad light, closed more than an hour early, West Indies led by 113 at 356–6, Richardson having just passed his hundred. The next morning, after DeFreitas had dismissed Marshall and Ambrose, Lawrence ended the innings by taking the final two wickets, Richardson the last to go, for 121, pulling another short ball to mid-wicket.

Since the Lawrence element of Gooch's 'high-risk' strategy had worked, it was appropriate, perhaps, that Stewart's undefeated 38 now took England from 80–4 to the 143 they required for victory. As makeshift wicket-keeper, standing up to Tufnell, he had also taken the key, difficult catch off Richards in the midst of the first- innings collapse. The success of these tactical ploys was, in the end, neither fortuitous nor inspired; it rested almost wholly on a confident belief in the professionalism the side had now achieved. This was confirmed by the ruthless efficiency with which, after batting with a collective sense of anticlimax in the first innings, England roused themseves to defeat Sri Lanka. Surging at 4.27 per over to a declaration on 364–3, Gooch set what, in Test terms, was the generous target of 423 in 131 overs. In reality, this represented more of an assessment of how long the bowlers would require to win – a miscalculation, in fact, since Tufnell's 5–94 brought victory four balls after tea!

When all aspects of a cricket team's performance are realised together, the impression left is of almost unstoppable power. When, on 3 February 1992, England completed a series victory over New Zealand by winning the opening two Tests of their subsequent winter tour, this was precisely the sensation which had been generated. It was the first time England had won four consecutive matches since 20 December 1978, during a period of similar apparent potency. As this analysis has attempted to trace, the decade which followed allowed that to prove an illusion. What, then, of the way ahead? Does the future of England Test cricket promise fulfilment or disenchantment?

8
Towards the Millennium

NEW ZEALAND v ENGLAND, 1991–92

Average England total: 384 *Average New Zealand total: 271*

Date	Venue	Result	Caps per Eng. player
18–22 Jan	Christchurch	*England* by an innings and 4 runs	28.27
30 Jan–3 Feb	Auckland	England by 168 runs	29.27
6–10 Feb	Wellington	Drawn	36.36

Tour party: G. A. Gooch (captain), I. T. Botham, P. A. J. DeFreitas, N. H. Fairbrother, G. A. Hick, R. K. Illingworth, A. J. Lamb, D. V. Lawrence, C. C. Lewis, D. R. Pringle, M. R. Ramprakash, D. A. Reeve, R. C. Russell (wicket-keeper), A. J. Stewart (wicket-keeper), R. A. Smith, P. C. R. Tufnell.

Selectors: E. R. Dexter (chairman), M. J. Stewart, G. A. Gooch (captain).

In sharing the honours with West Indies by winning at the Oval, England extended their record, since June 1990, to one series defeat in four consecutive contests. Even this apparently modest sequence represented the side's best run for eight years; and winning the series against New Zealand the following winter made it the most successful period since 1979. Yet there was still some way to go before the Greig/Brearley record of six wins and two draws in eight series could be rivalled. Indeed, to achieve the exacting standards of a three-year period in which England had been effectively second only to West Indies in the world, the side still needed to emerge successfully from twenty fascinating months of unbroken challenge ahead.

There are grounds for describing that period – from December 1976 to September 1979 – as England's finest in a modern era which began with the accession of India, Pakistan and, more recently, New Zealand to a genuinely competitive, first-rank status after 1970. England were undoubtedly flattered by defections to Packer in that time and by the absence of games against West Indies. This feeling was confirmed quite forcefully by comprehensive failure in the short, three-match series versus the post-Packer Australians during the winter of 1979–80. Statistically, though, the record stands, and England could hardly do more than inflict convincing defeat on the teams which were arranged against them. The test of the early 1990s for the side under Gooch – or under his successor perhaps – will be to establish a similar, if not better, standing in the world game.

The first two years of the decade brought an interesting realignment in the international balance. The core of the side which had sustained West Indian dominance for fifteen years moved on after the 1991 visit to England. The previous summer, Hadlee, Bracewell and Snedden had appeared for the last time in New Zealand's cause and Ian Smith and John Wright, too, at thirty-six, approached retirement. India still lacked any evident replacement for Kapil Dev, now in his thirties, and Sri Lanka were also sadly deficient in bowlers. For their part, South Africa, returning to the fold in 1992, would inevitably take time to establish their presence. However, Pakistan had found, in Waqar Younis, a new-ball partner for Wasim Akram who could compensate for the loss of Imran's venom, while Australia, in McDermott and Reid (when fit), had produced a spearhead worthy of their formidable batting strength. These were the powers – Pakistan and Australia – which, for two or three years at least, seemed set to succeed West Indies. These were also the powers destined to tour England in the two summers following the promise of 1991.

Having held West Indies and beaten Sri Lanka, England would, by the close of the 1993 season, have played each country, save South Africa, in turn. For Gooch, the prospect of a farewell as captain against an Australian side which had so upset his plans in 1990–91 would no doubt have considerable appeal. It would offer a chance to erase the memories of that tour by retiring with the Ashes regained. Potentially, it would also enable him to complete successful series against a near full-hand of international opponents. But he is known to be an increasingly reluctant tourist who values his domestic life highly. For that reason, perhaps, the outcome of the 1992 Pakistan series may have a significant bearing on his future. Ideally the captaincy would not be passed on until an heir apparent had emerged, who had both secured his place in the England side on relative merit and gained at least two seasons of leadership experience in the Championship. Moreover, it would be preferable for the new captain to undertake his first series abroad. If all this points to Gooch standing down in 1993, it is not necessarily the case that he would be prepared to alllow England's needs to override his family obligations, nor have we any right to ask that he should.

The key will be for the captain, and, indeed, the new manager, given Micky Stewart's pending retirement, to retain and continue Gooch's emphasis on basics, planning, preparation and attitude. For the essential question is not so much, 'Are England's playing resources in the forthcoming period equal to those of Pakistan and Australia?' but, 'Will England make the fullest use of the resources they have?' In the early 1980s, after all, the problem did not really concern ability; the side, then, probably had greater natural talent than the side which Gooch has developed. Certainly, in potential, it was as good as any other team in the world except West Indies.

The question of continuity in the selection policy was again thrown into doubt by the decision of the TCCB in March 1992, to add a fourth member to the successful selection committee and thereby threaten a return to the past. Few would doubt the competence of the newcomer, Dennis Amiss, chairman of Warwickshire's cricket committee, but an extra face seemed all the more unnecessary in the light of the evident benefits which streamlining had brought. Moved by panic to concede full powers to a wholly professional body in 1989, it is to be wondered, perhaps, whether the TCCB are now seeking to re-assert their influence.

With all players fit, Pakistan and Australia probably have a theoretical paper superiority over England which is rather more than marginal. At their strongest, they may even be better than the 1991 West Indians. But the difference is not so marked that it could negate with ease the advances made under Gooch in conviction and self-belief. That is, if England continue to display the qualities which have at last been restored to prominence, they will succumb, if at all, only after an extended fight characterised by dignity and pride.

While potentially, this promises more wonderfully enthralling cricket over the next five years, the proviso places a daunting burden upon the next captain.

The identity of that captain is complicated considerably by his need to be good enough to fill one of the evident playing gaps in the side. Moreover, such gaps may become ever fewer in number if certain cricketers, notably Ramprakash and Lewis perhaps, realise their full promise. At the end of the 1991 summer, the nucleus of the side for the next five years or so appeared to be Atherton, Hick, Smith and Russell. Fraser, if he regains fitness – which, sadly, is by no means certain – would immediately join that nucleus. So too, with certain other qualifications, would DeFreitas, Lewis and Tufnell. The ability of both DeFreitas and Tufnell is proven; what remains, admirably though each has responded to Gooch, is a doubt over their consistent commitment, which only further series will confirm or dispel. Lewis, too, would seem capable of an integral role but, after only nine caps, it is unfair to be categorical. If, to this contingent, are added Gooch and Lamb, then the places outstanding require either a middle-order batsman or, should Atherton drop down to three, an opener. A fast bowler would also be needed if Fraser's injury proves chronic.

By the end of the 1993 Ashes series, Gooch will be forty and Lamb thirty-nine. On the surface, this offers further places in the future, for an opener and a middle-order bat, but the new captain will need to have been well established in the side by then to justify his elevation. It is possible that Lamb will give way earlier and thus widen the room for manoeuvre, but even this space may immediately be closed by Lewis's development into a genuine all-rounder. Under Gooch, and Gatting before him, England adopted the modern realism of four-man attacks long accepted by all other sides in conditions where a daily Test quota of ninety overs has become the stipulated norm. This is not to say that, if resources were available, the more balanced five-man ideal, requiring a true all-rounder and adequate batting to at least eight, would be forsworn in all circumstances.

Preferably, the captain will be a batsman or a spinner. Tufnell is far too inexperienced, and as yet rather too eccentric, to be a credible candidate. Of the batsmen, Hick is an unassuming, even retiring, man who may require some time to attune himself to Test demands even as a player. Robin Smith, as a dedicated team professional with the highest personal standards, might be thought most appropriate, but his batting success is built upon such degrees of laudably obsessive devotion that it would be difficult for him to forget his own concerns when in a period of poor form. Like Gooch, he might well take to the role in his late career – towards the end of the decade, perhaps – but, at present, England would sacrifice a prime playing asset with little assurance of any compensating gain.

Of the three batsmen in the projected nucleus, this leaves Atherton, who did gain two years' captaincy experience at Cambridge. But in the context of even Championship play, university cricket – still, in an echo of those outmoded attitudes which so afflicted Test performance, quite absurdly deemed first-class – has little or no relevance. Initially, Atherton appeared to be Gooch's choice, perhaps because no other young player in his first, inexperienced sides began to fulfil the requirements of age, role, ability and temperament for the job. Despite an ideal outlook at the crease, however, there is arguably something too vague about Atherton's general approach to the game. Conscientious thoughtfulness as a batsman does not always translate into the strength of character required to lead teams, and the fear lingers that Atherton might prove more akin to Gower, say, than Gooch.

There is little doubt that England, knowing all too well how crucially important it would be to find the right successor, had still not resolved the dilemma of matching leadership potential to Test ability by the winter of 1991–92. Their options seemed to have narrowed, with much justification, to Alec Stewart and Martyn Moxon. Stewart was named as deputy for the New Zealand tour and even captained the side in a state game in which Gooch played as a batsman. With some significance, Moxon was given the task of leading the England A tour to West Indies with Keith Fletcher, the likeliest candidate for the full England role, as his manager. In fact, Moxon soon had to stand down through injury, the captaincy passing to Hugh Morris. Since England lacked a recognised opener to partner Gooch, it seemed odd that Moxon was not himself selected for New Zealand. With the World Cup following that short tour, however, and the need to establish whether or not Stewart could bat at number two, this might only have complicated matters unnecessarily.

Alec Stewart took the Surrey captaincy for 1992, by which time Moxon had been in charge at Headingley for two seasons. Stewart would certainly have the force of personality to sustain Gooch's developments, albeit with a tendency at first, perhaps, to be over-assertive with those players who might respond better to more subtle methods. Moxon, in an altogether more understated and quiet way, would also seem adequate to the task and would enjoy the respect of his fellow professionals. The doubt over both is whether they have the batting talent appropriate to Tests.

It must be emphasised again exactly what this specific judgement should entail. One of the many problems in the 1980s derived from continual indecision over who should fill those positions for which obvious, outstanding contenders were lacking. In contrast, the debate, for Gooch, has involved less an assessment of whether an individual will prove a roaring success – an unfair criterion – than an assessment of whether other cricketers are appreciably more deserving of long-term endorsement. As the opener, only the left-handed Darren Bicknell might seem a possible better bet than either Moxon or Stewart, and his claims are by no means irresistible. In the middle order, Stewart's rivals might be Hussain, Fairbrother and, most especially, Ramprakash who appears, at a very early stage, to be of the highest quality. The full development of Hick, Ramprakash and, in the context of a lower order strong enough to permit five bowlers, of Lewis would indeed compromise a middle-order captain with less than assured Test credentials.

It can hardly be assumed, alas, that the popular press's view of events will be as rational or analytical as that which continues to inform England discussions. Both because of the circumstances of his appointment and the results he immediately gained, Gooch has, for the most part, attracted ominously positive coverage. It would be naïve to believe that a new captain, struggling for his own runs against quality bowlers while the team suffers defeat, will be accorded much sympathy. Not only will the appointee face the pressure of following Gooch and keeping the side to his standards of conduct and commitment, he may soon confront the same atmosphere of malice which so soured England Test cricket in the 1980s. Structurally, the changes made will provide the confidence to respond to ignorance with contempt rather than panic and the side's attitude will continue, one hopes, to command public respect.

But there is little reason to expect any shift in the media from sensation to wisdom; indeed, the early evidence of their desire to convert Tufnell into a Bothamesque figure for the 1990s presages unsavoury developments to come.

If either Moxon or Stewart is seen as the future captain and both are thought of as openers, it will be important to keep one of them in the side in that position from the 1992 Pakistan series onwards. In Stewart's case, it would make most sense for him to become Bicknell's opening partner for Surrey at the Oval since Surrey lack an established number two. Beyond these two, an outside contender is perhaps Ramprakash, whose Middlesex transition from self-centred teenager to responsible team player has been impressive. However, Ramprakash will be only twenty-four by the close of the 1993 Ashes season and it is premature in the extreme to demand even consistent batting success from him, far less the maturity to lead his country. A more unexpected turn of events might follow any early lifting of the ban on 'rebel' cricketers which theoretically runs until February 1995.

The general stance of the vast majority of English professionals would be that the ban should stand, on the basis that all those involved knew the consequences of their actions and were well rewarded for the decision they took. Yet, should they be permitted to return, perhaps as early as July 1992, there is little doubt that selection would follow for any player genuinely believed to enhance the England side. This should probably not apply to Gatting, who will anyway be thirty-five before the start of the 1992–93 tour to India, if only because sufficient young middle-order talent exists to be encouraged for the long-term future. As we have observed, though, the absence of a confirmed opener either to accompany Gooch or, more relevantly, to replace him presents entirely other possibilities. For a three-year period, perhaps, it is likely that Broad would return though of the same age as Gatting, a decision which would constrain the captaincy options yet further. A man who might resolve both the question of the opener and of the leadership, and one who has ten years of respected county captaincy experience, is Kim Barnett. Gooch himself provides the precedent for a former 'rebel' being accepted by the TCCB as captain, and it is not inconceivable that, if the ban were dropped, Barnett, thirty-two in the summer of 1992, would be considered with care.

The decision will be discussed not only by Gooch, Micky Stewart, Dexter and Amiss, but by Stewart's own successor in a role which is almost as significant, that of England manager. Keith Fletcher was appointed to this post in May 1992 ahead, most probably, of Geoff Arnold. Fletcher's grasp of the game's tactics and mental requirements is the equal of Stewart's, but he is far less detailed and meticulous in his preparation for a tour or series. His ability to assess the strengths and weaknesses of an opponent's game on the evidence of a few overs is almost unparalleled and his aid, both technical and psychological, to A team players has been greatly valued. Yet there is a considerable difference between applying knowledge on the field in the county game and anticipating the key elements of another Test team's strategy, for example, or the likely implications of particular venues within a tour itinerary. The brief which the manager inherits from Stewart entails a degree of careful research and planning for which Fletcher may lack an immediate, intuitive feel.

We discussed in the last chapter one other evident area of potential difficulty in the composition of future England sides, the role of spearhead bowler. If, especially following Lawrence's horrific injury in New Zealand, neither he nor Malcolm quite proves able to fill this position through the next three or four years, there may perhaps be an eventual opportunity for Andy Pick. This is made all the more likely by the sad retirement of Ellcock just before the start of the 1992 season. Two months older than Lawrence, Pick can swing the ball at impressive pace, but has not quite made the progress he promised in 1990. And while a strike bowler can be allowed a certain degree of inaccuracy, the point that the quickest and most consistent candidate should be preferred has long been adhered to by Gooch. Again, if the 'rebels' are re-admitted, Paul Jarvis will have supporters, though there will be as many doubts over his attitude as over that of Matthew Maynard, the other young cricketer to surrender a possible Test career at an early age. Even by the official end of their bans, both players will be only twenty-nine, a fact which in itself makes the point.

Gooch has never evaded the task of getting the best from potentially difficult players. There is no reason to fear that, with self-belief and clear objectives maintained, his and Stewart's successors should prove less effective. Such a hope may most obviously be tested by the treatment of Tufnell. There is a thin line for the spinner between aggression and self-indulgence, both in outlook and performance. With a good action less prone to problems than those of, say, Afford and Medlycott, there is an opportunity for Tufnell to become not only an integral component of England sides, but an inspiration and role model for aspiring spinners throughout the decade. The need to control disappointment and ill-feeling towards the batsman is paramount in slow bowling; if the spinner returns to his mark thinking about the last ball rather than the next, his game will suffer. While it is an advantage to believe he can take a wicket with every ball, it is a fault to allow poor deliveries or fours conceded to prey upon his mind – a fault which good batsmen will exploit to the full.

Tufnell has matured markedly under Gooch, both in his own game and his appreciation of team dynamics. The burden of early success, Tufnell having been crucially instrumental in the first three of those four successive England victories, may become apparent when wickets fail to materialise so readily and doubts are cast upon his true ability. Yet he will enjoy the benefits of a fair selection policy and, perversely, he will also be assisted by the fact that good bowling alone will ensure his place. The essence of his development will be to keep faith with the methods which have brought such an exciting start and to avoid adjustments to his action or approach when Test cricket proves less rewarding.

The off-spin foil for Tufnell, on the Indian subcontinent, perhaps, or on those few Test occasions when the ball will turn elsewhere in the world, is less apparent. Indeed, the off-spin role for a bowler who cannot bat well has become even more limited at Test level than in the Championship. The right-arm equivalent of a bowler who, like Tufnell, has learned his art on covered pitches yet aspires to Test ability has not to date emerged – nor, sadly, is he likely to. Harvey Trump of Somerset, a spinner with strong hands and physique who delivers at some pace and fields well to his own bowling, is perhaps the nearest approximation to the type of player such a new breed of specialist would be. It is more likely though, that two slow left-armers would be preferred, with either Illingworth or Alex Barnett coming to the fore. Refreshingly, it is not inconceivable that the leg-spin of Ian Salisbury would provide the third slow bowling option on an Indian tour.

It is a further tribute to the continuity and intelligence of the

Gooch/Stewart period that the number of fringe players in the support seamer category has also narrowed. Given his age – twenty-three prior to the start of the 1992 season – Martin Bicknell would seem to have the chance of an important role in the 1990s, while Reeve's potential to take wickets on good Test pitches with varied and experimental attack bowling could make him an all-rounder with a specific, controlled, fourth seamer's remit. It is an unfair indulgence to speculate about players of little experience, as the modern era has so frequently demonstrated. The England management has rightly taken great care to avoid placing undue pressure on young cricketers by raising inappropriate expectations. Suffice it to say, then, that there seemed good reason to elevate someone as young as Dominic Cork, at only twenty, to an A team tour.

By the time these words appear, England will be engaged in a series against the Pakistan side which is probably now the best in the world. The task of preparing a plan of campaign for an English season will have been intrinsically more difficult than for a tour. The attack will still be asked to maintain control, in the hope that Pakistan's stroke-making middle-order can be persuaded into over-ambition. For the batsmen, facing swing at high pace, the prospect of collapse to a single bowler is probably even stronger than against West Indies and may determine a slight re-adjustment towards the offensive. Though Geoff Arnold and Alec Stewart will obviously speak at length about Waqar Younis – if, following his injury in February 1992, he lasts out the tour – and Alan Ormrod, perhaps, about Wasim Akram, for England to resist these two and draw the series would be a real achievement. Given the sequence of venues, it would again seem that the fourth Test at Headingley will have a critical bearing, while a series victory for England would probably require success on a seaming pitch in the first Test at Edgbaston.

After an Indian tour, possibly under a new captain, which will provide as stiff a test as any of the new-found patience and resilience of the attack – notably DeFreitas perhaps – England will then confront an Australian side which, conceivably, will also be under new leadership. Whether or not Border tours, the visitors' batting will, on paper, remain as strong as any team's in the world, and a new-ball attack of Reid, aged thirty, and McDermott, twenty-eight, would seem potentially almost as incisive as that of Waqar Younis and Wasim Akram. England's ability to regain the Ashes will rest largely on the results achieved in the preceding two series, and thereby the continuing development of their confidence, and the fitness of Australia's bowlers. At thirty-seven, it seems unlikely that Alderman will play and, tragically, each day's cricket which Reid completes is taken as something of an unexpected bonus, following the major surgery to his back.

In purely cricketing terms, these three series will provide answers to the twin questions upon which England's progress through the next five years seems to depend. First, for all the excellent fighting spirit shown by England batting line-ups through the length of the order, it is factually indisputable that each of the first five series under Gooch have involved a heavy reliance on runs from the captain himself, from Smith and, to a lesser degree, from Lamb. Continuing competitiveness thus entails one of two things: either that the remaining specialists advance consistently in the eighteen months after the New Zealand tour, or, if top-order runs still prove only adequate, the non-specialists discharge repeated batting duties without this affecting either their bowling or the team's cohesion. Second, given that England lack the consistently world-class bowlers presently available to Pakistan, Australia and West Indies, will the attack be able to maintain sufficient levels of committed professionalism to achieve as a unit what others achieve with match-winning individuals?

The achievement of Gooch has been to regain for his side a sense of identity and even of meaning. Nothing more can be asked of a team than that it plays to the fullest level of its talent. If England sides lose because their opponents are better cricketers, there can be grounds for disappointment alone, not reproof. Victory is a measure of ascendancy; it is not a measure of worth.

Appendix
England Test Averages 1981–92

West Indies v England, 1980–81

Batting

	T	I	NO	R	HS	100s	Avge
G. A. Gooch	4	8	0	460	153	2	57.50
D. I. Gower	4	8	1	376	154*	1	53.71
P. Willey	4	8	3	244	102*	1	48.80
G. Boycott	4	8	1	295	104*	1	42.14
R. O. Butcher	3	5	0	71	32	0	14.20
P. R. Downton	3	5	1	48	26*	0	12.00
I. T. Botham	4	7	0	73	26	0	10.42
J. E. Emburey	4	6	1	38	17*	0	7.60
R. D. Jackman	2	3	0	14	7	0	4.66
G. R. Dilley	4	6	3	11	7*	0	3.66
C. W. J. Athey	2	4	0	7	3	0	1.75

Played in one Test: D. L. Bairstow 0, 2; M. W. Gatting 2, 0; G. Miller 3, 8; C. M. Old 1, 0; B. C. Rose 10, 5; G. B. Stevenson 1.
**Signifies not out.*

Bowling

	O	M	R	W	BB	Avge
I. T. Botham	145.2	31	492	15	4–77	32.80
R. D. Jackman	73.2	15	198	6	3–65	33.00
G. R. Dilley	129.4	25	450	10	4–116	45.00
J. E. Emburey	185	62	419	7	5–124	59.85

Also bowled: G. Boycott 3–2–5–0; G. A. Gooch 14–5–36–0; G. Miller 18–4–42–1; C. M. Old 16–4–49–1; G. B. Stevenson 33–5–111–3; P. Willey 47–12–111–1.

England v Australia, 1981

Batting

	T	I	NO	R	HS	100s	Avge
A. P. E. Knott	2	4	1	178	70*	0	59.33
C. J. Tavaré	2	4	0	179	78	0	44.75
G. R. Dilley	3	6	2	150	56	0	37.50
I. T. Botham	6	12	1	399	149*	2	36.27
G. Boycott	6	12	0	392	137	1	32.66
M. W. Gatting	6	12	0	370	59	0	30.83
J. E. Emburey	4	7	2	134	57	0	26.80
D. I. Gower	5	10	0	250	89	0	25.00
P. Willey	4	8	0	179	82	0	22.37
C. M. Old	2	4	1	63	29	0	21.00
J. M. Brearley	4	8	0	141	51	0	17.62
G. A. Gooch	5	10	0	139	44	0	13.90
R. A. Woolmer	2	4	0	30	21	0	7.50
R. G. D. Willis	6	10	2	43	13	0	5.37
R. W. Taylor	3	6	0	23	9	0	3.83

Played in two Tests: M. Hendrick 6*, 0*, 0*. Played in one Test: P. J. W. Allott 52*, 14; P. R. Downton 8, 3; W. Larkins 34, 24; P. W. G. Parker 0, 13.
**Signifies not out.*

Bowling

	O	M	R	W	BB	Avge
G. R. Dilley	98	24	275	14	4–24	19.64
I. T. Botham	272.3	81	700	34	6–95	20.58
P. J. W. Allott	23	4	88	4	2–17	22.00
R. G. D. Willis	252.4	56	666	29	8–43	22.96
J. E. Emburey	193.5	58	399	12	4–43	33.25
C. M. Old	84	27	175	5	3–44	35.00
M. Hendrick	100.2	28	221	6	4–82	36.83

Also bowled: G. Boycott 3–2–2–0; M. W. Gatting 3–1–13–0; G. A. Gooch 10–4–28–0; P. Willey 16–3–35–1.

India v England, 1981–82

Batting

	T	I	NO	R	HS	100s	Avge
I. T. Botham	6	8	0	440	142	1	55.00
G. A. Gooch	6	10	1	487	127	1	54.11
D. I. Gower	6	9	1	375	85	0	46.87
G. Boycott	4	8	1	312	105	1	44.57
C. J. Tavaré	6	9	0	349	149	1	38.77
K. W. R. Fletcher	6	9	2	252	69	0	36.00
G. R. Dilley	4	5	0	70	52	0	14.00
M. W. Gatting	5	6	1	68	32	0	13.60
R. G. D. Willis	5	4	2	26	13	0	13.00
D. L. Underwood	6	7	4	38	13*	0	12.66
R. W. Taylor	6	7	1	57	33	0	9.50

Played in three Tests: J. E. Emburey 0, 1, 1, 2; in two Tests: J. K. Lever 1, 2; in one Test: P. J. W. Allott 6.
**Signifies not out.*

Bowling

	O	M	R	W	BB	Avge
J. K. Lever	73	16	204	7	5–100	29.14
R. G. D. Willis	129.1	29	381	12	3–75	31.75
J. E. Emburey	99	31	222	6	2–35	37.00
I. T. Botham	240.3	52	660	17	5–61	38.82
D. L. Underwood	228	99	438	10	3–45	43.80
G. R. Dilley	105	17	350	7	4–47	50.00

Also bowled: P. J. W. Allott 31–4–135–0; K. W. R. Fletcher 6–2–20–1; M. W. Gatting 1–0–4–0; G. A. Gooch 33.1–6–77–2; D. I. Gower 2–0–2–1; C. J. Tavaré 2–0–11–0; R. W. Taylor 2–0–6–0.

England v India, 1982

Batting

	T	I	NO	R	HS	100s	Avge
I. T. Botham	3	3	0	403	208	2	134.33
D. W. Randall	3	3	0	221	126	1	73.66
A. J. Lamb	3	5	1	207	107	1	51.75
C. J. Tavaré	3	5	1	178	75*	0	44.50
P. J. W. Allott	2	2	1	44	41*	0	44.00
D. I. Gower	3	5	1	152	47	0	38.00
P. H. Edmonds	3	3	0	90	64	0	30.00
G. Cook	3	5	0	138	66	0	27.60
R. G. D. Willis	3	3	1	35	28	0	17.50
D. R. Pringle	3	3	0	39	23	0	13.00
R. W. Taylor	3	4	1	36	31	0	12.00

Played in one Test: G. Miller 98.
**Signifies not out.*

Bowling

	O	M	R	W	BB	Avge
R. G. D. Willis	88	11	330	15	6–101	22.00
D. R. Pringle	82	22	219	7	2–16	31.28
I. T. Botham	93.3	16	320	9	5–46	35.55
P. H. Edmonds	102.2	35	261	6	3–89	43.50

Also bowled: P. J. W. Allott 49–9–147–2; G. Cook 1–0–4–0; G. Miller 16–4–51–1.

England v Pakistan, 1982

Batting

	T	I	NO	R	HS	100s	Avge
C. J. Tavaré	3	6	0	216	82	0	36.00
D. I. Gower	3	6	0	197	74	0	32.83
D. W. Randall	3	6	0	168	105	1	28.00
I. T. Botham	3	6	0	163	69	0	27.16
R. W. Taylor	3	6	2	108	54	0	27.00
M. W. Gatting	3	6	1	111	32*	0	22.20
E. E. Hemmings	2	4	0	41	19	0	10.25
R. D. Jackman	2	3	0	28	17	0	9.33
A. J. Lamb	3	6	0	48	33	0	8.00
I. A. Greig	2	4	0	26	14	0	6.50

Played in two Tests: R. G. D. Willis 0*, 28*, 1*. Played in one Test: G. Fowler, 9, 86; V. J. Marks 7, 12*; G. Miller 47, 5; D. R. Pringle 5, 14.
**Signifies not out.*

Bowling

	O	M	R	W	BB	Avge
R. G. D. Willis	74	14	222	10	3–55	22.20
I. T. Botham	150.5	33	478	18	5–74	26.55
I. A. Greig	31.2	6	114	4	4–53	28.50
R. D. Jackman	105	30	247	8	4–110	30.87

Also bowled: M. W. Gatting 10–3–21–0; E. E. Hemmings 56.1–12–149–3; V. J. Marks 7–1–31–1; G. Miller 9.4–2–27–2; D. R. Pringle 26–9–62–0.

Australia v England, 1982–83

Batting

	T	I	NO	R	HS	100s	Avge
D. W. Randall	4	8	0	365	115	1	45.62
D. I. Gower	5	10	0	441	114	1	44.10
A. J. Lamb	5	10	0	414	83	0	41.40
G. Fowler	3	6	0	207	83	0	34.50
E. E. Hemmings	3	6	1	157	95	0	31.40
I. T. Botham	5	10	0	270	58	0	27.00
D. R. Pringle	3	6	2	108	47	0	27.00
C. J. Tavaré	5	10	0	218	89	0	21.80
G. Miller	5	10	1	193	60	0	21.44
R. W. Taylor	5	10	3	135	37	0	19.28
N. G. Cowans	4	7	1	68	36	0	11.33
R. G. D. Willis	5	9	3	63	26	0	10.50
G. Cook	3	6	0	54	26	0	9.00

**Signifies not out.*

Bowling

	O	M	R	W	BB	Avge
R. G. D. Willis	166.3	28	486	18	5–66	27.00
G. Miller	171	50	397	13	4–70	30.53
N. G. Cowans	107	14	396	11	6–77	36.00
I. T. Botham	213.5	35	729	18	4–75	40.50
E. E. Hemmings	188.3	59	409	9	3–68	45.44
D. R. Pringle	73.5	12	214	4	2–97	53.50

Also bowled: G. Cook 6–3–23–0; A. J. Lamb 1–1–0–0.

England v New Zealand, 1983

Batting

	T	I	NO	R	HS	100s	Avge
A. J. Lamb	4	8	2	392	137*	2	65.33
D. I. Gower	4	8	1	404	112*	2	57.71
C. J. Tavaré	4	8	0	330	109	1	41.25
D. W. Randall	3	6	1	194	83	0	38.80
I. T. Botham	4	8	0	282	103	1	35.25
G. Fowler	2	4	0	134	105	1	33.50
M. W. Gatting	2	4	0	121	81	0	30.25
P. H. Edmonds	2	4	1	63	43*	0	21.00
C. L. Smith	2	4	0	78	43	0	19.50
R. G. D. Willis	4	7	2	67	25*	0	13.40
N. G. B. Cook	2	4	0	51	26	0	12.75
R. W. Taylor	4	7	1	63	21	0	10.50
N. G. Cowans	4	7	1	22	10	0	3.66

Played in one Test: G. R. Dilley 0, 15; N. A. Foster 10, 3; V. J. Marks 4, 2.
**Signifies not out.*

Bowling

	O	M	R	W	BB	Avge
R. G. D. Willis	123.3	38	273	20	5–35	13.65
N. G. B. Cook	135.2	56	275	17	5–35	16.17
I. T. Botham	112.5	27	340	10	4–50	34.00
N. G. Cowans	125	25	447	12	3–74	37.25
P. H. Edmonds	87.1	30	221	4	3–101	55.25

Also bowled: G. R. Dilley 25–6–52–0; N. A. Foster 28–5–75–1; M. W. Gatting 7–3–13–0; V. J. Marks 43–20–78–3; C. L. Smith 12–2–31–2.

New Zealand v England, 1983–84

Batting

	T	I	NO	R	HS	100s	Avge
C. L. Smith	2	3	1	148	91	0	74.00
D. W. Randall	3	4	0	293	164	2	73.25
I. T. Botham	3	4	0	226	138	1	56.50
A. J. Lamb	3	4	0	82	49	0	20.50
M. W. Gatting	2	3	1	38	19*	0	19.00
C. J. Tavaré	2	4	1	54	36*	0	18.00
D. I. Gower	3	4	0	69	33	0	17.25
R. W. Taylor	3	4	0	54	23	0	13.50
N. G. Cowans	2	3	0	32	21	0	10.66

Played in three Tests: R. G. D. Willis 5*, 6, 0, 3. Played in two Tests: N. A. Foster 10, 18*; G. Fowler 4, 10, 0. Played in one Test: N. G. B. Cook 7, V. J. Marks 6, A. C. S. Piggott 4, 8*.

**Signifies not out.*

Bowling

	O	M	R	W	BB	Avge
R. G. D. Willis	115.1	28	306	12	4–51	25.50
N. G. Cowans	52	14	154	5	3–52	30.80
V. J. Marks	40.2	9	115	3	3–115	38.33
N. G. B. Cook	89.3	37	196	4	3–153	49.00
I. T. Botham	109.4	25	354	7	5–59	50.57
N. A. Foster	91	29	229	4	2–91	57.25

Also bowled: M. W. Gatting 10–4–28–1; V. J. Marks 40.2–9–115–3; A. C. S. Pigott 17–7–75–2; C. L. Smith 3–1–6–0.

Pakistan v England, 1983–84

Batting

	T	*I*	*NO*	*R*	*HS*	*100s*	*Avge*
D. I. Gower	3	5	1	449	173*	2	112.25
G. Fowler	2	3	0	134	58	0	44.66
V. J. Marks	3	5	0	218	83	0	43.60
M. W. Gatting	3	5	0	158	75	0	31.60
C. L. Smith	3	5	0	132	66	0	26.40
D. W. Randall	3	5	0	103	65	0	20.60
A. J. Lamb	3	5	0	78	29	0	15.60
N. G. Cowans	2	4	3	7	3*	0	7.00
N. G. B. Cook	3	4	1	18	9	0	6.00
R. W. Taylor	3	5	0	29	19	0	5.80

Played in two Tests: N. A. Foster 6, 0. Played in one Test: I. T. Botham 22, 10; G. R. Dilley 2*; R. G. D. Willis 6, 2.

**Signifies not out.*

Bowling

	O	*M*	*R*	*W*	*BB*	*Avge*
N. G. Cowans	57.3	11	175	7	5–42	25.00
G. R. Dilley	37	6	142	5	3–101	28.40
N. G. B. Cook	178.3	54	444	14	6–65	31.71
N. A. Foster	82	20	230	7	5–67	32.85
V. J. Marks	90	24	260	4	1–23	65.00

Also bowled: I. T. Botham 30–5–90–2; G. Fowler 1–0–3–0; M. W. Gatting 5–0–35–1; C. L. Smith 2–1–2–1; R. G. D. Willis 19–6–46–2.

England v West Indies, 1984

Batting

	T	*I*	*NO*	*R*	*HS*	*100s*	*Avge*
A. J. Lamb	5	10	1	386	110	3	42.88
I. T. Botham	5	10	0	347	81	0	34.70
G. Fowler	5	10	0	260	106	1	26.00
B. C. Broad	4	8	0	195	55	0	24.37
P. R. Downton	5	10	1	210	56	0	23.33
R. G. D. Willis	3	5	3	43	22	0	21.50
D. I. Gower	5	10	1	171	57*	0	19.00
D. R. Pringle	3	6	1	81	46*	0	16.20
P. J. W. Allott	3	6	0	67	26	0	11.16
N. G. B. Cook	3	6	0	25	13	0	4.16

Played in two Tests: G. Miller 22, 11, 0, 9; V. P. Terry 8, 1, 7; P. I. Pocock 0, 0, 0, 0. Played in one Test: J. P. Agnew 5, 2*; N. G. Cowans 0, 14; R. M. Ellison 20*, 13; N. A. Foster 6, 9*; M. W. Gatting 1, 29; T. A. Lloyd 10*; D. W. Randall 0, 1; C. J. Tavaré 16, 49.

**Signifies not out.*

Bowling

	O	M	R	W	BB	Avge
R. M. Ellison	44	10	94	5	3–60	18.80
P. J. W. Allott	104.5	26	282	14	6–61	20.14
I. T. Botham	163.2	30	667	19	8–103	35.10
P. I. Pocock	53.3	17	145	4	4–121	36.25
D. R. Pringle	71.3	10	257	5	5–108	51.40
N. G. B. Cook	95	15	297	5	2–27	59.40
R. G. D. Willis	85	15	367	6	2–48	61.16

Also bowled: J. P. Agnew 26–4–97–2; N. G. Cowans 19–2–46–0; N. A. Foster 18–2–82–0; G. Miller 28–1–142–1.

India v England, 1984–85

Batting

	T	I	NO	R	HS	100s	Avge
M. W. Gatting	5	9	3	575	207	2	95.83
R. T. Robinson	5	9	2	444	160	1	63.42
P. R. Downton	5	6	3	183	74	0	61.00
G. Fowler	5	8	0	438	201	1	54.75
A. J. Lamb	5	7	1	241	67	0	40.16
P. H. Edmonds	5	6	0	175	49	0	29.16
D. I. Gower	5	7	1	167	78	0	27.83
C. S. Cowdrey	5	6	1	96	38	0	19.20
P. I. Pocock	5	5	2	39	22*	0	13.00
N. A. Foster	2	2	0	13	8	0	6.50
R. M. Ellison	3	4	0	12	10	0	3.00
N. G. Cowans	5	5	1	10	9	0	2.50

**Signifies not out.*

Bowling

	O	M	R	W	BB	Avge
N. A. Foster	87	18	286	14	6–104	20.42
P. H. Edmonds	276.1	104	584	14	4–60	41.71
N. G. Cowans	181.5	41	627	14	3–103	44.78
P. I. Pocock	237.5	53	655	13	4–93	50.38
C. S. Cowdrey	61	2	288	4	2–65	72.00
R. M. Ellison	105	24	289	4	4–66	72.25

Also bowled: G. Fowler 1–1–0–0; M. W. Gatting 13–1–36–0; D. I. Gower 3–0–13–0; A. J. Lamb 1–0–6–1; R. T. Robinson 1–1–0–0.

England v Australia, 1985

Batting

	T	I	NO	R	HS	100s	Avge
M. W. Gatting	6	9	3	527	160	2	87.83
D. I. Gower	6	9	0	732	215	3	81.33
R. T. Robinson	6	9	1	490	175	2	61.25
G. A. Gooch	6	9	0	487	196	1	54.11
A. J. Lamb	6	8	1	256	67	0	36.57
J. E. Emburey	6	6	2	130	33	0	32.50
I. T. Botham	6	8	0	250	85	0	31.25
P. R. Downton	6	7	1	114	54	0	19.00
P. H. Edmonds	5	5	0	47	21	0	9.40
P. J. W. Allott	4	5	1	27	12	0	6.75

Played in two Tests: R. M. Ellison 3; L. B. Taylor 1*. Played in one Test: J. P. Agnew 2*. N. G. Cowans 22*; N. A. Foster 3, 0; A. Sidebottom 2; P. Willey 36, 3*.

Bowling

	O	M	R	W	BB	Avge
R. M. Ellison	75.5	20	185	17	6–77	10.88
I. T. Botham	251.4	36	855	31	5–109	27.58
J. E. Emburey	248.4	75	544	19	5–82	28.63
P. H. Edmonds	225.5	59	549	15	4–40	36.60
P. J. W. Allott	113	22	297	5	2–74	59.40

Also bowled: J. P. Agnew 23–2–99–0; N. G. Cowans 33–6–128–2; N. A. Foster 23–1–83–1; M. W. Gatting 5–0–16–0; G. A. Gooch 41.2–10–102–2; A. J. Lamb 1–0–10–0; A. Sidebottom 18.4–3–65–1; L. B. Taylor 63.3–11–178–4.

West Indies v England, 1985–86

Batting

	T	I	NO	R	HS	100s	Avge
D. I. Gower	5	10	0	370	90	0	37.00
G. A. Gooch	5	10	0	276	53	0	27.60
A. J. Lamb	5	10	0	224	62	0	22.40
D. M. Smith	2	4	0	80	47	0	20.00
P. Willey	4	8	0	136	71	0	17.00
I. T. Botham	5	10	0	168	38	0	16.80
W. M. Slack	2	4	0	62	52	0	15.50
R. M. Ellison	3	6	0	82	36	0	13.66
J. G.Thomas	4	8	4	45	31*	0	11.25
J. E. Emburey	4	8	2	64	35*	0	10.66
P. R. Downton	5	10	1	91	26	0	10.11
R. T. Robinson	4	8	0	72	43	0	9.00
P. H. Edmonds	3	6	2	36	13	0	9.00
N. A. Foster	3	6	1	24	14	0	4.80

Played in one Test: M. W. Gatting 15, 1. *Signifies not out.*

Bowling

	O	M	R	W	BB	Avge
J. E. Emburey	153	34	448	14	5–78	32.00
N. A. Foster	83.5	8	285	7	3–76	40.71
R. M. Ellison	82.3	19	294	7	5–78	42.00
J. G. Thomas	86	13	364	8	4–70	45.50
I. T. Botham	134.5	16	535	11	5–71	48.63

Also bowled: P. H. Edmonds 92.3–16–260–3; G. A. Gooch 7–3–27–1; A. J. Lamb 0.0–0–1–0; P. Willey 4–0–15–1.
Note: A. J. Lamb's only delivery in the first Test was a no-ball.

England v India, 1986

Batting

	T	I	NO	R	HS	100s	Avge
M. W. Gatting	3	6	2	293	183*	1	73.25
G. A. Gooch	3	6	0	175	114	1	29.16
D. I. Gower	2	4	0	101	49	0	25.25
D. R. Pringle	3	6	0	136	63	0	22.66
C. W. J. Athey	2	4	0	78	38	0	19.50
A. J. Lamb	2	4	0	65	39	0	16.25
J. E. Emburey	3	6	1	74	38	0	14.80
P. H. Edmonds	2	4	1	42	18	0	14.00
G. R. Dilley	2	4	1	18	10	0	6.00
B. N. French	2	4	0	22	8	0	5.50

Played in one Test: M. R. Benson 21, 30; P. R. Downton 5, 29; R. M. Ellison 12, 19; N. A. Foster 17, 0; J. K. Lever 0*, 0; N. V. Radford 0, 1; R. T. Robinson 35, 11; W. N. Slack 0, 19; C. L. Smith 6, 28.
**Signifies not out.*

Bowling

	O	M	R	W	BB	Avge
D. R. Pringle	126.3	31	302	13	4–73	23.23
P. H. Edmonds	85	27	178	7	4–31	25.42
J. K. Lever	53	9	166	6	4–64	27.66
G. R. Dilley	85.2	19	299	10	4–146	29.90
J. E. Emburey	76.5	28	141	4	2–40	35.25
N. A. Foster	63	18	141	4	3–93	35.25

Also bowled: R. M. Ellison 35–11–80–1; M. W. Gatting 2–0–10–0; G. A. Gooch 13–2–31–1; N. V. Radford 38–3–148–2.

England v New Zealand, 1986

Batting

	T	I	NO	R	HS	100s	Avge
D. I. Gower	3	5	0	293	131	1	58.60
G. A. Gooch	3	5	0	268	183	1	53.60
J. E. Emburey	2	3	1	92	75	0	46.00
M. W. Gatting	3	5	0	170	121	1	34.00
B. N. French	3	3	2	33	21	0	33.00
M. D. Moxon	2	4	0	111	74	0	27.75
C. W. J. Athey	3	5	0	138	55	0	27.60
G. C. Small	2	2	1	14	12	0	14.00
P. H. Edmonds	3	4	1	35	20	0	11.66

Played in two Tests: G. R. Dilley 17. Played in one Test: I. T. Botham 59*; N. A. Foster 8; A. J. Lamb 0; D. R. Pringle 21, 9; N. V. Radford 12*; J. G. Thomas 28, 10; P. Willey 44, 42.
**Signifies not out.*

Bowling

	O	M	R	W	BB	Avge
G. R. Dilley	69.3	16	179	9	4–82	19.88
P. H. Edmonds	101	32	212	8	4–97	26.50
G. C. Small	64	20	134	4	3–88	33.50
J. E. Emburey	79.5	33	141	4	2–87	35.25

Also bowled: I. T. Botham 26–4–82–3; N. A. Foster 28–7–69–1; G. A. Gooch 19–9–38–1; D. I. Gower 1–0–5–0; D. R. Pringle 22–1–74–0; N. V. Radford 25–4–71–1; J. G. Thomas 43–5–140–2.

Australia v England, 1986–87

Batting

	T	I	NO	R	HS	100s	Avge
B. C. Broad	5	9	2	487	162	3	69.57
D. I. Gower	5	8	1	404	136	1	57.71
M. W. Gatting	5	9	0	393	100	1	43.66
C. J. Richards	5	7	0	264	133	1	37.71
J. E. Emburey	5	7	2	179	69	0	35.80
C. W. J. Athey	5	9	0	303	96	0	33.66
I. T. Botham	4	6	0	189	138	1	31.50
P. A. J. DeFreitas	4	5	1	77	40	0	19.25
A. J. Lamb	5	9	1	144	43	0	18.00
G. C. Small	2	3	1	35	21*	0	17.50
P. H. Edmonds	5	5	1	44	19	0	11.00
G. R. Dilley	4	4	2	6	4*	0	3.00

Played in one Test: J. J. Whitaker 11.
**Signifies not out.*

Bowling

	O	M	R	W	BB	Avge
G. C. Small	78.4	23	180	12	5–48	15.00
G. R. Dilley	176.1	38	511	16	5–68	31.93
I. T. Botham	106.2	24	296	9	5–41	32.88
P. H. Edmonds	261.4	78	538	15	3–45	35.86
J. E. Emburey	315.5	86	663	18	7–78	36.83
P. A. J. DeFreitas	141.4	24	446	9	3–62	49.55

Also bowled: M. W. Gatting 23–7–39–0; A. J. Lamb 1–1–0–0.

England v Pakistan, 1987

Batting

	T	I	NO	R	HS	100s	Avge
M. W. Gatting	5	8	1	445	150*	2	63.57
R. T. Robinson	5	8	0	299	166	1	37.37
C. W. J. Athey	4	6	1	186	123	1	37.20
I. T. Botham	5	8	1	232	51*	0	33.14
J. E. Emburey	4	5	0	162	58	0	32.40
D. I. Gower	5	8	0	236	61	0	29.50
B. C. Broad	4	7	0	193	55	0	27.57
B. N. French	4	5	1	103	59	0	25.75
P. H. Edmonds	5	7	4	66	24*	0	22.00
N. A. Foster	5	6	0	93	29	0	15.50
G. R. Dilley	4	5	2	20	17	0	6.66

Played in one Test: D. J. Capel 53, 28; P. A. J. DeFreitas 11; N. H. Fairbrother 0; M. D. Moxon 8, 15; C. J. Richards 6, 2.

**Signifies not out.*

Bowling

	O	M	R	W	BB	Avge
N. A. Foster	137.2	36	339	15	8–107	22.60
G. R. Dilley	133.3	26	388	14	6–154	27.71
P. H. Edmonds	92.3	36	219	4	1–2	54.75
I. T. Botham	134.3	30	433	7	3–217	61.85

Also bowled: D. J. Capel 18–1–64–0; P. A. J. DeFreitas 12–4–36–1; J. E. Emburey 107–21–222–0; M. W. Gatting 22–5–40–0; M. D. Moxon 6–2–27–0.

Pakistan v England, 1987–88

Batting

	T	*I*	*NO*	*R*	*HS*	*100s*	*Avge*
J. E. Emburey	3	6	3	207	74*	0	69.00
G. A. Gooch	3	6	0	225	93	0	37.50
B. C. Broad	3	6	0	204	116	1	34.00
M. W. Gatting	3	6	0	128	79	0	21.33
D. J. Capel	3	6	0	125	98	0	20.83
B. N. French	3	5	1	80	38*	0	20.00
C. W. J. Athey	3	6	0	92	27	0	15.33
N. A. Foster	2	4	0	40	39	0	10.00
P. A. J. DeFreitas	2	4	0	38	15	0	9.50
N. G. B. Cook	3	5	0	33	14	0	6.60
R. T. Robinson	2	4	1	16	7*	0	5.33

Played in one Test: G. R. Dilley 0*, 0*; N. H. Fairbrother 3, 1; E. E. Hemmings 1*.
**Signifies not out.*

Bowling

	O	*M*	*R*	*W*	*BB*	*Avge*
N. A. Foster	44	10	104	6	4–42	17.33
N. G. B. Cook	93.3	35	195	7	3–87	27.85
P. A. J. DeFreitas	52.5	10	170	6	5–86	28.33
J. E. Emburey	124	48	251	7	3–49	35.85

Also bowled: B. C. Broad 1–0–4–0; D. J. Capel 13–1–59–1; G. R. Dilley 21–2–102–1; G. A. Gooch 2–1–4–0; E. E. Hemmings 25–8–51–1.

New Zealand v England, 1987–88

Batting

	T	*I*	*NO*	*R*	*HS*	*100s*	*Avge*
M. D. Moxon	3	4	1	208	99	0	69.33
B. C. Broad	3	4	0	204	114	1	51.00
J. E. Emburey	3	3	0	106	45	0	35.33
M. W. Gatting	3	4	1	106	42	0	35.33
R. T. Robinson	3	4	0	126	70	0	31.50
G. R. Dilley	3	3	2	17	8*	0	17.00
P. W. Jarvis	2	3	1	34	14	0	17.00
P. A. J. DeFreitas	2	2	0	20	16	0	10.00
B. N. French	3	3	0	23	13	0	7.66
D. J. Capel	3	3	0	16	11	0	5.33

Played in two Tests: N. H. Fairbrother 1. Played in one Test: C. W. Athey 22, 19; N. V. Radford 8; E. E. Hemmings did not bat.
**Signifies not out.*

Bowling

	O	M	R	W	BB	Avge
G. R. Dilley	104.5	33	210	15	6–38	14.00
P. W. Jarvis	98	31	201	6	2–43	33.50
P. A. J. DeFreitas	91.1	33	175	4	2–39	43.75
D. J. Capel	109.2	22	274	5	2–57	54.80

Also bowled: J. E. Emburey 133.5–48–236–3; N. H. Fairbrother 2–0–9–0; M. W. Gatting 23–5–61–2; E. E. Hemmings 45–15–107–0; M. D. Moxon 2–0–3–0; N. V. Radford 50–8–132–1.

England v West Indies, 1988

Batting

	T	I	NO	R	HS	100s	Avge
G. A. Gooch	5	10	0	459	146	1	45.90
A. J. Lamb	4	8	2	254	113	1	42.33
D. I. Gower	4	8	1	211	88*	0	30.14
R. A. Smith	2	4	0	106	57	0	26.50
P. R. Downton	3	5	1	84	27	0	21.00
P. W. Jarvis	2	3	1	42	29*	0	21.00
B. C. Broad	2	4	0	71	54	0	17.75
T. S. Curtis	2	4	0	69	30	0	17.25
N. A. Foster	2	4	1	49	34	0	16.33
M. D. Moxon	2	4	0	55	26	0	13.75
G. R. Dilley	4	7	1	58	28	0	9.66
M. W. Gatting	2	4	0	38	29	0	9.50
J. E. Emburey	3	5	0	46	30	0	9.20
D. R. Pringle	4	7	0	52	39	0	7.42
D. J. Capel	2	4	0	29	16	0	7.25
P. A. J. DeFreitas	3	5	0	36	18	0	7.20
C. J. Richards	2	4	0	13	8	0	3.25
J. H. Childs	2	4	4	2	2*	0	0.00

Played in one Test: C. W. J. Athey 16, 11; R. J. Bailey 43, 3; C. S. Cowdrey 0, 5; M. P. Maynard 3, 10; G. C. Small 5*, 7.

**Signifies not out.*

Bowling

	O	M	R	W	BB	Avge
G. R. Dilley	136.1	26	403	15	5–55	26.86
N. A. Foster	73.2	12	250	9	5–64	27.77
D. R. Pringle	119	33	326	11	5–95	29.63
G. C. Small	37.5	6	140	4	4–64	35.00
P. W. Jarvis	57.1	6	217	6	4–107	36.16

Also bowled: D. J. Capel 22–2–79–1; J. H. Childs 86–29–183–3; C. S. Cowdrey 5.3–0–21–0; P. A. DeFreitas 92–16–253–3; J. E. Emburey 62–14–228–3.

England v Australia, 1989

Batting

	T	I	NO	R	HS	100s	Avge
R. A. Smith	5	10	1	553	143	2	61.44
R. C. Russell	6	11	3	314	128*	1	39.25
D. I. Gower	6	11	0	383	106	1	34.81
J. E. Emburey	3	5	1	131	64	0	32.75
K. J. Barnett	3	5	0	141	80	0	28.20
N. G. B. Cook	3	5	3	45	31	0	22.50
G. R. Dilley	2	3	1	42	24	0	21.00
B. C. Broad	2	4	0	82	37	0	20.50
G. A. Gooch	5	9	0	183	68	0	20.33
M. A. Atherton	2	4	0	73	47	0	18.25
N. A. Foster	3	6	2	68	39	0	17.00
I. T. Botham	3	4	0	62	46	0	15.50
T. S. Curtis	3	5	0	71	41	0	14.20
P. W. Jarvis	2	3	0	33	22	0	11.00
D. R. Pringle	2	3	0	33	22	0	11.00
A. R. C. Fraser	3	5	0	47	29	0	9.40

Played in one Test: D. J. Capel 4, 17; P. A. J. DeFreitas 1, 21; M. W. Gatting 0, 22; E. E. Hemmings 38, 35; A. P. Igglesden 2*; A. J. Lamb 125, 4; M. D. Moxon 0, 18; D. E. Malcolm 9, 5; P. J. Newport 36, 8; R. T. Robinson 0, 12; G. C. Small 59; J. P. Stephenson 25, 11; C. J. Tavaré 2.

**Signifies not out.*

Bowling

	O	M	R	W	BB	Avge
N. A. Foster	167	42	421	12	3–39	35.08
A. R. C. Fraser	144.2	30	323	9	4–63	35.88
J. E. Emburey	152	37	342	8	4–88	42.75
G. C. Small	60	12	198	4	3–141	49.50
N. G. B. Cook	103.5	23	282	5	3–91	56.40
D. R. Pringle	86.2	12	306	5	4–70	61.20
G. R. Dilley	85	12	318	5	2–123	63.60

Also bowled: M. A. Atherton 8–0–34–0; K. J. Barnett 6–0–32–0; I. T. Botham 80–15–241–3; D. J. Capel 24–2–101–2; T. S. Curtis 3–0–7–0; P. A. J. DeFreitas 63.3–10–216–3; G. A. Gooch 31–9–72–1; E. E. Hemmings 33–9–81–0; A. P. Igglesden 37–3–146–3; P. W. Jarvis 69.2–8–290–2; D. E. Malcolm 44–2–166–1; P. J. Newport 44–7–175–2.

West Indies v England, 1989–90

Batting

	T	I	NO	R	HS	100s	Avge
A. J. Lamb	4	7	0	390	132	2	55.71
G. A. Gooch	2	4	1	128	84	0	42.66
R. A. Smith	4	7	2	186	62	0	37.20
W. Larkins	4	8	1	176	54	0	25.14
A. J. Stewart	4	8	1	170	45	0	24.28
R. C. Russell	4	7	1	139	55	0	23.16
N. Hussain	3	5	0	100	35	0	20.00
D. J. Capel	4	7	1	81	40	0	13.50
A. R. C. Fraser	2	2	1	13	11	0	13.00
R. J. Bailey	3	6	0	73	42	0	12.16
P. A. J. DeFreitas	2	4	0	45	24	0	11.25
D. E. Malcolm	4	6	3	17	12	0	5.66
G. C. Small	4	6	1	17	8	0	3.40

**Signifies not out.*

Bowling

	O	M	R	W	BB	Avge
A. R. C. Fraser	71.1	19	161	11	5–28	14.63
G. C. Small	161	33	505	17	4–58	29.70
D. E. Malcolm	161.4	21	577	19	6–77	30.36
P. A. J. DeFreitas	78.5	11	242	6	3–69	40.33
D. J. Capel	124	17	436	9	3–88	48.44

England v New Zealand, 1990

Batting

	T	I	NO	R	HS	100s	Avge
M. A. Atherton	3	5	0	357	151	1	71.40
G. A. Gooch	3	5	0	306	154	1	61.20
G. C. Small	3	4	2	84	44*	0	42.00
A. J. Lamb	3	5	1	129	84*	0	32.25
R. A. Smith	3	5	0	152	64	0	30.40
A. J. Stewart	3	5	0	147	54	0	29.40
P. A. J. DeFreitas	2	2	0	52	38	0	26.00
R. C. Russell	3	4	0	84	43	0	21.00
N. H. Fairbrother	3	5	1	59	33*	0	14.75
E. E. Hemmings	3	4	1	33	20	0	11.00
D. E. Malcolm	3	4	2	4	4*	0	2.00

Played in one Test: C. C. Lewis 32, 1.
**Signifies not out.*

Bowling

	O	M	R	W	BB	Avge
D. E. Malcolm	118.4	38	269	15	5–46	17.93
E. E. Hemmings	107.3	44	215	10	6–58	21.50
P. A. J. DeFreitas	59.4	9	175	6	5–53	29.16
C. C. Lewis	41	8	127	4	3–76	31.75
G. C. Small	104	27	290	5	2–49	58.00

Also bowled: M. A. Atherton 10–6–17–0; G. A. Gooch 13–7–25–0.

England v India, 1990

Batting

	T	I	NO	R	HS	100s	Avge
R. A. Smith	3	6	4	361	121*	2	180.50
G. A. Gooch	3	6	0	752	333	3	125.33
D. I. Gower	3	6	2	291	157*	1	72.75
M. A. Atherton	3	6	0	378	131	1	63.00
A. J. Lamb	3	6	0	364	139	2	60.66
E. E. Hemmings	3	2	0	70	51	0	35.00
R. C. Russell	3	3	1	59	35	0	29.50
D. E. Malcolm	3	2	1	28	15*	0	28.00
J. E. Morris	3	5	2	71	32	0	23.66

Played in three Tests: A. R. C. Fraser 1, 0. Played in two Tests: C. C. Lewis 3. Played in one Test: N. F. Williams 38.
**Signifies not out.*

Bowling

	O	M	R	W	BB	Avge
A. R. C. Fraser	159.1	41	460	16	5–104	28.75
E. E. Hemmings	137.2	26	454	11	3–75	41.27
C. C. Lewis	65	8	281	5	2–26	56.20
D. E.Malcolm	110	16	436	7	2–65	62.28

Also bowled: M. A. Atherton 28–3–161–1; G. A. Gooch 18–4–70–1; N. F. Williams 41–5–148–2.

Australia v England, 1990–91

Batting

	T	*I*	*NO*	*R*	*HS*	*100s*	*Avge*
G. A. Gooch	4	8	0	426	117	1	53.25
D. I. Gower	5	10	1	407	123	2	45.22
A. J. Lamb	3	6	0	195	91	0	32.50
M. A. Atherton	5	10	1	279	105	1	31.00
R. A. Smith	5	10	2	238	58	0	29.75
W. Larkins	3	6	0	141	64	0	23.50
A. J. Stewart	5	10	0	224	91	0	22.40
R. C. Russell	3	5	1	77	30*	0	19.25
P. A. J. DeFreitas	3	6	1	77	45	0	15.40
G. C. Small	4	6	1	42	15	0	8.40
P. C. R. Tufnell	4	6	4	13	8	0	6.50
A. R. C. Fraser	3	5	0	27	24	0	5.40
D. E. Malcolm	5	7	1	27	7	0	4.50

Played in one Test: E. E. Hemmings 0; C. C. Lewis 20, 14; P. J. Newport 0, 40*.
**Signifies not out.*

Bowling

	O	*M*	*R*	*W*	*BB*	*Avge*
A. R. C. Fraser	143	31	311	11	6–82	28.27
P. A. J. DeFreitas	113.3	22	318	10	4–56	31.80
E. E. Hemmings	73	16	199	6	3–94	33.16
P. C. R. Tufnell	140	45	345	9	5–61	38.33
D. E. Malcolm	223.5	42	665	16	4–128	41.56
G. C. Small	149	33	424	9	3–34	47.11

Also bowled: M. A. Atherton 15–2–70–0; G. A. Gooch 23–5–69–2; C. C. Lewis 15–0–58–3; P. J. Newport 20–0–78–1.

England v West Indies, 1991

Batting

	T	I	NO	R	HS	100s	Avge
R. A. Smith	4	7	2	416	148*	2	83.20
G. A. Gooch	5	9	1	480	154*	1	60.00
M. R. Ramprakash	5	9	0	210	29	0	23.33
P. A. J. DeFreitas	5	8	1	134	55*	0	19.14
D. R. Pringle	4	7	0	128	45	0	18.28
R. K. Illingworth	2	4	2	31	13	0	15.50
A. J. Lamb	4	7	0	88	29	0	12.57
H. Morris	2	4	0	50	44	0	12.50
G. A. Hick	4	7	0	75	43	0	10.71
R. C. Russell	4	7	0	73	46	0	10.42
M. A. Atherton	5	9	0	79	32	0	8.77

Played in two Tests: D. V. Lawrence 4, 34, 9; C. C. Lewis 13, 65, 47*; D. E. Malcolm 5*, 4, 0; S. L. Watkin 2, 0, 6. Played in one Test: I. T. Botham 31, 4*; A. J. Stewart 31, 38*; P. C. R. Tufnell 2.

Signifies not out.

Bowling

	O	M	R	W	BB	Avge
P. A. J. DeFreitas	185.5	55	457	22	4–34	20.77
P. C. R. Tufnell	60.3	9	175	7	6–25	25.00
D. R. Pringle	128.1	33	322	12	5–100	26.83
S. L. Watkin	36	4	153	5	3–38	30.60
C. C. Lewis	79	30	201	6	6–111	33.50
D. V. Lawrence	78.1	7	350	10	5–106	35.00
R. K. Illingworth	56.4	10	213	4	3–110	53.25

Also bowled: I. T. Botham 27–8–67–3; G. A. Gooch 8–1–14–0; G. A. Hick 24–5–95–2; D. E. Malcolm 42.3–3–180–3.

New Zealand v England, 1991–92

Batting

	T	I	NO	R	HS	100s	Avge
A. J. Lamb	3	5	0	338	142	1	67.60
A. J. Stewart	3	5	0	330	148	2	66.00
R. A. Smith	3	5	0	213	96	0	42.60
C. C. Lewis	2	3	0	126	70	0	42.00
R. C. Russell	3	5	1	135	36	0	33.75
G. A. Gooch	3	5	0	161	114	1	32.20
G. A. Hick	3	5	0	134	43	0	26.80
D. A. Reeve	3	5	0	124	59	0	24.80
D. R. Pringle	2	3	0	53	41	0	17.66
P. A. J. DeFreitas	3	4	1	11	7*	0	3.66
P. C. R. Tufnell	3	3	3	8	6*	0	—

Played in one Test: I. T. Botham 15, 1; D. V. Lawrence 6.
**Signifies not out.*

Bowling

	O	M	R	W	BB	Avge
P. C. R. Tufnell	186.1	69	367	16	7–47	22.93
C. C. Lewis	100	23	249	10	5–31	24.90
P. A. J. DeFreitas	106.4	39	235	8	4–62	29.37
D. R. Pringle	58	16	162	5	2–21	32.40
G. A. Hick	87	36	148	4	4–126	37.00

Also bowled: I. T. Botham 22–5–76–3; D. V. Lawrence 29.1–8–71–1; D. A. Reeve 24.5–8–60–2; R. A. Smith 4–2–6–0.

Index

Abbreviations: Aus: Australia; Bar: Barbados; Derbys: Derbyshire; Dur: Durham; Eng: England; Glam: Glamorgan; Glos: Gloucestershire; Guy: Guyana; Hants: Hampshire; Jam: Jamaica; Lancs: Lancashire; Leics: Leicestershire; LI: Leeward Islands; Middx: Middlesex; Nor: Northamptonshire; Notts: Nottinghamshire; NSW: New South Wales; NZ: New Zealand; Pak: Pakistan; Qld: Queensland; SA: South Australia; Som: Somerset; Sur: Surrey; Sus: Sussex; Tas: Tasmania; TCCB: Test and County Cricket Board; Trin: Trinidad and Tobago; Vic: Victoria; WA: Western Australia; Warks: Warwickshire; WI: West Indies; WnI: Windward Islands; Wor: Worcestershire; Yorks: Yorkshire.